# Praise for *The Wild Wh*

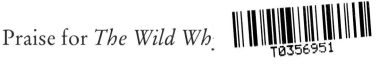

"In *The Wild Why*, Laura Munson invites readers to answer 'the most powerful and wonder-full question' for themselves: 'What can I create?' This book is an open-hearted invitation to explore the connections between wonder and empathy, intuition and serendipity, self-compassion and creativity— and to live a bigger, braver life."
—MAGGIE SMITH, *New York Times* best-selling author of
*You Could Make This Place Beautiful*

"The ability to feel wonder is part of the human experience, but life moves us further from that childlike state. *The Wild Why* is part memoir, part self-exploration, workbook, and tutorial on how we can reach inside and use our own sense of wonder to remove barriers, quiet naysayers, and enrich our lives."
—LEE WOODRUFF, #1 *New York Times* best-selling author

"In *The Wild Why*, Laura Munson deploys self-exploration, self-sabotage, confession, contrition, 'bonfires,' undying love for Montana, and her own line of full-fledged writing retreats, all aimed at healing the familial, cultural, and inter-relational wounds that curtail our sense of wonder. The wonder I felt in finishing Laura's epic? Her recipe worked!"
—DAVID JAMES DUNCAN, author of *The River Why*,
*The Brothers K*, and *Sun House*

"*The Wild Why* will inspire you to re-discover your wonder, find your true voice, and bring back the pieces of yourself you lost along the way. This book not only reminds us about the importance of our one precious life—but helps us understand *how* to live it well."
—AMY B. SCHER, best-selling author of *This Is How I Save My Life* and *How To Heal Yourself When No One Else Can*

"Laura Munson's exuberant book *The Wild Why* is for anyone seeking to heal their wonder wound and reclaim their wild wonder. Rich with serendipitous adventures and a fresh perspective on personal vulnerability, this book contributes a welcome voice to the growing literature on wonder. Get this book and get your magic back."
—JEFFREY DAVIS, author of *Tracking Wonder: Reclaiming a Life of Meaning and Possibility in a World Obsessed with Productivity*

"The late great William Kittredge said that acts of imagination lead to acts of empathy. This wise, generous, and dazzling craft-book for the soul does just that, and in so doing resurrects in the reader the state of wonder that is so vital to our survival."
—CHRIS DOMBROWSKI, author of *The River You Touch*

"*The Wild Why* is an invitation and a permission slip, a beckoning and a reckoning. It's more than a book—it's a chill-giving, tear-inducing, wide-grinning experience. Laura Munson writes with astonishing generosity and authenticity, like she's raising the velvet curtain to her own heart. This book is a gift to those who know there's more to life than following rules and checking boxes. There is medicine and magic in these pages. Devour them."
—JJ ELLIOTT, author of *There Are No Rules for This*

"*The Wild Why* is a heart-opening invitation to rediscover a braver life filled with the simplicity and power of awe. The uniquely powerful part of this invitation is that Laura brilliantly offers it through two tools needed most for a life of wonder—storytelling and your own unmasked humanity. Read it, now, and ponder it often."
—TANMEET SETHI MD., author of *Joy Is My Justice*

"I believe that it takes one person to open your heart, to inspire you, to encourage you, to make you believe that nothing is impossible. Laura Munson is that ONE person. Take this *The Wild Why* ride with her. She will make sure you land safely and she will encourage you to find the wonder, never give up, and seek the folks who make you swoon. You will feel like you made a new friend who you will never, ever want to let go of."

—AMY FERRIS, author of *Mighty Gorgeous: A Little Book About Messy Love*

# the wild why

# the wild why

## Stories and Teachings to Uncover Your Wonder

LAURA MUNSON

SHE WRITES PRESS

Published 2025
Printed in the United States of America
Print ISBN: 978-1-64742-838-9
E-ISBN: 978-1-64742-839-6
Library of Congress Control Number: 2024925805

For information, address:
She Writes Press
1569 Solano Ave #546
Berkeley, CA 94707

Interior Design by Tabitha Lahr

She Writes Press is a division of SparkPoint Studio, LLC.

Names and identifying characteristics have been changed to protect the privacy of certain individuals.

This book is for anyone who
has ever said, "I don't have a voice."

You do. I promise.
You just lost it for a while.

Come with me.
Let's find it again.

# Contents

## part III: wonder-lost

## part IV: wonder-found

*part I*

wonder-wounded

# my wondering:
# have you lost your wild why?

> "I talk too much. I ask too many questions.
> I cry too easily. I laugh too loud.
> I'm too sensitive (I'm not sure what that means).
> And I feel bad about all of it."
> —LAURA MUNSON (fourth-grade journal)

What happened when you asked why the sky is blue? What makes a rainbow? If there is a God. Why people die. Why you weren't being protected. Why you weren't being loved.

Maybe you weren't taken seriously for your questions. Or maybe your elders considered your feral questions an honor to answer. Maybe they lingered in their answering, trying their best to illuminate your questions.

Be honest with yourself: How were you treated for your questions? Were your questions considered an annoyance? Were you placated for your asking? Were you told that you were rude for your asking? Were you even punished? Did you ever get an answer that you could live with? Or did the answers just make you find more *why* inside of you that you decided wasn't safe to share? Maybe you took your wild, wonder-full why and hid it so deep inside you that even you couldn't find it. And you stopped asking. And traded your wild why for what fast became your wonder wound.

Maybe you forgot about your wild why altogether.

If you have this book in your hands, somewhere along the line, it's likely that someone hurt you for asking questions or for how you expressed yourself. My hurt came in early and strong from family, friends, teachers, authority figures, adults in general. Not all. Not by any stretch. But enough to matter.

When I wrote those words in my fourth-grade journal, it's clear that my wonder wound was already festering. But somehow, I never let the wound *kill* my wonder, and that's why I've written this book. I want to explore this "somehow."

What if you could go back to the genesis of your own wonder wound and tell that version of yourself, likely a little child, that your questions and feelings don't make you bad? What if I could have known back then how to not "feel bad about all of it"? The talking, the asking, the crying, the laughing, the feeling? What if I had known how to tell myself to feel *good* about all of it? *Good* about the way I wondered and expressed myself. Especially when my whys landed in an exasperated "Because I said so!" That's when I knew I was in big trouble. And when I was in big trouble, I never felt *good*. Instead, I felt very, very *bad*.

When I was in big trouble for my wonder, I would hide. Maybe you did too. I had all kinds of hiding places. In a dusty spare bedroom closet under blankets and pillows. In the upper, thin branches of my tree house, where no adult could climb. Under the skirts of the blue spruce that abutted our backyard. In deciduous-leaf-pile forts I'd make in the small swath of forest behind my suburban Chicago home. And in my journal.

In my hiding places, I could ask *why why why* as much as I wanted and never get into trouble because no one ever found me. I was a good hider when I wanted to be. When I needed to cry and laugh and be sensitive and feel safe. And say no. In my hiding places I felt pure delight. Butterflies in my stomach. Holding on to those thin branches, sometimes in the wind, looking over my house and into our village with a bird's-eye view, I felt like anything was possible and every question was there for the asking.

*Maybe I can even fly! Do I have the power? What if I do and just don't know it? What if I live my whole life with the ability to fly but never know that I can . . . unless I try? Maybe I should try.*

That was the wildest why I knew. I can still feel the power gathering and surging in my chest for what would surely send me winging through the sky.

I'm glad I never tried. Not from that altitude. Sometimes wondering is better kept inside than put into action. I did try a few times closer to the ground, proved that I was human, and instead flew in my dreams. Always low, skimming the earth, feeling the heat and the cold and the dew. I still fly like that in my dreams.

It took writing this book to consciously understand that I've spent my adult life finding my way back to my hiding places in one way or another. Finding my way back to that girl and telling her that she doesn't need to feel bad about her wonder. That she can feel *good* about it. That it's time to come out of hiding and to find places in the world where her wonder is safe. In fact, she can't live without it. No one can.

Imagine what it would take to feel good about your questions and the way you ask them as the adult you are. What if you felt good about the voice you express and the thoughts and feelings behind it? What if you knew how to find safe places for your wonder, regardless of the challenges you face? And what if those safe places didn't feel like hiding but, instead, felt like liberation? This book is my effort to restore your butterflies. It's an invitation to return to your wonder, reclaim it, and go forward with it fully intact.

I'll admit my fear here, because it doesn't serve either of us for me to pretend, especially in light of my own wonder wound. I know that I must step into that light, however daunting it is, by sharing my truth.

In these pages, I've invited myself to exhaust myself with my wonder. To talk. To tell stories. To ask a lot of questions. To cry and laugh and be highly sensitive. There's no other way if I am to shed the inner terrorism whose enemy is wonder most of all.

I hope you will join me. Isn't it time to come out of our cocoons and fly? Isn't it time for us to return to our wild whys?

# you and me and the 4:00 a.m. haunt

This is you. And me. This is all of us. Without our wonder. In a crisis of truth and lies. And by the end . . . hope. I hope. For me it happens at 4:00 a.m. Maybe for you it happens in the middle of the day in a rash of anxiety, just when you least expect it. But I know that at whatever time, and in whatever form, as adults, we can all lose the liberation of our wonder to our world of woe.

Let's get real. We can't afford not to—not for one more second. Do you lie in bed at 4:00 a.m., paralyzed by fear and shame and self-loathing and worry? Do you lie there creating movies in your mind of doom and dread? Do you feel the power running out of you, like water through your fingers? Your tired fingers, tired from all of that *tap tap tap* on all of those buttons. And your eyes stinging and blurry from all of those screens. Your voice scratchy from all that talking and persuading and strategizing and reasoning with everyone in your life—kids, husband, wasband, aging parent, that one sibling who breaks your heart relentlessly, your boss who isn't much different, that friend you always thought would be there for you and who just . . . isn't.

And your brain. Your poor, tired brain. It's 4:00 a.m., and it's still on, working every angle of your semi (or fully) screwed-up life, trying so hard to get it right. How and why did you get here? You were "supposed" to be so "successful." So "perfect." But you know, deep down in a place too scary for even the wee hours, that you're here because you haven't allowed yourself to be your true self, and to have that true self be your best self, no matter what society thinks of you. No matter what the people in your life think of you. Somehow you've allowed yourself to be completely defined by everyone but . . . you.

You've got to let your truth out, but the problem is that you don't even know what your truth is anymore, so how can you find the words to tell it? Did you ever know what your truth was? Yes, you did. When you were a small child, you did. If you think hard enough, you can remember her. She was honest. She was playful. She was happy and curious and full of awe. She chased fireflies and butterflies just to feel them tickling her fingers. She picked up rocks and shells and kept them in her pockets to play with and wonder about. Maybe she put them on her windowsill like friends.

When I was a small child, I charmed birds right into my hands as if they were living nests. And then let them go so I could watch them take flight and try to be as free as they were, flying through the sky. Maybe you did too. Maybe you knew who you were then. And there's a strong likelihood that you weren't afraid to express it. Not when you were very young. That's because your wonder was intact. Before everything happened to you. And to it. Before the world started to say, "All that childhood wonder was cute, but now it's time to buck up and become a successful part of society. People with their heads in the clouds don't get anywhere."

Lying in the dark at 4:00 a.m., sweating into your sheets, you know you shouldn't have believed that lie. You know you need to get back to that wonder-filled version of yourself.

Your life depends on it. But how, with all that is currently on your shoulders? How can you let go of everyone else's version of what your truth is, and what's best for you, and find your own?

Why not let your wonder lead you? Ask what *you* want from you, never mind the world. Are you even capable of separating yourself out of the life you've let run you? Of course you are.

So keep going. Ask more questions. And I don't mean questions like "What are the best workout shoes for the best price?" If you want to find your *true* truth, you must awaken to your true questions. Because your questions, especially the ones you ask yourself, are the loyal and loving gatekeepers to your truth. And your truth needs you to ask in the voice that only you have. You know it, just like you know that you must find what it is that you truly want from your life. And even if you've fought it with all your bony might for years, you know . . . it's time.

Dare it. Dare your voice to ask, "What do I truly want for my life?"

If it's too much right now, instead, in the quiet, lonely, dark, dare *this* question: "How did I lose my voice? My truth? My questions? Myself?"

Maybe you can't even begin to remember the origin of this whole crisis of self. Because that's what you're in: A giant crisis. Of. Self.

Implore yourself to remember.

As a child, you might have heard some version of these phrases from an authority figure who was supposed to love you: "Stop asking so many questions!" "Be quiet!"

And if you asked why it was bad to ask and talk, you might have heard: "Don't talk back to me or you'll be punished!"

If you started to cry, you might have heard: "You're so sensitive." "You're so dramatic." "You're too much."

And if your whys were met with infuriated ultimatums, and you said "no" in response, maybe you heard an iteration of: "Don't you dare say 'no' to me, you disrespectful child! You will pay for this!"

If you're nodding, then somewhere long ago, your own version of these poisonous words got injected into the veins of your self-perception and your self-expression. And at 4:00 a.m., you hear, in your own voice, an echo of those early messages telling you that you're not worthy of your wonder.

Stuff like: *If you were capable of even finding your truth in the first place, you wouldn't be creative enough to know how to express it. You don't have a voice. Not one that's important, anyway. You should just give up . . . and shut up . . . and . . . go . . . back . . . to . . . sleep so that you can get back to your miserable life when the alarm goes off.*

You stare at the ceiling. You feel like a failure at your life even though no one would know it because you're so good at saying that you're "fine." But what's behind those words is the deep belief that you should have become what you were *supposed* to become. And these personal myths (because that's what they are, you know) are not just in your thinking or speaking or writing. They're quite possibly in your movement and the way you dress and what you say to your friends and family. In your cooking and even in your acts of service. It's been a lifetime of blocking your true self-expression on all fronts, and tonight . . . you're just so sick and tired of it. Truly sick and tired. You lie there and stare into the dark and think:

*What has happened to me?*

*I want to rip myself up and start all over again.*

*I want my joy back. I know what joy is still, don't I?*

And you scan your memory for the feeling of joy. But you can barely touch its shadowy toe. So you try for one butterfly. Nothing comes but more darkness and a lonely truck out on the road.

This is dire. We are in crisis. I know, because I'm in it too. In fact, it might just be the fight of our lives. Everything about us is at stake except our physical lives, but maybe those too. Does a breaking emotional heart make a breaking physical one? My *God*, how can we get this life thing *right*? We're *not* screwups. We *know* we're not. We have people who love us. We have people whom we love. We have mortgages. Or rent. We vote. We get called in for jury duty. AARP wants to send us "modern felt" tote bags! That must make us upstanding citizens! We *must* have the ability to win at this thing called "life"! We must have voices and ways to make them matter! Shit—*other* people seem to have it figured out. What are we *missing*? Why are we getting it all wrong? What is our *problem*? We have mugs that say CREATE YOUR LIFE. We must know what the hell that means. We *bought* them for ourselves, for crying out crazy.

And that's how we feel at 4:00 a.m. Crazy.

We think and we think. And we think. And our thoughts ping-pong back and forth from being so *mean* to so *desperate* with nothing in between.

Until, finally, we're just . . . done. The crazy runs out with that last trickle of power that pools in our palms and leaks over our pinkie fingers.

And we hope for sleep to release us from our apparent lack of ability to make our mugs come true. For all of our best efforts, in the end, it turns out that we suck at creating our lives, so how can we possibly find our truths, never mind our voices? All we can seem to land on is what we were/are supposed to be. That distant "supposed to be."

Let's be brutally honest, because we have to be, and let's do it with some wonder:

Is anyone in our current lives actually telling us this nonsense about who we are? Or is it just we who say these things to ourselves? Are *we* our own worst enemies? Perhaps we have internalized our early messages and allowed them to translate into our adult lives as lies like: *I don't have a voice. I don't know what's true anymore. I don't know who I am or what I want. I'm stuck in my life. I can't see my future. I'm completely lost. I belong to everyone around me but myself.*

The child who held on to the high, thin branches thinking she could fly—she knows the answer, and it's quite likely yes. We are in fact our own worst enemies.

So where did our liberated, wise, self-accepting child go? That stunning child who treated each moment as a potential for magic and miracles? That child who had so many questions and longed to enter into the open field of them? She longed for answers, but the questions alone were what she really cared about. Did we allow her to die? Can we resuscitate her? Or is she lost to us forever? What would it take to lovingly bring her back?

Can we please try? The world needs us to try. Everyone who loves us needs us to try. *We* need us to try. The child in us, let's call her our Free Child, needs us to try—so she can return to her wonder and have a joyful future. Isn't that what we all want? When we get real? At 4:00 a.m., it feels like there's no other choice. It's daylight that's the problem. It's in daylight that we forget the haunt and live in the lie that the world needs us to go, go, go. Away from ourselves.

And then, in our sweating and groaning and bemoaning, we hear a voice. A kind voice. A knowing voice. A familiar voice that we haven't heard for a long, long time:

*I want you to return to your Free Child. What you've forgotten is your wonder. That's all. Trust me. You used to trust me, back when we were an us. Let's tuck into a safe, warm place together, just like when we were little, and find our wonder again. Only this time, we won't be hiding. This time we'll declare a free zone. A quiet, screenless, buttonless place where we get to be guts-out raw. Where we get to look at the stories of our wonder and where it went away. Let's find* that *girl again. She's not scared or dogged by anything, really. She's a little, wild, tree-climbing, barefoot, bird-charming child who is begging us to come back to her. And play. She is calling us back . . . to our wonder.*

"She is?" I whisper. "I can't see her. I'm not sure she ever existed."

*Of course she did. I'll see her for you, for us, for now. All you have to do is open your arms. You're standing in a fresh, green, wide-open meadow full of wildflowers. She's running at you. Catch her. Twirl her in the air and see her beautiful smile beaming into your twin beautiful eyes. Smile back. Remember that smile? It's time you two take a good, long look into each other's eyes. And a good long twirl together. I want us to be* an us *again.*

"But how?"

*Just take in a deep breath and let out a deep sigh. Ready?*

"No. Maybe. Okay . . . yeah."

*On your mark . . . get set . . . go.*

And then, dawn breaks. And we think, *Am I going to be true in this new day?*

I wonder.

# what is wonder?

L et's start with something that connects even a cynic to wonder: a rainbow. When you see a rainbow, what do you feel? What do you think? What do you do? Do you stop in your tracks? Do you lift your head to the sky? Do you look to see where it starts and finishes? Do you look to see if it's a double rainbow? Do you think about pots of gold? Do you have a secret promise to yourself that you will stand there until it disappears? In other words, do you stand in awe?

Or do you catch the rainbow out of the corner of your eye and keep doing whatever you're doing because whatever you're doing is way more important than an illusionary color spectrum in the atmosphere that's just going to fade away in a matter of moments? Why give it your attention when there are so many more important things going on?

When I see a rainbow, I think of a book I loved as a child called *Ant and Bee and the Rainbow*. Ant and Bee like to do things together. Create things. One day, Ant and Bee see a rainbow and want to play on it but figure they can't play on a rainbow. So they find an old tractor tire buried halfway in the ground, get some paint, and paint the tire to look like a

*14*

rainbow. They hang out playing on their own private rainbow until the rain washes it back to a plain old tire. And then they do it all over again. This book always made me sad that beautiful things have to leave us, but it also reminded me to consider the possibilities of the moment. To think: *How can I play with this moment?* This wonder-full question lends its curiosity, triggered by awe, to creativity. But the word "creativity" scares a lot of people.

Somewhere along the line too many of us were told that we weren't creative. We were put into slots like "jock," "brainy," "artsy." "Artsy" equals "creative." The opposite being: "not creative." Which is nonsense. The day you were told that you weren't creative was the start of your wonder wound and the beginning of the end of your wild why.

People tell me all the time that they're not creative. It's just not true. It's one of those personal myths people carry. Everything we do is an act of creation. The way we dress, the way we decorate our living rooms, every word that comes out of our mouths, every thought we think . . . it's all an act of creation. When I make this point to people who insist they're not creative, their eyes glaze over. They can't get past the word "creativity." Too much wounding around it. I knew I had to find another way to express this concept, especially as a writing teacher.

One day, I was walking in the woods, where I do my best thinking, and I thought: *What's* behind *creativity?* The answer came fast: wonder. *Is* wonder *scary for people? What* is *wonder anyway? It's curiosity but not* just *curiosity. It's awe too. Curiosity mixed with awe. Like Ant and Bee and their rainbow!*

I sat down on a stump to think about it. *Has society lost its wonder?* If the answer was yes, then we were doomed. Fear shot down my spine, stumpward, and I looked deeply into the trees for help. They'd seen hundreds of years but likely only a smattering of stump sitters. More like stump makers. Were the trees curious? Humans most definitely had *not* lost their curiosity. Curiosity and the gleaning of answers was what created and had sustained the internet. Plenty of us see rainbows and quickly google, "What makes a rainbow?" The problem is that we're looking at our screens and not at the rainbow!

The more I sat there, the clearer it became: The key element of wonder that seems to be lost is awe. Awe requires stopping and truly taking something in. Not rushing to find answers. Just stopping and making room for the awe. To *be* in it. Without questions or answers. The *not* knowing is the magic of awe. Awe doesn't care what you think or know. In fact, it wants us *not* to think or know . . . and to just *be*. I suspected it was the same for the trees.

So I challenged myself to sit there on that stump and not think. Not think about how old the tree was when it was felled. Not count its rings. To abandon my curiosity and instead just stare into the old firs and larch and ponderosa pines and let them give themselves to my awe. I looked up, as if to find awe itself in their branches. Instead, I saw mushrooms. Whole mushrooms, placed perfectly on the boughs of a grand fir, like Christmas tree ornaments. My curiosity surged. It couldn't help itself. Was it some sort of art installation? A portal into another world? But I took in a deep breath and invited myself to simply behold this forest treasure and not defer to my wild whys. And the answer presented itself in a small, busy, chattering squirrel, skittering up the trunk with a mushroom in its mouth, dashing out to a bough, and, yes, placing it there. In the sun. And it was clear then: the squirrel was drying mushrooms for the winter. But the answer was far less interesting than the moment of discovery.

I needed to sit on stumps more often. All of society needed to sit and gaze into the wild world more often. Would a person out on a hike with their Fitbit on, counting steps, think it was strange behavior if they saw a woman sitting on a stump far off the main trail? Likely, yes. Is our modern civilization so driven by finding answers that adults don't long for this exact, wonderous moment when curiosity stops us in awe? Begs us to bear witness to what's right before our eyes? Begs us to stop?

There's nothing wrong with answers, but as long as we see awe as gratuitous and not vital, we'll abandon it for our screens, where we think the answers live. But do they really? Aren't they a lesser answer than what's actually in the world? Do you think that ancient civilizations were studying and tracking the night sky and the moon and sun out of gratuitous foolishness? Of course not. It was how they sustained themselves and made sense of the mystery of living on this planet. They knew their lives depended on it. When to sow. When to harvest. And a whole lot more. They had questions, yes. But in order to find answers, they *had* to be in awe of the natural world. That's all they really had and they knew it. They held their wonder at their essence. Their curiosity wasn't enough. It needed to be mixed with awe if they were going to survive. How is it possible that we have "evolved" out of living by this fact? I can say that I've never learned more from a screen than what I've learned sitting on a stump.

Consider a baby. I suspect that the ancients would agree with my belief that we are born with our wonder intact. It's as innate as our will to live. And our will to live can't exist without wonder. Why? Because wonder is behind everything a baby does. Wonder is how we learn to crawl and walk and eat and speak and thrive.

Since so many people feel that they have no voice, let's focus on the thinking piece here. If you could translate a baby's running thoughts, they would go something to the tune of: *Look at that smiling face with the same voice I've been hearing but haven't seen. I want to touch it so that I know it's close*

*by and I feel safe. Her mouth is kissing my cheek and it feels
good. I want to kiss it back. Oh listen! She's making sounds
that I like. I want to make those sounds too. When I make
those sounds, she smiles. I want to smile. When I smile, I get
more kisses. I like kisses. I want more. How do I get more?*

Once that baby can talk, it all comes spilling out. Sometimes
in song. Sometimes in tantrums. Sometimes in words. Sometimes
in pointing or grasping or grabbing or hitting or hugging. And
always in wonder. Extreme wonder. Life-dependent wonder.
Because without an adult, a baby isn't going to live. And the way
to live is in the asking and wanting and watching.

Wonder begets the creativity that begets our self-expression.
Self-expression begets a sense of connection, safety, purpose,
meaning, value, self-worth, authenticity, achievement, and even
survival. But wonder is where it all begins. Wonder is what's
*behind* creativity. And creativity is how we apply wonder and
grow our personalities and our lives. Finding our wonder is how
we find our voices—and let the story of our lives flow.

**EMPATHY**

Wonder is a vital life force not just for our personal devel-
opment but for the continuation of our civilization. Why?
Because without wonder, we abandon empathy. And without
empathy, we would have no civilization at all.

When we approach the world and its creatures with open
curiosity—*Who are you? How are you? What are you? I really
want to know. I need to understand*—we begin to understand
our essential sameness versus our essential differences. This is
how humanity bridges oceans and mountains, social groups,
gender, age, race, religion, politics, land, all of it. This is how
wars are avoided but not likely won.

When we recognize that wonder drives empathy, and
when we accept that empathy will save our civilization, then
we get a whole lot more serious about it. And if we're being

honest with ourselves in this department, if we really want to return to our wonder, then we must first confront our pain. If we don't look at our wounds, we will never heal them enough to remember what's behind them: the essence of who we are. If we're not willing to look at our wounds, we actually can't find the essence of who someone *else* is either. It's one thing to be able to identify with people's joy, but we have to be willing to identify with their pain and what's behind it in order to share in the full experience of empathy. If we can't or won't, then we are rendered empathy-less. Is that the legacy of our civilization that we want to pass on? I hold that there will be no future civilization if we don't put empathy at the center of ours now.

When we *feel* our pain and want to heal from it, free from the distractions of the charades that drive our daily lives, that's when we stand a chance at getting back to the engine behind it all: wonder. So we need to *feel* that pain. Feeling it will lead us *out* of it. I have found that quite often, our pain is rooted in our wonder wound.

Having the courage to look at our wonder wound, and the gumption to heal our way to the wonder that still lives in us, leads us to see the wonder in others. When we wonder on the other side of our belief systems, we ask questions: *What makes these people who are so different from me tick? How can I learn from them, no matter how nefarious they are?* Enter not just empathy but radical, civilization-saving empathy. What if radical *empathy* became our driving force? Especially for the people and things we don't understand?

My father used to say, "People are the same everywhere." I've spent my life testing his philosophy because I've wanted it to be true. After much questioning, and even radical empathy, putting myself in places and situations where I am way outside of my comfort zone, I have no doubt that people are the same everywhere in the way he meant: We all want to love and be loved. We all want to be valued and do something of value. What if we all lived in this wonderous, empathy-seeking way? What if we wondered our way into wild and supreme empathy? And what if all of it brought us into our purest form of self-expression, wonder wound healed? Wild whys back intact. I want to live in *that* world. Don't you?

If you're nodding, then we need to begin with a serious commitment to empathy. Not to make people right or wrong. Not to set yourself up to be made right or wrong. But to live the Rumi quote: "Out beyond ideas of wrongdoing and right-doing, / there is a field. I'll meet you there."

Can we try to meet in this field, even and especially when we hold opposing opinions and beliefs? Can we imagine both of us in this field, holding our Free Child close? Can we ask questions of others without trying to be right but instead trying to simply wonder together? To stand in curiosity and awe of our essential sameness instead of our differences? Because when we apply this level of wonder, it becomes possible to see ourselves in each other or at least to understand what motivates another person and what causes them to see the world the way they do.

## THE POWER OF THE QUESTION

While practicing radical empathy and exploring the wonder that spawns it, pay attention to the power of questions. The *external* questions in this instance, not the ones that live inside us. Asking questions of others can be loaded. It's important to be pure about it. It's important to check in with your intention when you ask a question of another. Consider the following questions about questions:

*Am I trying to make a point by putting someone else on the spot with my question?*

*Am I trying to tease out an answer so that I am in a position of power or so that I can have dominion over it with my response?*

*Do I want to answer more than ask?*

*When I ask someone how they are, do I really want the true answer? Or do I hope that they'll just tell me they're fine even if they aren't?*

If the answer is yes to any of these, you are not practicing empathy. Be kind to yourself instead of feeling bad about it. It's just an awareness exercise so that you can work harder at finding a pure, empathetic question. Look to the playground. See how quickly kids who are strangers play together. "Do you want to swing? Play in the sandbox? Climb on the jungle gym?" They're looking for ways to connect with each other and play. Not for what makes them different.

Question asking is a fine art. And so is answering, especially if the question is a personal one. Answering often means that you're being called upon or invited to tell a personal story. Where do we begin in the sharing of our stories? It can feel too vulnerable. Do we really owe others our stories? We get to decide. But if we are compelled to tell our stories, how do we find our true voice to share them in the first place?

## YOUR TRUE STORIES

Finding your true voice starts with finding the central question that lives and burns in you *because* of your stories. By finding the central *wondering* within you. Notice how true connection happens, human-to-human, when we say, "I have that question too. I've been afraid to ask it or admit it . . . but I do have stories around it. And you're willing to tell me yours? How rare! Why don't we sit down on this park bench and tell each other our stories?"

Sounds like the playground, doesn't it? We have a lot to learn from the playground.

Rare are the people who make the time to pause and share their stories. Instead, we've trained ourselves to say things like, "Enough about me. How about you?" Or "The long and short of it is . . . ." Most little kids don't do that. They *want* to tell their stories. If that's the case, then often it's because the world hasn't given them the message that their stories aren't good, or right, or interesting, or important, or that they don't have the voice to tell them.

In other words, most young children don't have a wonder wound yet.

Typically the wonder wounding starts in our teens. But tragically, it can happen from the very start of some people's lives due to abuse. Earlier generations were masters at wonder wounding: "You shall speak only when spoken to." "You should be seen but not heard." "Go outside and pick a switch from the willow tree for your beating." "Go to your room without dinner for asking why!"

A child should be heard, be seen, and have the freedom to speak when the spirit moves them! Within respectful boundaries of course. But where there's clear room to share, a child will often take it. Unless . . . they've already been too hurt just for opening their mouth. Those generational messages of invisibility as "appropriate" behavior have trickled down into an adult gag order for so many people in our current culture. So we say "I'm fine" when asked how we are, even when we're bashed and bloodied inside. If this is true for you, I hope you'll receive this very real possibility: You're not fine. And it's not doing you any good to pretend that you are.

In trying to parse this cultural reality, it's helpful to ask: Why do we think that we need to tidy up our truth and clip off our musings? Why is our adult world so prone to this sort of messaging? Why do we succumb to the lie that has us saying, "Sorry, I talked too long." "Sorry, I shouldn't have shared that." "Sorry, I'll be brief." Cutting to the chase. Fast-forwarding. Telling untrue stories. Some of us even speak lies to appease people. To get them off our backs. To try to get them to like us or approve of us. White lies or otherwise.

Why would the adult world advocate for this? I believe it's because we stop listening for the wild why in others. The wonder. And instead, we learn to listen only for answers. The adult world loves its answers, even when they don't amount to much.

This guts me and enrages me because the less we tell our true stories and the central questions and conflicts that make those stories important to us, the more we skip to the point, and the more we lose our essential connection with one another. Skipping to the point is just that—*skipping* the human experience. Spouting talking points. A photo or phrase or hashtag on social media that "says it all." Ten easy steps. Tips and tricks. No wonder we buy into the nonsense that we "don't have a voice."

Tips and tricks just . . . don't . . . stick. Even on a sticky note adhered to your desk. They might stick for a time. But think about it: It's the stories you remember. It's the stories that help you not feel so alone. Not the bullet points. It's the stories that live in you deeply, earnestly, honestly, vibrantly. Fearlessly. And that's where your voice lives. If you think you don't have a unique voice, or a voice at all, ask yourself: *Do I have stories?* Of course you do. And no one can tell them like you can.

If you saw a speaker on a stage five years ago who made a lasting impression on you, it's likely the stories that you remember. Not the bullet points. Maybe you were able to conjure those up for a few weeks or months after the speech, but it's the stories that stick. The Sunday supper they described and how safe they felt in their grandmother's kitchen. I bet you can still hear that grandmother talking while she rolled out her biscuits and made her gravy. I bet you can remember how she smelled and what color apron she wore . . . all because it was delivered to you through story. It activated your imagination. It invited you to connect and empathize.

It's through story that we join in the *collective* human story. When I tell you about something I've experienced, it helps you know you're not alone. And vice versa. Maybe you've been having the same or similar experience as mine, but you've been too ashamed or afraid to admit it. When you hear my story, suddenly you know it's okay to share your own. That's how to heal the world, and yourself in it. Not by skipping to the point. Not by hoarding your story. Not by spouting bullet points.

## NOTICING BOTH SIDES

We must notice where we fall on both sides of the question-asking and story-sharing experience. Notice how others monologue. Notice if you do. Notice if others make room for question asking and story sharing, and notice if you do. It usually feels good to be asked a question about yourself when someone genuinely seems to want to know the answer, so we must cultivate this in our own conversation too. What if asking deep and curious questions of one another (when it's emotionally safe) and sharing personal stories abundantly was the norm? Not the "I'm fine" and the "Long story short...." Seriously. Think about it. How would the world be different? How would the world be better? How would your life be better? How would 4:00 a.m. be better?

My favorite question to ask people is "What do you like to do?" This is not the rote question most of us ask and get asked—the "What do you do?" question (meaning work), but rather the "What makes you *you*?" question. People's eyes go from autopilot, so used to being asked what they do for a living, to suddenly digesting the question and lighting up. "What do I *like* to do? I like to kayak! I like to hike! I like to ride horses! I like to sing! I like to read books! I like to travel!" And there is almost always a story that they then share, and with vigor! Through a simple question, you open connection—and usually this connection sparks sharing, empathy, more curiosity, and, you guessed it, wonder.

Wonder is at the root of a functional society. If you have ever looked at our world and thought, *How can I help?* there's proof of your wonder. It's *wondering* about our world and the people in it that *sustains* our world. It's valuing connection versus division. We simply have to be *connected* to, and invested in, our world, and that starts in our own community. That's the perfect place to practice non-polarity. Practice at the grocery store. On the soccer sidelines. In the office elevator. At the dinner table. Practice, practice, practice.

If we are going to survive as a civilization, we need to stop looking at our differences as bad and instead get *curious* about those differences and even stand in awe of those differences. We need to try to understand that which feels radically separate from us and swallow whole the fact that we are all connected, whether we like it or not. Leading with wonder will get us there because, through the lens of wonder, we look for sameness, not difference. And when we do all that, we know what to say. The words emerge, sometimes without even thinking about them first. We express ourselves freely. We are in our voice. Our curiosity. Our awe. Our empathy. And it's entirely available to you, right where you are. Right now.

## WONDER AS NECESSITY

In our departure from wonder, we start to think about the *results* of what we've created, but we forget what generated those results in the first place. As we get older, we let our wonder go dormant. But I don't believe our wonder ever truly leaves us. We can think it does. But it's still in us. Somewhere.

Meanwhile, wonder killers are all around us. That said, we have to *agree* to let them try to kill our wonder. And when we allow that to happen, we lose the self-expressed voice that has sustained our life and our happiness since the beginning. We lose our ability to tell our true stories and help others know that they're not alone. We lose touch with the collective of humanity.

Why do we let our wonder go dormant? Is it because we forget that wonder is life force and instead tell ourselves that wonder is foolish folly or self-indulgent or a thing for children? If this is what you think about wonder, I'm asking you to revise that personal narrative. It's just not true. And it doesn't serve you at all. Or our world. In fact, it hurts you. And it.

Wonder tends to evoke a spectrum of feelings. Like its arching arm, the rainbow. I've learned to invite all of it, because there are always lessons there, calling us to ask what it would take to keep our wonder intact. Sometimes it's a clear call. Sometimes it's blurry. And sometimes, it's much easier to turn away from wonder altogether and fall in line. I don't want that for any of us.

What if we think of wonder as on par with sleeping, eating, and drinking water? What if wonder is how we survive? And if so, what happens if we try to kill our wonder? Who do we become? And where do we find ourselves later in life? Looking for our "voice"? Feeling "stuck"? Tossing and turning in a torturous night haunt? Going on pilgrimages when all the answers are already inside us? Returning home and not being able to access what we found when we were far away?

In observing self-ascribed "wonderless," "voiceless" people in my own life, I've noticed there's a common thread: people try to find their "voice" by starting with the goal of "success" by society's standards. Achievement. And then, usually very quickly, those people get "stuck." They can't see their way. They compare themselves to others and it takes them down.

Those people are using the wrong measuring stick.

The only measuring stick that matters is the one the child in them cares about.

My wonder has been challenged many times, and sometimes I've even forgotten about it for a spell. But the wonder stories of my life have always been present, trying to bring me back, no matter what is going on. Sometimes I keep them private, for my eyes only, in my journal. But I've learned how to know when it's worth the risk to share those stories with others. This book itself is a risk, because it addresses my own childhood wonder wound: "I talk too much. I ask too many questions. I cry too easily. I laugh too loud. I'm too sensitive. And I feel bad about all of it."

But it's worth the risk if I can help you find your stories, the wonder behind them, the empathy they create in sharing them in the voice that only you can. And to learn how to discern which of your stories are true. And which of your stories never were.

I know my wonder stories, lost and found, by heart. But it's been a while since I've spent time with them, and I miss them, even the hard ones to hold. So I'll go first. I may be a tiny bit braver than you, but if so . . . not by much. At least I can attempt to hold the torch in hopes that you will follow and then take the lead in your life.

You tell me: Is that story I told myself in my fourth-grade journal true? Or was it more likely something told to me that I *took* as truth and then lived by? What I *didn't* write in that fourth-grade journal but what I now read between the lines is this: "Everybody says I talk too much. Everybody says I ask too many questions. Everybody says I cry too easily. Everybody says I laugh too loud. Everybody says I'm too sensitive." Was any of that true? Did *everybody* really say those things? Or were there only a few key people who said those things, and those were the judgments and rejections that I believed? Likely, yes. And these became the beliefs that have haunted me and defined me and hurt me. I think a lot of us have been run by personal myths spun by people and institutions in our lives, whether or not they were ever true at all.

It's tragic to me that those untrue stories are often the ones that we let shape our lives, our personalities, our questions, our wonder. Maybe I talked a lot and asked a lot of questions and had a lot of tears that came easily and had a big, loud voice, but if other people thought I was "too much," that was their point of view. That didn't—and doesn't—have to be my truth. We get to decide what is or isn't our truth. And how we let the actions and words of others affect our hearts and minds.

I invite you to tell your true stories, not the memorized, caustic ones that were perhaps told to you and that you believed. Maybe some of those untrue stories live in you: *I'm not smart. I'm not creative. I don't have anything to say. I should just shut up. I don't matter. I'm not original.*

It's time to shed those untrue stories and give voice to the stories that live inside you in *truth*. Those need to come out. Those need to be honored. Which is why throughout this book, at the end of these chapters, you will find a section called "Your Wild Why . . ." with a writing prompt. I invite you to play with these prompts. This is a safe place for you to practice, and then, if it feels good to you, if it feels worth it to you, you might share your new or refound truth with others, whether verbally or written.

My hope is that you will use the reading and writing in this book to help you rejoin the child that I believe is still in you. The one who woke up in the morning with butterflies in her stomach. Especially if you forgot that she was ever there to begin with. I promise you: she was. Hold her and don't let her go. She has missed you. And she has so much to teach you.

## your wild why . . .

List your top childhood memories of your wonder and where it was safe. A tree you climbed and the branches that held you. A leaf fort in the woods under the skirts of a spruce tree. A pillow fort in a closet. The first time you flew a kite. The first time you held a puppy. A baby. Maybe it was with a trusted family member who loved your wild whys and your long stories. The longer the list, the better. No wonder list can be too long. (Note: For this exercise, it's important to focus only on where your wonder and your wild whys were intact. Not your wonder wound. That will come later.)

Now pick the memory on your list that holds the most positive charge for you in this moment, and write about what it felt like in your body to be in that place of wonder. What your thoughts were like in this state of being. What your senses felt like. What words might have come out of your mouth, and, if there was a trusted person with you, what words might have come out of theirs.

You don't have to write in complete sentences. You can make a list of words and phrases if that works better for you. The point is to find the language to express the feeling of wonder in you from childhood. Even if your childhood wonder was highly challenged, try to capture a feeling, a state of mind, a moment where your wonder was alive and well.

Allow yourself to dwell in this safe and wonder-full place for as long as you can. Let your wonder words flow. Think of it like a treasure hunt. If other voices come in and say that it's foolish or a waste of time, please tell them that they are not invited into your memory or this exercise. It's all yours. This is your baseline wonder place. Hold it close.

Now that you've remembered, find the *core truths* of what you found in your safe wonder place, and write them down. At least three of them. More if you'd like. Freedom? Relief? Joy? Safety? Long-lost butterflies in your ribcage?

Keep those words close as you read this book and as you live your life. They will be your guide as you return to what you already know: your wonder.

# the wonder time line

Now let's take a more in-depth look at your key wonder moments from childhood into early adulthood. In keeping with my promise to go first, I've written my own time line of wonder moments to help you imagine yours. I dug deep to find what inspired my wonder, met it, challenged it, wounded it, and even tried to kill it. And then at the end of the chapter, I'll invite you to share yours for your eyes only.

This can be a daunting exercise because it requires that you take an honest scan of your life, looking for places where your wonder was alive and where it was crushed. This exercise was excruciating for me. At first, I skimmed through, noting a few things here and there, and called it good. But then I got real, and my Wonder Time Line got long, painful, and honest. I wept as I wrote because I couldn't believe how much my wonder has been challenged all my life. I'd always thought that it was sublimely intact against the odds. If this happens to you, you might as well let those tears flow. I have found that tears are not always about sorrow but often about truth that needs to move through us. And wonder is truth's voice.

This exercise also surprised me, and it may surprise you too. I discovered that my key wonder memories didn't land on my hiding places as a child, writing in my journal and feeling safe, wild, and free. Instead, the places my mind and heart wanted to revisit were *out* of hiding. Out in the world where I believed wonder existed in the shiny, dreamy great beyond . . . only to discover that wonder, for the most part, wasn't what the world wanted.

In creating this Wonder Time Line, I also couldn't believe how much my wonder had ignited my dreams, which had ignited my ambition and expectations and a whole imagined future that, for the most part, didn't come true. What my gut has known all along, and what I didn't want to look at, was how consistently my wonder dreams were dashed in the clutches of the world . . . and that *I* let it happen. That's what was most disheartening.

Once I saw my wonder dreams for what they were, however, it was a gift to see how they've played out—in many cases in *spite* of my sometimes self-sabotaging efforts to keep those dreams from coming true. My dreams took surprise turns, sometimes inconvenient and sometimes gutting. I'm glad, then, that I was willing to let wonder take those turns and allow them to create the dreams that have ultimately fed me. In staring it all down, I realized that wonder has been at the helm. That has been the unspoken pact.

For the cynics, this Wonder Time Line exercise isn't a flowery, self-helpy, guru-y concept. I can be an extreme cynic when it comes to branded wonder. No, this is *vital* work. We need to stare it all down, especially if our wonder is in jeopardy and especially if we are avoiding taking our wonder as seriously as we should. Yes, *should*. We need to figure this out. We need to put it in one place and take a long look at it. To see what once flowed in the field of wonder and what interrupted that flow. To see where our untrue stories were born. To see where the true ones lived and still live.

Ease into this exercise. Allow your thoughts and memories to flow honestly. Keep in mind that the wonder moments you land on might be quite different from my own. And to be very clear: This exercise isn't meant to get you stuck in your past. It's meant to awaken you to your past in an intentional way, as an archeologist of your life looking for truth that you can work with in your present. If you resist it, perhaps it's because you hear this in your head: *I don't have wonder. I never did. I don't remember ever having a wild why. I don't even think I have a wonder wound.*

You wouldn't be reading this if you didn't.

## MY WONDER TIME LINE

The perfect place to begin my Wonder Time Line is with an excerpt from Luisa's opening monologue/song in the musical *The Fantasticks*. I played this role in high school, and it changed the course of my life. It was perhaps my most important invitation into my wonder at the height of adolescence, when the wonder-kills are so often fierce, cruel, and relentless, as if the world is taking back everything it promised. My theater teacher knew that I was Luisa in real life, and he invited me to embody her.

Here is her opening monologue. I can still recite it:

This morning a bird woke me up.
It was a lark or a peacock
Or something like that.
Some strange sort of bird that I'd never heard.
And I said "hello"
And it vanished: flew away.
The very minute that I said "hello."
It was mysterious.

So do you know what I did?
I went over to my mirror

And brushed my hair two hundred times without stopping.
And as I was brushing it,
my hair turned mauve.

No, honestly! Mauve!
And then red.
And then sort of a deep blue when the sun hit it.

I'm sixteen years old,
and every day something happens to me.
I don't know what to make of it.
When I get up in the morning to get dressed,
I can tell:
Something's different.
I like to touch my eyelids
Because they're never quite the same.

Oh! Oh! Oh!

I hug myself till my arms turn blue,
Then I close my eyes and I cry and cry
Till the tears come down
And I taste them. Ah!
I love to taste my tears!
I am special!
I am special!

Please, God, please!
Don't—let—me—be—normal!

In many ways, I have never stopped being Luisa.

## WILLIE WONKA

Remember when you saw *Willie Wonka & the Chocolate Factory*? The one where Gene Wilder kicked yoga-ball-sized hard candy and sipped tea out of a candy daffodil cup and then ate the cup? Remember when he looked at those lusty, greedy kids and said, "We are the music makers. We are the dreamers of dreams"?

I saw that movie twelve times the summer it came out. It was 1971. I was five. It was playing in our local movie theater. The old kind with the organ and the balcony and the plaster escutcheons that no longer held chandeliers, and thank goodness because the whole thing felt like it was about to fall down with all of its ancient stories, before the cell phone and personal computer and internet took over and falsely placated our central loneliness. I miss those old movie theaters and the community of them, observing the other moviegoers and their wide eyes and wonderous smiles. Willie Wonka thirty feet tall and floating in the dark! I just couldn't get enough of it. I'd found a new place to hide, and it was in that theater, watching *Willie Wonka* with all those other curious people.

That summer, I was the charge of various adults and teens in my life, as both my parents worked. Two were my grandmothers. One was my ten-years-older sister, someone who always listened to me with supreme love and patience. Another was a cranky nanny who did not. All of them took me to the movies that summer, specifically *Willie Wonka*. It's all I wanted to do.

"Can we see *Willie Wonka* again?" I'd ask my grandmothers.

"Maybe I could teach you how to make my southern lemon chiffon pie." Or: "Why don't I teach you how to crochet?"

"Can we see *Willie Wonka* again?" I'd ask my sister.

"Why don't I teach you tennis? We can practice off the garage door."

"Can we see *Willie Wonka* again?" I'd ask my nanny. She had a lethal scowl, as a rule (never around my parents of course), and it would increase at the edges if I dared to ask if we could go see *Willie Wonka*. I'd brave it anyway, and even she would eventually give in, but not without calling me "spoiled" at least a handful of times. It was worth it. Even if I believed her.

A matinee back then cost one dollar, which wasn't cheap. And I think my parents funded this decadence just to occupy my mind over my mouth. On the outside, we looked like we had money. But compared to the other people in our affluent WASPy suburb, we really didn't. As the cultural vernacular goes: "all blue and no green." So it's quite likely that they acquiesced to Shut. Me. Up. Maybe they wanted me to learn about what happens to children who don't obey the rules. (They drown in chocolate . . . .)

But there was collateral damage: the more I saw that movie, the more I couldn't stop talking about it. The glass elevator! The bad kids! The good kid! The kind grandfather! The burping and the bubbles. The scary tunnel that the adults hid from my eyes but that I peeked at through the spaces between their fingers. It was as if *Willie Wonka* had given me the words that had been living inside me, like pre–Ice Age seeds from bogs and forest floors. Ancient words from ancient little girls. Just like me. Maybe there were little girls from the beginning of time just like me. I had so much to say and so many questions that the grown-up world really didn't want to listen to, never mind answer.

## THE WONDER-KILLS START TO CIRCLE

That summer my family drove the station wagon to Disneyworld. We were all finally together, despite our significant age gaps and all the usual social engagements that had me left alone in the musty rec room, playing with puzzles missing pieces and toys missing parts. Plus, my big sister was about to leave for boarding school. She'd been the "mother" who had held me in her lap for long, listening, lollygagging expanses of time, rubbing my back, stroking my hair, folding me into her safety and love, and I was about to lose her.

For now, I had them all in one place. I was ecstatic. This wasn't the Wisconsin of our summer vacations, where we'd water-ski and eat Friday-night fish fry and sit on the dock chatting with other tan midwesterners, slathered in Sea & Ski, reading magazines. This was the Magic *Kingdom*!

In preparation, I'd made up a song called "The Whole Family" to the tune of "He's Got the Whole World in His Hands," and I cajoled them into a limping sing-along from Chicago to Champaign until I was upstaged by the Harry Belafonte 8-track. But I got them to sing along to that too. "Jamaica Farewell." "Matilda, Matilda." "Jump in the Line." All of it and for hours. The whole family. All was right with my little world, and to *boot*, I was about to see Cinderella's castle!

There it was! The towering, glistening lavender place where dreams were made. I broke free from my parents' hands, and I ran into what was sure to be the most enchanted world of wonder ever! The Magic Kingdom was going to deliver me my first slice of *real live* magic, not just magic hanging on a screen in the movie theater.

*But wait! What's this tunnel? I'm on the other side of the castle! Where are the crystal chandeliers and the marble ballrooms and the gold ceilings and the mice turned horses and the horse turned coachman?*

The whole thing was a Disney-spun ruse! If castles were fake, then maybe princesses were too. But what about dreams? Was Jiminy Cricket full of it? I didn't want to look my parents or sister in the eye. Not because they were liars but because they had held this ruse for me and asked me to believe. I'm sure it was because they knew full well that the world would take it away soon enough and I would have to believe in other things. But that day it felt like a grand injustice.

Now I had questions that weren't as much about winged things but more about that which clipped wings so that questions could never fly.

## SAYING NO

I was suspicious, and the questions erupted, hot and effusive.

*What about Santa? What about the Easter Bunny? What about the Tooth Fairy* while we were at it, even though I always knew she was a ruse. (And a weird one. Money for lost teeth? I didn't get it. Still, I took the quarters and saved them for the movies.) *What about God?* I'd always had a lot of questions about God, most of them having to do with church. Those answers usually landed in: "Because it's the right thing to do."

"But *why*? *Why* do we have to go to church? Can't God be *anywhere*? Isn't God in my *tree house*?"

Apparently that was the wall, and I'd hit it. No more answers. Now my questions were met with words like "disobedient." "Impertinent." One "why" and the gauntlet was thrown. And there were consequences. "Stop asking so many questions. Or else." It didn't stop me. Instead, the "or else" usually elicited a hard "no" from my end. And that was problematic. Enter: the wonder wound.

"No" became a partner in "crime" to "why." No to holding hands across the street. No to wearing scratchy "party pants" over my underwear at church. No to *going* to church. No to eating soft, lukewarm leftover peas and gray liver and onions in soulless Pyrex dishes, heated up the next day, and the next day, and the next day in the oven, without a lid, so that it all came out like jerky. "No! No! No!" Even in the face of "or else." Having my wild whys silenced seemed a much worse crime.

The big ones were the nos to my mother's nos. Those Mother nos resulted in a lot of soap and Tabasco in my mouth to wash and burn the no away. Sometimes a leather dog collar, called "the strap," on a bare bottom. Sometimes a wire wig brush.

It didn't work. I'd suffer the punishment and flee to my hiding places and stay there until the grown-ups went from mad to worried. I'd hide until I heard that worry mount to a come-in-for-dinner white flag. I'd won.

So it was back to the movie theater with the various grown-ups whose job it was to keep an eye on me. I was lucky in that way. I could have been locked in a closet under the stairway like the orphaned children in the books I read. Instead, I was sent to *Willy Wonka*. It was a beyond-magical asylum. Wonka's factory was a wonderland I could trust, even if Disney was a lie. And even if the factory was in my own mind. So what? My mind was the safest, most sacred ground I knew.

My father seemed to love that sacred ground. I'd lie there at bedtime and go on and on about *Willie Wonka*, and he'd listen and smile, smelling like newspaper and grass clippings, in full, astonished joy that his little girl had so much wonder. He didn't have the words, but I knew he felt it in his heart. When I'd risk a why, he'd just smile and say, "Tell me more." That worked for me. My whys always longed for listening, and his ears were wide open, no matter how long bedtime took, even if we got into trouble for it.

"And then there was this mean, spoiled, rich girl in a red dress, and she wanted a goose, a goose who laid golden eggs, and I think her daddy shouldn't have given it to her. Because it killed her. And I know you would never give me a goose that was bad for me. Even if I wanted it. And then there was this boy who was good and kind and he had this good and kind grandfather who loved him and wanted him to have his dreams come true even if the boy wasn't so sure . . . and . . . also, am I spoiled? I don't want to be spoiled."

My father would finally put his warm, thick, dry hand on my forehead and say, "Time to fold into the arms of Morpheus, my little Laura Munson. And no. You are not spoiled. You are blessed." And he'd sing "Bye, Baby Bunting," say the "Now

I lay me" prayer, and give me ten kisses on my forehead for good dreams. It was the other safest ground I knew.

My father told me throughout my life how I talked and talked about that movie. How I had stars in my eyes like Charlie. That I would have *been* the Charlie character in *Willie Wonka*. That I would never have been the other nasty children. That I was a *good* girl. *I* was a good girl. I *was* a good girl.

I believed him. Well, mostly.

We truly are blessed if we have at least one person who believes in our goodness. Who honors the wonder that gives it wings. Who feeds our wonder for exactly this winged reason. My father saw that my wonder was what made me, well, *me*. And he championed it against the soapy, spicy, scowling odds, especially with the word "no" being so dangerous to my wild whys.

My father was born in 1918, was raised during the Depression, and served in World War II. I'm not sure how much wonder he had left by the time I came onto the scene in his fifties, but there was a hidden pact between us: in his bedtime stories, and in listening (mostly) to mine, I gave him something that was new, or lost, to him. "Tell me about the olden days," I'd beg, knowing somehow that he needed to talk too.

"Well . . . all right," he'd say. "But it's past your bedtime. We're going to get into trouble." It seemed like past-my-bedtime was one of the few places wherein he took that risk.

He had a handful of stories from his childhood that he loved to share, and they always brought tears to his eyes: tying flies with his father, chasing the ice truck and licking the sawdust off the big cubes, shooting marbles with his buddy Art, playing telephone with tin cans and a string stretched from his attic to his buddy Dick's across the street, building rock forts in a vacant lot where they'd puff on a corncob pipe, going to the movies with his buddy Dot, and getting a chocolate soda afterward, all for a dime.

But the rest of it was bleak, and I knew not to ask. Maybe

my wonder was a free zone for him too—a time when he could dream about the good things from his past that didn't have to do with war, or his disabled brother, or his father working long shifts at the corn syrup factory, or his mother waiting in line for bread instead of taking the opera stages of her dreams. His generation had been told not to bother with dreams. Keep quiet. Work hard. Never complain. Don't make waves. I suspect that the subject of wonder never came up at all.

When I talked and questioned, my father's eyes truly twinkled. It showed me that I was loved and valued. It vouchsafed a confidence and a quest-full-ness in me that I've never completely abandoned. Like he was making a silent and verboten promise to me in those magical bedtime moments: *I will carry your confidence in the field of wonder as long as I possibly can, because as we all well know . . . the world won't carry it for us.*

That's when my mother started putting me to bed. I must have gotten him into trouble with my endless requests of "Just one more story. *Pleeeeeeease?*"

Looking back from an adult's perspective, I can see why my wonder was so intriguing to him. He was sensitive and stoic, for the most part out of necessity. His life was a matriarchal curation where rules reined. His mother had been forced out of her dreams and into her rules—stringent rules that called for thin margins that you didn't test. My mother's margins were the same. I was heartbroken that the twinkle in his eyes lost out to rules in the end. I was *not* going to let that happen to me.

My mother's bedtimes were expeditious. One short book. Maybe a short memory from her childhood if I asked just right. Always one prayer and one lullaby. Ten kisses on the forehead. "Sweet dreams. God bless." No questions. No discussion. Door left ajar.

"Please leave the hall light on. I'm scared," I'd tell her. I'd never been scared of the dark before, but now I was scared every single night without my father's end-of-the-day calming countenance. I wished I could ask her, "Can't you tell me about the olden days? Just one story?"

But her rules were not to be broken. Bedtime was bedtime. Nonnegotiable. I was left with my own imagination. Good. And bad. I had, and still have, a very active imagination. Especially at bedtime. And at 4:00 a.m.

My bedtime was at seven thirty until sixth grade. I was not to leave my room, no matter what. No place to run. No place to hide. My hiding had to be in my mind. I had to answer my questions. And it wasn't just *Willie Wonka* that I wanted to talk about. It was the whole wide world and beyond!

As those years moved along, I got a lot of "*Shhhhh!*" "Stop *talking!*" And when my siblings were home from boarding school, even "*Shut up!*" Maybe I wasn't such a good girl after all. Or maybe it was my questions that were somehow wrong. Or bad. I started to feel like I was bad.

And then a report card came to prove it: "Laura excels in all of her classes but is sometimes disruptive by asking too many questions. It would behoove her to keep her hand down and do more conscientious listening. Otherwise, she is a delight." Reading, Writing, and Social Science: A+. Math and Athletics: NI. Classroom Behavior: NI.

Needs improvement.

Even my father didn't defend me.

I was so confused. All the grown-ups had been so *nice* when I was little. They'd prodded and prompted me to sing and play the piano and tell stories. They'd done so much *listening*, and *smiling*, and saying that I was so "cute." Until they didn't. Now I wasn't supposed to "draw attention" to myself. Now I was supposed to have "social graces." There were new rules, and I was supposed to understand them. What I understood was this: the rules were anti-wonder . . . even though back then I didn't have the words.

It hurt to the bone.

## A SAFE PLACE FOR MY WORDS

My maternal grandmother, the polar opposite of my paternal grandmother, was full of flourish. She'd been a flapper in the Roaring Twenties who drank champagne out of her dancing slippers. We called her Gogo. Gogo would regularly take me aside, and with the lily of the valley scent of Diorissimo wafting from her every pore and her Arkansas accent (even though she'd lived in the North for four decades), she'd say, "We all know that *you* are going to be the *staaah* of the family."

I sensed dangerous ground. Yet interesting and maybe sad. Because if they all thought I was going to be the star of the family (and what exactly did that even mean?), why didn't anyone want to hear what I had to say? Didn't stars take *stages*? Didn't people pay *money* to listen to stars *talk*? That sounded like the sort of arrangement they'd approve of. Good, hardworking, midwestern sorts. Maybe they wanted me on a stage. Just not at the dinner table. Or in our family recreation room during the news. Or *The Lawrence Welk Show*. Or *The NBC Mystery Movie*. Or Disney. Or the moon walk. (I deserved that one. But I mean . . . so many *questions*!)

I asked my paternal grandmother Mimi. She'd taken me to see *Willie Wonka* plenty of times. She'd wanted to be on stages. Maybe she had an answer. But Mimi didn't want to talk about her failed opera days. Something about a bad professor. Quick subject change to the afghan she was crocheting and not *La bohème*.

The message: Stages are better left alone. If you follow your dreams, be sure they're practical ones. She lived out her life in a small, hot apartment, alone, watching Billy Graham and reading *Reader's Digest* with a magnifying glass, humming to herself. "Practical" looked miserable. But apparently being a star was too.

My confusion grew. I knew that parental discussion on this topic was off the table. If they really thought that I was going to be the "*staaah* of the family," it sure didn't seem like it. It seemed like they were more concerned with keeping my elbows off the table and my mouth shut, unless I was reading the Nicene Creed.

Was I special? Or normal? Which one was it? The adult world made no sense at all. This was one of those things I would have to figure out on my own.

I didn't want to be practical. I knew that much. And it itched all over. How could I keep from scratching? Even if it got me into trouble? I was getting tall. Smart. Unpunishable by their old measures. Only where to hide now? The thin branches were getting too thin even for me.

I took to my bedroom and listened to the *Free to Be . . . You and Me* album from beginning to end and back again. It was 1975 and I was nine. Every kid I knew was listening to that album in their bedrooms. We couldn't get enough of it. Boys could have dolls and cry. Girls didn't have to boost men's egos or do housework alone. Babies had a secret language and wondered why adults were so confusing. Positive illumination! The message was all about expressing yourself. Being exactly who you were. Delighting in it! We even sang some of those songs in school, so they must have been adult approved! Maybe this was the way to my parents! I mean, they'd given me the album for my birthday. Maybe they were finally saying that it was okay to be in my wonder!

So one night I took a risk. I cued it up on their enshrined Magnavox console in the adults-only living room and blared the theme song, "Free to Be . . . You and Me." Maybe my parents and I would have a sing-along, just like back when we were a whole family! Maybe we'd even dance like we did to Lawrence Welk!

After their initial confusion about why I was in the living room, they offered blank stares. "Where did you get that *record*?" they said in unison.

It all became clear: they'd never even listened to it! They wouldn't have given it to me if they had. The whole album was about saying no to the things they stood for and saying yes to the things they didn't. I quickly put it back in my bedroom before they could take it away.

I was striking out with the adults. I needed new refuge.

Then it occurred to me: I'd seen my big sister write in a journal. She looked so captivated by it. So soothed. Was that her grown-up way of hiding? Did she need to hide too? I missed her so deeply, devastatingly—our relationship now confined to conversations from her boarding school pay phone and our kitchen wall phone. Neither place good for sharing heart language. Maybe a journal was the way. Maybe I could even be *with* her somehow if I wrote in a journal too. Maybe it would be a secret language that only she and I spoke. None of the other grown-ups wrote in journals.

Plus, I was curious. What was a blank page all about? Was it a safe place for all the wild whys? What did she write in that pretty book? Were those pages *listening* to her? What were *written* words all about? Did written words want you to be the star of the family in one breath but tell you that you had to follow the rules and be appropriate and have social graces in the next? Or did those pages not care? Maybe I'd find the wild why world of *Willie Wonka* in a blank page but for my eyes only. That seemed like a safe new hiding place. Or maybe those blank pages were just like a good friend playing on a swing set, chatting the day away. I had a few of those good friends in real life. But sometimes friends could hurt. The truth was that no one was as safe as my father and sister had been. But I wasn't little anymore. Maybe a journal could take their place.

So in fourth grade, I picked out my first journal at the local and beloved stationery store. It was pink and patent leather, and it said "Private" on the front. With a lock. And I had the key. It was sexy. So sexy. The sexiest, most wonder-full thing I knew. And it was all mine. My journal became my best friend. Never mind my Snoopy. (I still have my Snoopy. Don't tell anyone.) At least those pages could be my witness. I suspected that I would be free of rules there.

## SLEEPOVERS AND SLUMBER PARTIES

Sleepovers began to take up the bulk of my weekends. I went on a lot of them. I was always the last one talking, my friend lightly snoring in the dark. That hurt too. But it didn't stop me. And they didn't seem to mind. And they didn't tell me to "*Shhhhh!*" They even seemed to *like* my talking. Maybe it was because I wanted to talk about things that other kids didn't want to talk about. Like God. And the stuff parents did. And older siblings. They had stories, too, but it turned out that nobody had asked them to tell them. So when I asked them questions, they talked too. And I listened. Turned out that I loved listening. Report card be darned!

It occurred to me: Maybe I hadn't given my friends, or even my elders, the chance to tell their stories. Maybe I really *did* talk too much. So I started asking my friends a lot of questions and gave them a lot of chances to answer, and they took them.

Sleepovers turned to slumber parties—the perfect place to try out my new method, now on multiple friends at a time. It took courage. But those parties were a natural trajectory, especially with my family life being so spare. At slumber parties, there were a lot of chances to ask and listen and be asked and answer. And my life was really happy for a few years in the realm of friendship and self-expression.

And then . . . .

Directly from my journal: "How could my best friends put a garden hose in my ear while I was still asleep and turn it on? I went outside because they were snoring. I wanted to see the sunrise. I've never seen the sunrise. I woke up to this horrible cold feeling in my ear. They were all standing over me, pointing at me and laughing. I thought they loved me."

Had I talked too much? Asked too many questions? Now with my *friends* and not just with my family and at school?

I ran home that morning, the better part of a mile on a busy suburban Chicago road, in my wet nightgown, barefoot, holding my Snoopy, my wet sleeping bag over my shoulder, bawling. Apparently a girl who asked wonder-full questions about God, parents, older siblings, and life and death, and who wanted to listen to other girls talk about those things, deserved to be deaf, or at least to have her ears washed out with ice-cold hose water.

That day, I hid in the high, thin branches of my tree house until my mother insisted that I come down. My white flag this time. I told her I felt sick. She put me to bed without any questions. I *wanted* her to ask questions. Instead, I wrote in my journal all day. I told no one except my journal about the incident. That seemed like the only safe place for my words.

**THE STAR OF THE FAMILY**

Now I was ten and my family was on the East Coast visiting my siblings at boarding school, and we went to see *Annie* on Broadway. I'd memorized every word of every song while lying on my bedroom rug between my canopy beds, listening to the record until it scratched and skipped, mimicking the actress, Andrea McArdle, with everything I had. Annie was a dreamer. She believed in *tomorrow*. In infinite possibility—that she was special enough to have all her dreams come true. And she wasn't even a real person. She was a cartoon character being portrayed by an actress. On a stage. It seemed that questions could turn into dreams if you let them.

I sat in that audience, with my mouth slack and my heart buzzing, envying Annie. People *wanted* her to take that stage and dream on it. With all my heart, I wanted a safe place to dream like that, outside of my journal.

Then and there, with the alto vibrato winging Annie's dreams, I decided that if Annie could voice her dreams, I could too. I was going to *be* Annie on Broadway one day. Somehow. That was what I was going to do with the rest of my life. I wanted to be the deliverer of some supreme message, and I wondered what it would take. I was living in a comfortable home with stable parents, not in an orphanage with a drunk, abusive lady running the show. The stakes were stacked in my favor. I wondered: Could I be good enough to be the messenger that Andrea McCardle was?

I told my pink patent-leather journal: "As God as my witness . . . as GOD as my witness . . . I will become an actress!"

I'd watched a lot of *Gone with the Wind* with Gogo.

Then sixth grade hit. And all those hormones. Nice girls became mean girls, and the adult world lost its luster. It all broke my heart and began to silence me. Nobody wanted to talk about the things I wanted to talk about anymore. Or listen. Not the adults. Not the siblings. Not the friends. The teachers seemed more interested in smoking in the teacher's lounge than teaching. Plus, they never called on me anymore, no matter how long I kept my hand raised, propping it up with my other hand at the elbow until my fingers tingled. "Let's give someone else a chance to talk, Laura," they would tell me. Wondering hurt.

Now I put myself to bed, and not much past seven thirty. I needed a break from the world in much the same way that the world had needed a break from me. I had my journal, and I liked it that way. At least that's what I told myself.

### RIGHTEOUS INDIGNATION

My journal heard it all: "How could _____ be so mean? How could _____ have told my secret to the whole school? She promised! She swore on the Holy Bible!" Was there simply no safe place for self-expression? Seemed to me that Broadway held the key.

Now I begged for the *A Chorus Line* album. I'd heard it at a friend's house. Her mother was a singer and a dancer and something called a "lesbian." Her house was filled with lots of macramé and bell-bottoms and smoke that smelled like skunks and incense that smelled like garden dirt. I liked being in their house. My parents didn't listen to music unless it was at one of their dinner parties when they all listened to Lester Lanin, the society band leader, danced in the living room, and wore little beanies they got at debut parties and weddings. That smoke smelled like rancid cantaloupe, mothballs, and mink coats. My house felt wonderless in comparison to a house that freely listened to a song about tits and ass.

"Isn't *A Chorus Line* a bit old for you?" my mother asked, like she was trying to make up for the *Free to Be . . . You and Me* debacle in the way of morality.

"No!"

Apparently *that* no was okay, or maybe I'd just gotten better at my nos because I got the album for Christmas that year.

Night after night, I lay on my bedroom rug and listened to *A Chorus Line*. I felt all of the *something* that the actress who sang "Nothing" didn't. I also felt her crippling passion. Her crippling longing. I felt it in the bottom of my shoes—the soles of the tortured artists in that chorus line. I wasn't even in high school yet. Their words, "God, I hope I get it. / I hope I get it," rang in my head as I tried out for every play I could—at school, community theater, summer camp in Wisconsin. The sorts of plays where they had to take you. Put you in the back. Get you excited to play a tree or a flying monkey. I knew that dancing was out. I was a knock-kneed, pigeon-toed, athletic failure with scoliosis and a heart murmur. So that meant I had to up the ante on my singing.

I sang in every choir that would have me, even the adult church choir, and now I didn't have to wear scratchy party pants over my underwear. The idea of being the star of the family had engraved itself in my being but had escaped my mind altogether.

Now it was just a *drive* I had. A ferocious drive. I *wanted* those stages. I wanted them with everything I had. I didn't stop to wonder why. Dreaming had taken my wonder and run amok.

I auditioned and auditioned. I played a lot of trees and flying monkeys. But along the way I started getting leads. Character roles. Apparently I was funny and my alto was passable. The problem was that I wanted to play the ingenue. The innocent one who sang the sweet, wonder-full songs. The one who the audience rooted for. Not the bad, berating antihero. But I just didn't have the voice. I knew I had the innocence. But wonder didn't get you those roles. Being a skilled soprano did. Not a pitchy alto. I tried for those roles anyway. Dorothy! Maria von Trapp! Marian the librarian! Now I heard no from other elders. It hurt like a slumber party.

Maybe being a Broadway actress wasn't quite it. Maybe I needed a different dream. I didn't know what it should or could be. The coulds sounded more interesting than the shoulds. But who to ask for help? The adults, even my sister, were engaged in higher-stakes problems. My journal was limited in its guidance—more a hefty vessel for my growing woe.

What I did know was this: there was something in me that needed to come out in the way of self-expression, and it needed to come out big and bold and indelible. Not in having my training bra snapped in the school hallways for wearing clothes like our friend's lesbian mother: tapestry skirts, Chinese shoes, peasant blouses from India, and a middle part. And not in being told, "*Shhhhh,*" at the dinner table. Sixth graders didn't get their mouths washed out with soap or Tabasco. The punishments had morphed into psychological ones. And they used variations of "should" as their threat, usually having something to do with popularity, which apparently *was* a contest. And I was supposed to do my best to win it. Couldn't I play sports like the other girls instead of act in plays? Couldn't I wear a prettier dress to school? Couldn't I wear pink? Like the other girls?

That's when orange became my color.

But no matter how much orange I wore, I had the feeling in my gut that I was wrong for having my dreams, which I was fast learning to keep mum. The adult world had always liked to ask, "What do you want to be when you grow up?" I'd always taken a stab at it: "A painter!" "A pianist!" They'd always smiled and politely clapped their hands. *Hooray for your dreams!* But now that my answer was "An actress!" they didn't look so enthused. I switched to "I don't know." Much safer.

I can see it all clearly now. It wasn't really fame that I wanted. It was a ferocious longing to express myself and build that bridge to an audience that would listen lovingly and even accept me. Even *applaud* my way of expressing myself. That's what I was truly after. Acceptance. Even though at the time I would have fought the idea as fallacy. Being told that you are special is not necessarily a gift. Sometimes it can be a plague. I'm sad that I had a fight in me for battles that weren't worth my wonder. I'm sad that I was so wonder wounded that I didn't know how to applaud for myself. Yet.

I was twelve. The year the Inner Critic, the ultimate wonder-kill, takes court and attempts to blow wonder into smithereens. More and more, dreaming started to feel dangerous.

If singing and acting weren't my calling, what *was*? I'd write and write about it in my journal with such torture and craving: "Please please please . . . tell me what I'm going to be! I want to be something special! Not just like everybody else. I don't want to play tennis and field hockey like the other girls." What was this burning, churning feeling so deep inside me?

I had to ask someone. So I went to the adults, carefully, using polite and laundered questions like "What do *you* think I should be when I grow up?" I mean, their language, right? "Should" and all. Still . . . no one seemed to have answers that had anything to do with me. An accountant? Me? Who "needs improvement" in Math?

The adults seemed peeved that I was asking in the first place. What was wrong with going to college, getting a decent job, getting married, having kids, volunteering, and growing old with grandchildren and a good rocking chair? This included unspoken details like being a debutante and joining private city and country clubs. The *right* private clubs. For which I was born. "Like everybody else" in my peer group. But I didn't feel like *everybody else*. Did everybody else feel like *everybody else*?

I risked it and asked my friends. I had friends. Good ones. It's just that they hadn't proved necessarily safe after the slumber party attack and a few other instances that had to do with boys. I asked anyway. Maybe they'd go back to being the way they were when they had liked to ask and answer questions, swinging alongside each other for hours or building leaf forts in the woods. Questions like "Who made God?" and "Why do all the parents seem so unhappy at the end of the day?" and "Why are there starving people in Africa, and why should I feel guilty that I don't want to eat my liver and onions?" and "What do you want to play?" and "What do you want to do?" and "Who do you want to be when you grow up?" Those kids had such great things to talk about! But the sixth-grade version of themselves? Not so much.

In fact, they were starting to *agree* with the adults, like they were joining a club I didn't want to be in. It was crushing. Where was everyone's wonder going?

"You want to come over after school and listen to *A Chorus Line*?" I'd ask.

Blank stares. Sneers even. (If you were that twelve-year-old listening to *A Chorus Line* alone in your room and knowing that world was so far away from the age that bound you, feeling like the only kid in the world singing "Nothing," I wish we could have found each other and started our *own* club.)

Hail to the gods for the PBS TV show *Zoom!* Now *those* kids . . . I got. Only I wasn't lucky enough to live in the 02134 zip code. I lived in the "you need to learn how to have a better tennis serve" zip code. And the "stop wearing those hippie skirts and put on your Lilly Pulitzer pink and green" zip code. The "appropriate," "social graces" zip code. This was all compounded by the fact that when I wanted to, I fit in. I fit in well. That is, on the outside. But my insides didn't want to fit in. At all. And that was the worst no I could offer and the worst trouble I could possibly get into.

So I wrote and wrote about it. Just what was the liability of growing up? Did you have to lose that burning, churning feeling deep inside you? Did you have to lose your questions? The questions that had hatched your big dreams? Did you have to climb down from the high, thin branches and start walking on "normal" ground? No way. But a twelve-year-old going off on the wonders of *Willie Wonka & the Chocolate Factory* lacked appeal in the get-a-job sort of way. And what happened to *Free to Be . . . You and Me*? What about the song we'd all sung together about growing up and not having to change? At all?

Nope. Time to start thinking about sensible things. Like boarding school only three years away. There was a course, and all my peers were on it, and it required a specific trajectory that we were fully aware of. From an East Coast boarding school, we'd be accepted into a good college. And from a good college, we'd land a good job and, better yet, a *husband* with a good job, if we were girls. And we'd live in a city. Have kids. Move to the suburbs. Throw perfect parties. Do volunteer work. Perfect our tennis serve. Send our offspring off on the exact same trajectory. (Even in the late 1970s. Even with women's lib. Even with *Free to Be . . . You and Me*.)

Everything and everyone in my life started to aim that arrow, and the target was supposed to be bull's-eye exact. We'd follow in the steps of our parents and gratefully so. They'd worked hard to pave the way. Rinse, repeat. No questions asked. Why? Respect. And respect was not a thing to challenge. Even I knew that.

I didn't even need to ask anymore. Now I could hear their responses in my head without even uttering a why. Words like "ungrateful." "Rude." "Privileged." It had been hammered into us that we were the lucky few who had what other people wanted. Which meant that there would be no more asking. No more answering. And no more hiding. Even if you didn't want what you were supposed to want.

If I couldn't ask the adults, then I could at least study them. Did all that privilege make them happy? It looked more like a curse. Like my grandmother's "practical." There really wasn't a lot of twinkle in their eyes when they went off to work in the morning and came home in the evening. At the dinner table, my father talked about work and volunteer work. My mother talked about work and volunteer work. They both talked about what parties they were going to that weekend and what the hosts and hostesses did for work and volunteer work.

Was this where we were all headed? Was this what "supposed to" looked like when we grew up? Was this going to happen to my friends too? Was this going to happen to *me*? And, moreover, were we ever going to *play* again?

### IN SHORT, LIFE STARTED TO SUCK

The kids didn't want to play anymore—not the way we used to. Now they wanted to be divided into opposing teams and fight each other with balls of all shapes and sizes. I wanted to make up plays and pillage our mothers' closets for costumes and perform them in the woods. *No. No. No.* And there was this thing called "booze" that all the older siblings had taken a liking to, so we tried it too. When people drank it, they suddenly liked to play again. Was that why the adult world liked booze so much? Was that why the living room was adults-only? Was that living?

My parents called me "Pitiful Pearl," which was a doll who used her sad story to avoid doing what she was supposed to be doing. No one could understand why I was so sad. Why I didn't want to go to school. Why I didn't want to show off my budding breasts and long legs and wear party dresses to dancing school or the country club. Why I didn't want to play tennis and paddle tennis and squash like the other girls. Why my nose was in a book or my journal. And as I grew taller and filled out and had boys chasing me, no one could understand why I dressed in oversized T-shirts and didn't wear makeup like the everybody elses. Didn't I understand how lucky I was to live the life of an affluent suburban girl? Sure, we didn't have the money most of the other families did, but we had the pedigree. Pedigree was the ultimate currency where I came from. And it was not for sale. How could I possibly not want to deal in that currency?

Enter: shame. Shame that I didn't want to live the life of a *Mayflower*-spawned suburban girl. But I had no other role models—nobody telling me I could be anything I wanted. Gogo had seemed to change her tune because, apparently, sullen teens didn't become stars of the family. Mimi had died from what looked like practicality. My father seemed stressed out about money. My mother was busy. My sister was now at college and had her own life to live. Life was becoming a plot to steal vodka from our parents' liquor cabinets and cigarettes from our babysitters' purses. And the actors in *A Chorus Line* weren't exactly a helpful set of mentors. I suspected they did those shady things called "drugs." At that place called Studio 54. In New York City. Where, frankly, I wanted to be. Chicago was, after all, the second city . . . .

Record scratch. I was *supposed* to be the girl on the Christmas card, clad in pink and green, getting rapturously

ready for her first year at a New England prep school. There
didn't seem to be any other viable choices. So I kept my head
down. Maybe they'd leave me alone. I wasn't asking any questions anymore. A lot about those years is pretty much blank
in my mind. Makes sense.

Except for perhaps one of the greatest gifts my mother
ever gave me. She knew I was deeply unhappy, and she knew
she didn't have the ability to change that for me. So she pooled
her resources from her interior design jobs and sent me to a
backpacking camp in Colorado for the summer. Other wayward kids from our town had gone there. I think she was
desperate to give my wonder to a place that understood it. Or
maybe she was just desperate to get rid of me for a few months.

I could write a whole book about my experiences that
summer, sleeping in a covered wagon on a thin pad with a
small drawerful of clothing and 14,000-foot mountains to
climb. I was completely out of my comfort zone but as close
to my wonder zone as I'd ever been. At the end of the summer
of camping by mountain lakes, glissading down snowfields,
singing John Denver by campfire light with girls so much like
me in their laughing and crying and questioning and wondering, writing our names in hiker's logs at the top of hard-won
peaks, each camper had a requisite twenty-four-hour solo,
wherein we were dropped off on a mountainside. Alone. We
got a canteen of water, a tarp, some twine, a sleeping bag, a
bag of granola, a whistle, a pad of paper, and a pen. We didn't
know where the other campers were or where the counselors
were either. As far as we knew, we were alone in the Rocky
Mountains. The rain was coming in, and there was lightning
and thunder in the distance. I filled every page. This was the
opposite of hiding.

I wrote: "Solo Journal, Rocky Mountain National Park,
1979. As I sit here alone, I wonder at the trees, the flowers,
the birds, even the slightest hum of a bee. I marvel at the

bounteous limbs of the aspen tree which gives me shelter from the thunder and rain. I gaze at the Rockies standing brave and strong over the hills. I am alone out here, away from the noise of home and all the things that make me so sad. I am not sad here, nor am I scared. I sit here among the bugs and flowers and rain and I feel joyful. Rocky Mountain high heaven!"

Such lofty thoughts and loftier language. I love that I used the word *wonder* in my first sentence. I doubt anyone had ever really brought that word, or state of being, to my attention before that wonder-full camp. I spent eight weeks being in nothing *but* wonder, especially on that solo. And I remember being scared to return home, where I would surely find my sadness waiting for me. I cried uncontrollably as the bus drove us to the Denver airport, on the airplane all the way to Chicago, and all the way home in the station wagon. My parents were concerned. This wasn't what they'd planned. I wouldn't talk to them about it. They wanted to know if I'd improved my tennis serve at camp. They didn't get it. They'd likely researched that camp as much as they'd researched *Free to Be . . . You and Me.*

I told my sister about my feelings, and so that year for my birthday she sent me the exact gift I didn't know I needed: a new journal, this time a big one in brown leather with gold borders and blank pages. I wrote. And I wrote. Life had different mountains for me to climb. And I wasn't going to escape them. I just wasn't. I was just too sad.

Thanks to a few good teachers who seemed to see something in me that would one day soar, I got switched into higher-level English classes with higher-achieving kids, and the writing and speaking awards started to come. Still, I didn't feel like I deserved them. It was a fluke. They assured me that it wasn't. I had talent. But was that the talent I was *supposed* to have?

Those teachers saw me in a way that I couldn't, for all my sadness. So I figured I'd do it for them, especially my

Spanish teacher, who told me that when I went to college, in no uncertain terms, I needed to spend a year abroad. It seemed so exotic and unattainable. I promised her that I'd put that in my future arsenal, but for now I just had to walk the line for all the grown-ups who were in charge of my life . . . until I could leave. I just needed to steer clear of verbal question-asking for the most part, follow the rules, and hide my feelings in my journal. Maybe I'd have to be the goddamn debutante I was raised to be. Maybe it would be the acting role of my life. I'd be good at it. Too good. Smile. Shake hands. Ask the right questions. Stay off the wrong topics. Practice my boarding school admissions-ready handshake. What if, when it all came down to it, I didn't have the courage to fly?

Still, in my journal, I'd hold hope: maybe one day, when I was older, I could take my wonder and fly far away, where it was safe. Maybe even to the Rocky Mountains. I'd take the memory of my Free Child, still perched high in those thin branches of my tree house, and finally fly. Like Charlie blasting through the ceiling in his glass elevator, winging through the sky of possibility. Like life would become a perpetual twenty-four-hour solo.

**BOARDING SCHOOL**

Prep school in Connecticut. By the time it arrived, I couldn't wait. I still had no idea who I was going to be or what I was going to dream. No one knew my family in the far regions of Connecticut, and no one wanted me to be the star of it. Now was my chance to fly—whatever that meant. I'd soon find out. Maybe I'd find that New England prep schools, the stepping-off places for the Ivy Leagues, were the places where all the wondering was happening. New adults. New friends. New questions. Maybe I would finally be on that playing field where all the big questions were allowed to be asked. The place where dreams were made. The hallowed halls of the liberal arts!

What I learned immediately was that success was built on a straight-A report card (no NIs), chasing balls around on fields, and something called "extracurricular activities" if you wanted to get into a good college. Getting into a good college was the end goal. I was allergic to balls. I was even more allergic to numbers and thus horrible at math and the math section of the SATs. A flunker at multiple-choice aptitude tests. Wasn't everything a story? Wasn't everything subjective? Couldn't the liberal arts agree with me? Maybe they weren't so liberal after all.

At first blush, it seemed that my boarding school wasn't that much different from home. Same currency. Same clothes. Same sorts of faces. Different names. I had three years to put this extolled machine of higher education to work, but I needed to find *my* dream, not that of my parents. There was a lot of hope at that school. Teachers who seemed to get me. Friends too. It was much better than being back in the clutches of my parents. And since they were paying for it, I knew that it was my duty to do my best, at least in the way that they wanted. Respectfully. Maybe the burning, churning feeling would come back in this new, exotic, East Coast place.

So when I was invited to go to New York City with a new friend and her parents to see a musical called *Pippin*, I was ecstatic. But I was also still a bit sullen, arms crossed in front of me, the Broadway dream in the rearview mirror. Once bitten, twice shy being what it is.

Lights down. Curtain up. These words slayed me: "Why do I feel I don't fit in anywhere I go?"

I leaned forward. Uncrossed my arms and legs.

And this happened . . . .

So many men seem destined
To settle for something small
But I won't rest until I know I'll have it all
So don't ask where I'm going
Just listen when I'm gone
And far away you'll hear me singing
Softly to the dawn:

Rivers belong where they can ramble
Eagles belong where they can fly
I've got to be where my spirit can run free
Got to find my corner of the sky.

There it was! My wild why! I had to find my corner of the sky! Permission at last! Even if it brought shame on the family name. Even if it made my life very difficult.

It didn't matter. I'd suffer the consequences. In that moment, I knew: I needed to leave the currency of my origin in order for my spirit to run free. I'd have to leave who I had been groomed to be altogether. Just like Pippin. And frankly: fuck 'em all for trying. I was pissed. Being pissed was new. It was easier than just plain heartbroken. Being pissed was a new way to hide. And I was going to stay pissed until I figured my way out of all of it. The ruses. The pressure. The acting on the outside to meet everyone's expectations. The betrayal of my utmost self in the name of being so "lucky." I just wanted to be *me*!

But where, oh where, was my corner of the sky?

The second the movie *Fame* came out, I dragged my new friends to see it in the local movie theater. It didn't help at all. It *warned* against big dreams. I didn't know what mine were, and already I was daunted by them. On the first day, the teacher tells her students, "You got big dreams. You want fame. Well, fame costs. And right here is where you start paying in sweat."

I supposed that I could pay in sweat if only I knew what I wanted to pay *for*.

### FLASHDANCE

For the next two years, I fastened myself to mad on the inside and all smiles and due diligence on the outside. More acting. It wasn't worth being an outward rebel yet. I had a lot to figure out. And it was true: I was lucky. I had the handshake. The straight teeth. The clothes. And frankly, the pearls. I was asked to be the head of the tour guide club. Poster child. And it wasn't without gratitude. There was so much to love about my school. I was happy to show prospective students and their parents around campus. Maybe they would find their corner of the sky here. I wondered what tour guide would show me mine.

Fast-forward to junior year—1983. The year when college admission was paramount to all other things.

I went to see *Flashdance* with some friends. As usual I inwardly prepared to hate it because all the wonderless everybody elses loved it. Instead, sitting in that Connecticut movie theater, with my feet on the chair in front of me and my elbows on my knees, tears streaming down my cheeks, I *felt* it again. That unstoppable, starved craving to dream big had manna that I could swallow whole if I just had the courage. That angsty dancer in leg warmers was me, just like Pippin! I would live in a loft like that and do whatever it took, weld even, to go after my dream. I just wasn't sure yet what dream I should dream, and I knew that I had better figure it out fast.

When these words came, they slayed me even more than Pippin's corner of the sky: "If you lose your dream, you're dead." After the movie, I went directly to my journal and wrote those words at the top of a fresh blank page. Even if I didn't have a dream, once I found it, I was *not* going to lose it. Not me. I was not going to die that death. *So what* if dreaming was a gamble? It was worth it. Whatever it took, I was going to dream alive a big dream, even if the castles were fake and you had to live in Pittsburgh. But if not acting and singing and dancing . . . then what?

Journal: "What am I put on earth to do? Or be? Or become? I don't get it! Help me to get it! Where is my corner of the sky? What is my dream?"

Surely a human with so much passion for life, and with so many deep questions, was supposed to do something *important*. So I started to dig deeply into spirituality. I might not have been a fan of church, but I'd always wondered about the divine. Surely the divine would have some answers. And hadn't I been making deals with the divine all along? If not in church, well, in hiding in those leaf piles and closets and thin branches? In charming those birds? In singing about the *whole family* "in his hands"? In asking those questions? It seemed to me that God was a lot more interested in my wonder than in the clothes I wore to church. And it felt like a good bet to assume that God knew all about the stuff that dreams were made of. And that dreams began on the inside of a person.

### SEEKING AND READING

My insides knew how to write and how to read. Since my writing was full of a lot of the same ol', same ol', it seemed that reading was a better place to start. But not the du jour Danielle Steel romance novels that my peers were reading. I wanted to read books whose authors asked questions.

So on school breaks back in my hometown, I'd go to the little local indie bookstore and say, "Give me the books I need to read. Please! I have questions!"

Those bookstore ladies loved my young seeking mind, and they took that nonathletic ball that they seemed to know well and ran. They ran straight for the section of the bookstore that held the mystics from every world religion. They told me to start with *Letters to a Young Poet* by Rilke. I nodded with tears in my eyes as I read his sage advice to the young seeker: "Be patient toward all that is unsolved in your heart and try to love the questions themselves."

It was all in the questions! Was I a good enough question-asker? According to that fourth-grade report card, no. Was this why the everybody elses ran in the other direction when I started asking questions? Maybe it was all on me!

They loaded me up with the poetry of Rumi, Hafiz, Neruda, E. E. Cummings. I could feel a longing in these authors' words, deep in the depths of their being, just like me. The longing for *truth*. The relentless dance with *curiosity*. Awe. Not necessarily dreaming about the future but more about living in the present. I stockpiled those books for later when maybe I'd had enough life experience to understand. Same with Joni Mitchell's *Blue* album, which later became the soundtrack of my twenties. *She* had what I had, and she had it *bad*. *And* she had the pipes. I just had the longing. And the true fear of losing my wonder in order to live as an adult in this world. My greatest fear was that I would wake up wonderless. Like the everybody elses.

I wanted to believe Joni when she promised that there would be new dreams and maybe even better ones before it was all over. "The Circle Game" was my favorite song back then. It began with a boy going out to wander. I thought it was to "wonder." Either way, the lyrics made it abundantly clear: if you lose your wonder, you lose your ability to dream, and you lose your future to the "supposed to be." I was *not* going to let that happen. It hadn't occurred to me yet that if we lose our wonder, we lose our empathy. I was seventeen. I wasn't thinking about the sustainability of our civilization. I was thinking about myself. Duh. I was still thinking that I was *bad* for all of my wondering and winging ways in the first place.

Perhaps this Wonder Time Line life-scan, then, is my effort to *finally* believe in my goodness, especially since my father is long gone. Thanks to the powers that be, my sister is not.

## LET'S TAKE A BREAK AND A BREATH FROM HIGH SCHOOL

So far, I hope my collage of memories has your mind percolating with your own wonder moments, intact and challenged. But since I'm at the high school mark, I suspect that it's bringing up some of your own highly charged and even triggering memories from the past. And it's possible that they are causing you angst. That's how I feel, anyway. Hence the break and the breath. We have to be kind to ourselves in the pursuit of uncovering our wonder.

So let's do some reflecting from the vantage point of who we are now, far, far away from our high school days. If you haven't already, take out your journal and grab a pen. It's time to officially start. To begin, write down the main wonder moments of your life up until age seventeen. Go as far back as you can—to your earliest wonder-filled memories. Focus on when your wonder was alive and well, not when it was in danger. That said, I have found that the memories of my intact wonder are often imprinted on my mind precisely *because* my wonder was in danger. Regardless, try to return to at least three distinct moments from your formative years when your wonder was intact. List them in your journal. Use as many words as you want to breathe them alive. (I.e., "The first time I climbed to the top, thin, windy branches of my tree house and discovered that I could look over my house and into the village, and felt free. Like there was a world out there far outside the constraints of my homelife, beckoning me into it, with new fresh air to breathe and a future of wild-why possibility.") These are moments in time, not extended moments like "that summer when my father built me a tree house." Choose specific moments in time.

If you're drawing a blank, it's probably because you've learned to push those memories aside. Be gentle with yourself. Invite yourself to return to them knowing that you have a purpose. Promise yourself that you will not get stuck there.

You're only returning to these memories so that you can finally move on. So that you can learn something new that maybe you're ready to see.

As you're allowing yourself to lovingly and gently return to these wonder-full moments, it's helpful to think in terms of key scenes. After all, these moments played out like mini movies in your life. So think: Where were you? Were you with anyone, or were you alone? What were the physical and sensory details of your surroundings? How did you feel? What did you think? What did you say? What was said to you?

If there are more than three key scenes where your wonder was intact, then let your list be long. Honor what wants to flow out of your memory. But choose at least three key moments for now. Focus on your early memories. And remember to stop at age seventeen. You can add to your Wonder Time Line in the exercise at the end of this chapter.

Now pick the most defining scene from your list. It's the wonder that's important to relive, so choose the one that holds the most charge for you in this moment. Write the scene. Maybe you're resisting this exercise. Maybe you don't like to write. Let that go. This is a powerful exercise, and it's just for you. Maybe this scene brings pain along with it. Maybe you were having your wonder-full moment as a response to something ugly in your life. Like my hiding examples. Maybe revisiting this scene, the wonder and the pain, is old news— something you've unpacked and let go of long ago. But what if you haven't? What if you've just buried it deep inside you and gotten used to it? Maybe it's hiding . . . in *you*? So try it. See what you can learn from this uncovering. Maybe now is the time. Maybe in reliving this scene, you will finally learn from it and let it go once and for all.

Or maybe returning to this scene will be *all* wonder for you! *Zero* pain! *Total* delight, joy, freedom! If so, be sure to squeeze every drop out of it. I wear my baseline wonder scene like a badge and sometimes like a shield, especially when life gets hard and my wonder is challenged. I am that girl in the thin branches, swaying in the wind. It's exhilarating, safe, life-affirming. No one can get to me there. It's my domain. Mine and the birds' and butterflies'. That place and those feelings were a magnet to me. I couldn't get there fast enough. I daydreamed about those branches at school. I longed for them even from my own bed in my own bedroom, where people could still get to me easily enough. Not in my tree. There, I was free. Sometimes I picture my father mowing the lawn under the tree, looking up at me so high in the branches. His face was one of worry. "Be careful," he'd yell up. But then, always, he'd wink. He knew what I was doing up there. He saw that girl.

The loss of that girl is heartbreaking to me. I've almost lost her a few times in my life. I know, though, that ultimately I will *not* lose her, and I have full faith that you won't either.

So be honest with yourself, even if it's hard. Bring in as much as you can remember—people, place, action, dialogue, your thoughts, feelings, sensory detail. And here's a great tip: Write it in the present tense, as if it's unfolding as you write. As if you don't know what happens next. (I.e., I am standing in the thin branches of my tree house, holding on in the wind. I can see over my house and into our village. Etc.) Just feel what there is to feel in that moment of return. Bring yourself into that exact time of your life. Keep very focused on what your wonder felt like in that exact moment of your life. If you're doubting your ability to relive this moment, ask the child that I hope you're still holding in your arms. She knows. And she needs you to remember.

When you feel like you've really written into this moment, really rolled around in it so that you can feel it in your core, close your eyes and bring this feeling into your *current* moment. Breathe into the wonder of it, even if it feels very far away from who you are right now. This moment of pure, intact wonder is life force. And it's still in you, right where you are.

Now write about how you *feel* in this moment, as the human you are today, having relived this wonder-filled moment from your past. What does it feel like in your body right now? Are you calm or agitated? Are you filled with delight and possibility, or is it dread or regret that you feel? Is your brain busy or still? Are you frustrated, angry, lonely, sad? Do you feel complete with your wonder-return scene, or do you feel like you need to go back into your scene and add more? If that's the case, please do. You are linking arms with the essence of your wonder. It's vital work. All you have to do is remember. And reclaim.

We'll be adding to this exercise at the end of this Wonder Time Line section, so keep your journal close.

## BACK TO HIGH SCHOOL

It was unspoken but understood. I had a debt to pay to my parents, and it began with getting into a noteworthy college. They'd been clear about their vision for me in this regard. Mine was a bit different: I needed to get into a noteworthy college because I wanted to do something remarkable with my life. I kept it to myself, where it was safe.

So I hunted the remarkable, and on my terms, which usually landed in the arts. I was told by my school advisors that I needed to try some extracurriculars. I had the grades, but it was extracurriculars that set a student apart for college acceptance. Reading and writing weren't considered extracurriculars. I was a failure at sports. But theater . . . was considered a legitimate pursuit. The winter play had just been announced. *The Fantasticks.* Maybe I would try acting again.

My choir teacher told me that my singing voice had matured and encouraged me to audition, even though it was a soprano role. It brought up every failed audition of my life. I was terrified. But the minute I read the main lead's opening monologue and the words, "Please, God, please! /

Don't—let—me—be—normal!" I knew that I needed to be Luisa. I *was* Luisa. It was a primordial pull of epic proportions that I had never felt before. A confluence of *Annie*, every member of the chorus line, *Pippin*, *Fame*, *Flashdance*. This was what I'd longed for. This very role, Luisa.

I auditioned. And I got it. Well, sort of. I was cast as Luisa's understudy, but still . . . I couldn't believe it! I would get to be the main character, Luisa, even if I never got to perform! I'd still walk in Luisa's shoes with everything I had, just in case. I understood Luisa. She was made of longing. She was made of wondering. She was dearly judged, and punished, for her wild whys. She wanted to dream! And she wanted *out*! Even if the world brought her pain. It was worth it.

The second I walked into that theater, I knew that I'd found my people. All those late-night play practices and trust falls and deep breathing techniques and "Yes, and . . ." improvisation and geeky techie guys who wanted to talk about quantum physics and girls who wanted to be Annie when they grew up . . . these were the kids who had been singing along with *A Chorus Line* alone in their bedrooms! I'd finally found them! I could see my future! I'd go to the School of Drama at Yale like Meryl Streep! I felt that burning, churning deep inside me again.

I got to play Luisa once. I still count it as one of the most honest moments of my life. From then on, I put everything I had into all things theater, full steam ahead into my future as an actress. My journal was full of my dreaming, and my dreams were coming true! I got the grades I was supposed to get, had the admiration and praise from all of my teachers, and even starred as an impressive Adelaide in *Guys and Dolls*. Maybe ingenues were overrated. Adelaide had complicated issues, and they were interesting to me. Some of them involved stripping, which probably had something to do with the whole football team showing up at one performance. Who was in the limelight *now*? And I'd done it without, well, *balls*. I was hell-bent. *School of Drama at Yale, here I come!*

Until . . . .

One afternoon, the dean of students invited me into his office and advised me against taking any more theater classes. Instead, I had to take calculus if I was to get into a decent college. Which meant "live a decent future." I filled in the blank even more: *And be like everybody else.*

Red-faced and lovelorn, I said, "But I want to go to the School of Drama at Yale! I know what I want to do with my life. I'm going to be an actress. An actress needs to take theater classes. Not calculus!"

He laid down the law: the dream was a nice dream, but the reality required calculus.

I just couldn't take it. It was like the entire adult world and the institutions it upheld were against me being my own person in my own way. I left evening study hall that night and, for some reason, chose to walk in the dark around the playing fields—my most *un*happy place. I lost it. Erupted into tears. I cried to the moon and maybe to God, "Why doesn't anyone believe in my dream? Is that all I am? A *dreamer*? Am I destined to become one of the everybody elses? Is there anyone who can help me?" I didn't get any answers. And even though Rilke said to love the questions . . . I wanted answers, and I wanted them *stat*!

I walked into my dorm an hour late (a highly punishable sin in boarding school), and right there in the middle of the coveted chocolate chip cookie dough "feed," all the girls in their flannel Lanz nightgowns, wool rag socks, and pearls, I screamed at my corridor master, "I don't care if I get expelled! I'm *not* going to class tomorrow. I'm taking the day off from all of this . . . total . . . *bullshit*! I want to be an actress, and you all want me to be a wife! Or a CEO. Or both! I'm an *artist*! What is this 'liberal arts' *bullshit*?" I burst into tears, took one last look at my corridor master—who had the power, and the just cause, to expel me on the spot—and slammed my dorm room door. We didn't have locks. But my journal did. I wrote in it all night.

The next morning there was a knock on the door. It was my corridor master. I was in the biggest sort of trouble with nowhere to hide. My parents had sacrificed so much to get me to this institute of higher learning, and what had I done? I felt as bad as I had ever felt in my entire life. I deserved my punishment.

He had a book in his hand. "Read this," he said. And he left.

It was a novel called *The Razor's Edge*. About a young man who couldn't bear his wonder either. He had it so bad that he dropped out all the way to the Himalayas. He was from my exact hometown. There's a scene from my country club in the book. My second home. The place where I'd ditched tennis lessons and hid in the woods and written in my journal. The place where I had watched people and paid attention to the "lucky." I had never related so much to a character in my life. More than Luisa. Larry got *out* to find his corner of the sky! If he could do it, maybe I could too. And maybe there were other Larrys out there. Maybe I wasn't alone. Maybe I belonged somewhere.

So, against popular opinion, I took the theater class. Not calculus. The dean wasn't happy. And I didn't care.

I didn't end up applying to the School of Drama at Yale. Instead, I got wooed away by a full-ride theater scholarship from a small liberal arts college in Ohio with the caveat that I applied early decision. It was my backup, but after everything my parents had done for me financially, it seemed like the right thing to do. Maybe it was my debt to pay for all my nos. Either way, I took it and ran.

On graduation day, it was my corridor master that I thanked. I've thanked him since. He knew exactly what he was doing. They say it only takes one person. I've been lucky, then, to have a host of "persons" in my life. And right where I didn't think to look.

## MY CRINGE STORY

Not a lot of people know this next part. But I'd be remiss not to include this in my public Wonder Time Line. Sharing this makes me cringe, but cringeworthy stories are often the most important in the way of uncovering our wonder. And it features another "person."

One of my mother's and grandmother's dreams for me, as they had dreamed for my sister, was to be a debutante. To "come out." To be "presented" into society. To wear the white dress. To go to the black-tie parties. To maybe even find the right man. To flare the charm for which I had been groomed. And I had plenty of it. Against my nubile convictions, I didn't know how to say no to this distaff dream. It would have been the ultimate insult. And insulting my mother wasn't my goal. It never had been. I'd just needed room from her reign, and I'd finally gotten some. My dream was in place, and with that security came true gratitude for what she'd given me. Seemed like I could suffer through whatever being a debutante entailed to make her happy. I'd pretend I was in a play! It was a play that, according to her, a lot of people would have done anything to be in. It would be my ultimate role.

What happened next, however, was not in the plan. I didn't mean to get the *starring* role. But at the beginning of my sophomore year in college, *Town & Country* magazine asked me to be the "Debutante of the Year." The magazine assigned a writer to interview me, with plans to publish the piece in their magazine with my face on the cover. My mind reeled through the decadent high-society scenes. What would I tell her? It was all so unrelatable to 99.9 percent of the world. And frankly, to me, embarrassing. Was she going to take a satirical spin on it all? I knew that I would if I were writing that article. Maybe I could act my way through the interview too. This was the premier opportunity to leave my mother's dreams for me in the rearview mirror and to do it with grace and gratitude.

But what would I divulge? That I'd been to countless debut parties up and down the North Shore of Chicago and in New York and Boston, all at country clubs or city clubs or under big white tents in people's backyards, revving up for the big winter cotillion? Danced to sixteen-piece big band orchestras? Eaten this newfangled thing called "sushi" under a pagoda with a man-made river flowing upstream along a golf course, just for this occasion? That I'd had my own *Gone with the Wind*–themed party with three other girls? Toasted our parents for raising us with all of this privilege? Danced with our fathers like brides? That we'd shaken all the right hands and worn our great-grandmother's pearls? Been courted by ruddy, dapper boys in black tie? Dabbled in cigarettes and cocaine? Would I up the ante on the drama and divulge that I'd gone to a debut party where we were taken to a hidden room and greeted by a long glass table with young men and women in black tie and gowns seated on the floor around it, crystal champagne flutes at each place filled with Dom Pérignon, little crystal bowls holding whole strawberries—and one white, thick, powdery line down the middle? That I'd taken my place and watched the protocol? Picked up a strawberry, rolled it in the white powder, dropped it into the champagne, and drank? And then talked a lot about myself? Even about my dreams?

I steeled myself, and the interviewer began.

"So, Laura. Tell me all about being a debutante. You are, after all, the Debutante of the Year!"

I started in. "Well, it's a privilege, first of all. And I'm proud that at our cotillion, we raise money for a hospital. My mother and sister and grandmother did it. And my grandmother was from the South, where it's a bigger deal." I paused. "And she always said that I was going to be the '*staaah* of the family.' Maybe having my face on the cover of *Town & Country* magazine was what she meant!" I paused for comedic relief.

She didn't laugh. "Interesting. Tell me: What does that mean to you? Being the star of the family? Being a debutante?"

It blindsided me. I burst into tears. Hot, mad tears. They were a complete surprise, like they'd been waiting at the gates for a long time for just this minute. I held the words they fueled at bay, until I didn't.

What I said to her went something along the lines of this: "I really don't fucking know. The whole thing . . . is . . . is . . . well, it's like a fucking dog show. Only the dogs are young women in ball gowns, being paraded around like commodities for these wealthy young society men to marry. And to bear their children. And throw their parties and spin their social calendars. And, Jesus. I mean, didn't women fight for equal rights years ago? The whole debutante thing should have met with an abrupt finale with the right to vote! I'm a part of something that's attempting to take back the women's movement, for Christ's sake! I don't get it. These families spend more than what most people spend on a whole *wedding*. I feel totally objectified! I feel used! I want to do something with my life other than marry a rich WASP and live in the suburbs of some city. Have you ever seen the play *The Fantasticks*? Or *A Chorus Line*? Or *Pippin*? Did you ever listen to *Free to Be . . . You and Me*? Or read *The Razor's Edge*?"

Cue the bawling. Cue the shortness of breath. I was betraying my mother. My grandmother. My world of origin. For real. Not just in my journal. This was possibly the worst "trouble" I could get into. Was I ready for it? Was my freedom ready for it?

"It sounds like you don't want to be the Debutante of the Year, Laura," the writer said, ever so kindly. And then she added in a hush: "You don't *have* to, you know. It's *your* choice."

It was like the heavens opened right there on my dorm room floor. I took a breath. "No, I really don't want to be Debutante of the Year. Thank you." Another breath. "But I do know just the person for you. Promise me that you won't tell her I sent you. I don't want her to be embarrassed."

That person ended up on the cover of *Town & Country*, with an interview flanked by photos of her and her mother shopping for shoes on Oak Street. I saw the magazine on my mother's coffee table when I was home for winter break. My mother never knew what could have been on her coffee table instead, because I didn't tell her. I didn't tell anyone. It was better that way. My freedom felt like my own business.

To that writer, I owe a great debt. Those words of permission she gave me changed my life and paved my way to freedom. But that day, my anger went from internal to external. And when that happens, hiding places are hard to find.

## THE PORTRAIT

As if they were conspiring, another "person" came into my life soon thereafter, holding a permission slip in his hand for my exit from "supposed to be." This time not a writer but a society portrait artist.

It was customary in my world to capture the blush of your daughter's departure from youth into her well-procured womanhood in an oil painting. There was a portrait artist that everyone gushed about, and his work was hanging in prominent living rooms all over town. When my mother told me that she'd hired him, I balked. We'd always been taught to be frugal. If we were frugal, we could have nice things, like the everybody elses. The rule was to not go overboard. This felt like overboard. Especially after all things debutante. I mean, I was on a full-ride scholarship at a school I didn't love as an act of gratitude for all my parents had given me. It felt like frugality was the one thing we agreed upon. Plus, how could I

ever be an actress, and likely a "starving" one, when there was
an oil painting hanging in a suburban Chicago living room,
strongly (and wrongly) suggesting that I had a trust fund? It
was another brain tangle.

"We don't need a portrait of me! It's too expensive! You
didn't do it for the other kids. I feel weird," I told them. I knew
to keep the rest to myself. It would just be yet another nail in
the coffin of "disrespect," no matter how many A-plusses I
got in school and how many leads I landed.

I lamented in my journal. Why were we spending money
we didn't have on these lavish things when my mother was still
darning socks she'd made for my father in the 1950s? When
we were told to always "order the chicken" in the proverbial
purchases of life? Even my debutante dress was a hand-
me-down. I'd been proud of that. *We* were proud of that. I
liked being proud together. In our world, just because you
"belonged" didn't mean that you had the dough. It seemed
like a family badge and one I could wear with, yes, respect.
This portrait thing seemed off-brand.

I imagined my life past college, living in some crummy
apartment in New York City, going to auditions. What if people
caught wind of this past of mine? Surely they'd misinterpret it.
Surely I'd be called all the bad names even if I'd successfully
left it. That wouldn't be looked at like a triumph. My God,
what if I was called "*spoiled*," per my bitter childhood nanny?
One thing I couldn't bear was to be called "spoiled." If people
only knew. I'd be judged for things I'd never even wanted and
didn't even fully have. Things I'd said no to and been punished
for accordingly. I realized that saying no to those things was a
privilege. Even more confusing. The last thing I wanted was an
expensive oil painting hanging in our family living room. Now
I'd be fair game. It was the opposite of hiding. I'd worn the
white dress. I'd done the swanlike dancing figures. I'd shaken
the hands and done the curtsies. Now I just wanted to execute

my exit strategy, which I knew would be full of barbed wire and thorns. This painting was a wire on which I was sure to trip. I had to find a very specific no on this one.

I failed.

"He's coming tomorrow," she confessed, as if she'd known that the only way to pull this off was by surprise. She told me to wear my costume of belonging: the de rigueur Laura Ashley dress, pearl earrings and necklace, gold family-crest ring, gold family bracelets. She wasn't sure what to do with my hair. I'd recently cut it short from a neat bob. I was pale and gaunt and wore chunky shoes and baggy clothes—mostly black, and sometimes a bit of orange just to stake my claim: *I've paid my dues with as much grace as I can conjure, and I am going to pick my own road now and walk it, even if I will suffer.*

"Shape up," was what she said.

So I showed up in ripped blue jeans, a white T-shirt, and bare feet. No jewelry. It wasn't the most mature thing I've ever done. My mother was not happy.

The painter met with us in our adults-only living room. My mother offered him tea from her best sterling tea service. We sat in powder-blue chairs on either side of the fireplace. She told him about the way my hair "normally" looked and showed him the dress, which she'd grabbed from my closet and which "matched" the chair upholstery. She told him to paint me in the dress. And to paint pearls in my ears and around my neck. She showed him her matching gold crest ring and bracelets. "Paint these in too. She normally wears them." She glared at me.

I stared out the window, looking for ballast, my eyes landing on the blue spruce tree with its skirt of long branches where I'd hidden as a child.

"Mrs. Munson, could you please excuse us?" the artist asked. "I'd like to speak with Laura alone."

My mother's whole body gave a little lurch, but she submitted. Perhaps this was just what quirky artist types did. I felt a boulder roll off my back and watched it follow her down the marble hallway, not like it wanted to knock her down but like she was pulling it with her, part of her arsenal to begin with. I knew it would return. I was genuinely scared.

He looked at me. "You don't want this portrait to be painted. Do you?"

"I'm sorry, and I don't mean to be disrespectful to you in any way . . . but we really don't have the money for this. I know it looks like we do. But we really don't. And I feel awful about it. I know you've painted my friends. You're a great artist for sure. I hope you don't take offense. I just . . . ."

He looked at me like he was already painting my face. At least my eyes.

"Let's be honest, Laura. It's not about the money. You just don't want to be painted right now in your life. And for the painting to be hanging on a wall for people to see."

Either this was some sort of outsider ploy to persuade the sullen late-teen, or this guy was a gift from the gods. It didn't matter. My mouth opened, and my truth spilled. The last time had been to the freelance writer. Why these strangers?

"I don't get it. What is she trying to *prove*? That we *belong*? She's always talking about how we *belong* in one way or another. Fourteen ancestors that came over on the *Mayflower*. The plaque in the Old South Church in Boston that my ancestors founded. One New England–gravestone rubbing after the next. The family-crest rings. The needlepoint crests. The genealogy books. I'm sick of needing to prove that we belong. If we belong, why do we need so much *proof*? Plus . . . proof is expensive!"

He squinted at me but kindly. "Couldn't it just be a way of saying that your parents are proud of you?"

The thought was too heartbreaking because, in my deepest place, I wanted them to be proud of me. But not for who they wanted me to be. For who I *really* was. No, I was sure of it: they were proud of who I could *become*, but only if I played by the rules. Seemed like this portrait was a way of pinning me into those rules, and under them, until I suffocated in the fabric. The powder-blue chintz fabric that matched the dress I wasn't wearing.

I started bawling. "I feel like such an asshole! I'm so sorry that you have to deal with this bullshit. I mean, you're an artist. The last thing you probably want to paint are young WASPs!"

He waited, like the more I spilled, the more of a painting he could paint.

I couldn't help myself. Maybe he understood me. I wanted to be an artist too. "I mean . . . those ancestors were fighting for their *freedom*! *That's* the legacy I care about. *That's* what I want to claim as my own. *That's* the belonging I want! I want to belong to a fight for freedom. Not for my dress to match the upholstery in their living room! What happened to the fight? Where did it get lost? Do you really think those pilgrims cared about which fork went where? They were fighting for their beliefs and their liberation from old, stifling, corrupt ways!"

He looked at me sideways as if he'd read every page of every one of my journals from the beginning. "Grab that chair. We're going outside."

"Uh. My mother would *not* allow this chair to be taken outside. I can tell you that. We'd get in *big* trouble."

He was deadpan. "Take the chair. Go outside. Pick a spot that means something to you. A place where you want to be."

Was he serious? Did he understand that he was about to be *fired*?

But I wasn't going to say no to this one. I'd never had a partner in crime before. Not in the adults-only living room!

I grabbed the chair as if it begged to be released from its divots in the carpeting after so many years of standing sentry to cocktails and cups of tea. The fine wind of rebellion pushed me out the sliding glass door, across the patio, and into the backyard to my spruce tree. I eyed the oak tree that held my tree house across the yard. If I'd have been able to haul the chair up the rope ladder to the thin branches, I would have. Like my own nest. I'd sit in it. I'd be painted there. Ready to fledge.

"Here," I said, next to the spruce.

"Why here?" he said.

"This is a special tree for me."

"It's a beauty. What meaning does it have for you?"

"I used to hide under its boughs when I was little. When I got in trouble. No one would ever find me."

He smiled. "I used to hide in the woods when I was little too."

Now I smiled. "You *did*?" I sat. Maybe I could give them what they wanted. I put my hands politely in my ripped-denim lap like they were awaiting a Communion wafer.

"That doesn't look like you. Sit in the chair the way *you'd* like."

"Uh. I've actually never even sat in this chair. I'm not allowed in the living room unless we have guests. Or if I'm listening to my parents' stereo, but only their records—"

"Just sit in it. However you'd like. Here in your special place, in front of your tree. Pretend you're hiding." He was so serious. Nothing playful in his eyes. He was already working. He had the face of a theater teacher.

"Hiding?" Who *was* this guy? So I slung one leg over an arm of the chair. "She'll never go for this. Not in a million years."

"You don't look comfortable. Put the other leg over too. And your hands. Loosen them. Drape them over your knee. Like you're in your hiding place and no one can find you, and you're comfortable."

He took out his camera and started snapping shots.

"Shouldn't I smile or something?"

He didn't answer. He pulled out his paints and a small easel, arranged a canvas, and started painting.

We were all there for the unveiling. In the living room. My parents were excited. I was afraid.

Off came the sheet. And there I was. Sitting in the powder-blue chair with my legs and hands over the arm. In the Laura Ashley dress. With the neat bob. And the pearls. And the gold bracelets, and the gold crest ring poised on a hand that disappeared into the end of the painting. Then I noticed the blue spruce behind me, with golden light shining from within its low boughs.

I looked at him. I didn't know whether to be betrayed or blown away.

My parents gushed. They talked about where it should go. In what corner of the living room. Over the clivia plants? Next to the secretary?

And when it was time for the artist to leave, he took me aside. "See how your hand goes out of the frame, resting on your knee? Like it's pointing at something?"

I didn't know what to say. I was overwhelmed being this seen.

"That's to remind you that no matter where that painting hangs, and it may end up being yours one day, that you are controlling your future. No one else." He gave me a kiss on the cheek. "And don't forget that there are spruce trees wherever you go. You belong outside."

That portrait hangs in my office now in Montana, at my back as I write. One person.

## THE TRAVEL CURE

I hatched a new dream: I would travel. Like Larry. I would make good on my promise to my grade school Spanish teacher. It was common for liberal arts college students to take a semester abroad in their junior year. I wanted the *whole* year. My scholarship would cover it, and I had enough credits in my major to allow me to leave for two semesters. To see what I was really made of. It was one thing to rebel but another to have the courage to come home to your true self. That was my mission.

The truth was: I had made a mistake. This college was not for me. I fit in, but in all the ways I didn't want to fit in. Because this little college, back in the 1980s, despite its theater department, was prep school all over again. Heavy on the Greek system. Low on the arts. And being a token drama student wasn't all that appealing. The theater people seemed like outcasts, and while I wanted to be an actress, I also wanted to be part of something that was actively thriving. I was preparing to leave a lot, and I wanted to plug into a lot. And the Greek system didn't cut it. What was I doing in this small school in this small town in Ohio? Had I cut off my nose to spite my face?

One night I was lying in my bunk bed, bawling yet again. It was a Saturday night, and everyone else was getting ready for frat parties. Maybe if I'd taken calculus, maybe if I hadn't taken the scholarship, I'd be getting ready for a party full of New York–bound budding actors at Yale. The tears wouldn't stop. I'd realized how incongruent I was being with my dreams, thanks to the journalist from *Town & Country*, so I'd deactivated from my sorority and was paying the price. My car was being vandalized by someone obviously in my peer group, based on her particular style of abuse: dirty gym socks in my car (people knew I was allergic to sports), mean-ass graffiti on my license plate bearing my nickname, Lulu. (A surprise gift from my parents—not the car. The car was on loan.). Slashing all my tires the day I was headed east on a road trip to see my sister in Boston (all on my dime, cleaning houses and working at the school bookstore). I figured that was my punishment for going against the current. The truth was that I was a walking conundrum. If I couldn't figure out who I was, how could I expect anyone else to? But did they have to punish me for it?

I supposed I was hiding from that, too, when a few friends walked in and saw me bawling in my bottom bunk. One of them frowned, but sadly, and said, "What's *wrong* with you, Lulu? Why are you so *miserable*? You've got everything you could possibly *want*! Why can't you stop fighting who you *are*? Why can't you just *accept* who you are?"

I found words between sobs. "I just . . . don't think . . . that . . . who I *really* am . . . is anything close to . . . who people *think* I am. And . . . what everyone . . . wants me to be."

They left in silence but maybe with scorn too. I knew I was clumsy with my words. I didn't want them to think that I was rejecting them. I was rejecting *myself* in our world, and I couldn't see very far past my tears to be able to explain it. I was just simply miserable and felt entirely misunderstood and alone. What made it worse was that I knew full well that if I snapped into shape, I could go out with them and right back to being the life of the party. But I couldn't bear it. Which made me the weak link. So I kept hiding that night. And crying— likely the tears I didn't know how to cry the day my sister left for boarding school and left me alone with all the non-listeners and non-wonderers.

Just then, a girl I'd seen around campus popped her head into my dorm room. I didn't know her well. She wore red lipstick and funky thrift shop dresses. I'd admired that about her from afar. She looked like she'd seen some stuff. "What are you doing all alone on a Saturday night?" she asked.

"Writing in my journal about how much I loathe frat parties."

She laughed. It sounded like a whole bell choir lived in her throat. She had a bottle of red wine. No one drank red wine in college in 1985—not at this college, at least. They drank beer. Cheap beer. That came out of warm kegs. "I'm on my way to a party that isn't anything close to a frat party," she said. "Want to come?"

I said yes. She took me to an off-campus house party full of a bunch of seniors who didn't belong to frats and who'd all just spent their junior years abroad. Their whole years. Who were these people? We spent the whole night drinking Chianti and talking about travel. She'd just spent a year in Florence, Italy. She'd used it as a launchpad to go to places like Portugal. The Greek Islands. Tunisia. Morocco. Yugoslavia. Turkey. She was so exotic and sophisticated and experienced. I wanted what she had.

"What do you want to do after college?" I asked her, hoping she'd say something close to my heart. Maybe she wanted to be an actress.

"All I know is what I *don't* want to be!" she said. Her whole face radiated joy. It occurred to me then that none of the theater majors radiated joy. Neither did the theater teachers. In fact, I'd never seen an interview with an actor who seemed joyful at all. They all looked sort of . . . miserable. And the movie stars: *skinny* and miserable. Maybe I didn't have to know what I wanted at all. Maybe that was the dream to dream.

The next day I went into the study-abroad office, and the next fall I was in Florence, Italy, living with a family who made their own Chianti and olive oil, grew figs, and loved life and each other in a way I'd never seen. And I got to be part of that family for a whole year! Had I dreamed this? It didn't matter. I was living it. Sitting around a long table all Sunday afternoon, eating and laughing and talking and wondering and snoozing in the sun.

I was the American girl obsessively writing in her journal, now a handmade marbleized paper-covered journal with leather binding. Hopping on trains without knowing the destination. Standing before ancient sculptures, wondering what it must have been like to live in the wonder of the Renaissance. I would have *belonged* in Renaissance times. I was nineteen. Grandiosity was what it took to survive rebellion, especially from such a stringent demographic, which did not forgive its rebels easily.

## THE PIVOT

And here is where it all took the turn that became the road that I would stay on for the rest of my life. The road that became the bridge. The bridge to myself.

It was 1987. I was studying film and art history in Florence and living with that lovely Italian family, who I would have done anything for and vice versa. I didn't speak the language. I knew it was better for me to look into kind eyes and allow them to look into mine—without words. While most of the students spent their free time traveling to Paris and London and Salzburg, I fulfilled my personal pact and took trains to Poland. Prague. A Yugoslavia on the brink of revolution. I wasn't interested in the "easy places," as I called them.

But the place I wanted to go to most was the Blue Mosque in Istanbul. I was obsessed with ceramic tiles and had been told that exact color blue existed nowhere but there—and that it was one of the most sacred, inspiring places on earth. The Blue Mosque became my Everest. So at Christmas break, instead of going home to Chicago, I got a train ticket to Turkey for a month. My parents begged me to be sensible and come back home. I didn't want to. My wonder had come back, and I couldn't risk losing track of it again.

A friend gave me Salinger's *Nine Stories* and *Franny and Zooey* to read on the train. "Franny reminds me of you," he'd said with a grin. He'd been to Kenya for his junior year abroad. He wasn't going to go home at all. He was going to be a professional traveler. Maybe that's what my future held. I'd find odd jobs along the way. I didn't care about being rich. I just wanted to be curious. He was spot-on: Franny hit me like Luisa and Larry, all needing so badly to leave home, common sense be darned. I needed to get to the Blue Mosque now more than ever.

The second my train pulled into the Istanbul station, I grabbed my backpack and went directly to the Blue Mosque. Standing there, I'd never felt such wonder. Those minarets were real, not Disney-spun. There was the promise of truly sacred space inside those doors. I was going to leave my anger there. Refind my wonder there. And go forward with my life on my own wonderous terms.

I ascended those steps, ready to cover my head and slip off my shoes to behold this ancient, sacred blue and dreamy place. To listen for my soul's knowing.

The door was shut. There was a sign on it in Arabic and English. The mosque was closed. Renovation. I was crushed. And I couldn't help but believe that it was all because I wasn't ready for this knowing. Maybe I'd have to climb Everest after all.

Instead, I spent the afternoon sitting on a step outside the mosque, writing in my journal. But this time . . . it wasn't about me. It was about someone *else*. Someone *like* me but not *exactly* me. Someone made up. It was about all the Larrys of the world. The Pippins. The Luisas and Frannys. *Of* me. But not *really* me. It was positively freeing. Better than any blue could ever be. My pen moved across those pages, pursuing this "she" like a lost lover. That "she" wasn't me. Yet it was the truest thing I'd ever expressed to anyone, especially myself.

What came out sounded a lot like a novel about a young woman with undreamed dreams, awash in her wonder. Huh.

I looked up into the spiring minarets and thought: *Maybe I could write books. Not just read them.*

With that thought, a warm, wonderous wave of joy surged inside of me. A world of possibility. Something I hadn't felt since I was a little girl. I exhaled all my angst away. I'd found it. Books. Who needed the truest blue when you could use *words* to show the color of wonder? And not just words in a journal. Words that someone might read. Someone a lot like me.

## THE EXIT

Senior year I returned from Europe and saw that my college offered a screenwriting class. Maybe that would be my first real attempt at writing. We were supposed to write a thirty-minute scene. I wrote a two-hour, full-length screenplay, half in Italian. I stayed up all night in the computer room on the VAX. Think *2001: A Space Odyssey*. We didn't have personal computers yet. I had never been more obsessed with anything in my life, even though the tech guy had narcolepsy and kept falling asleep when I asked him for help.

Suffice it to say that I figured out the VAX and took my dot-matrix stack of pages to the film department, only to have my professor look it over, smile at me, write a D-plus in red Sharpie, and say in a faux British accent, "Ms. Munson. This is not cinema! Take this to the fools in the English department!"

I took that stack of papers to the "fools" in the English department, and the dean said, "Where have you been for the last three years? You're a writer," and then slapped me into the advanced creative writing class for writing majors. (One person times two.)

Suddenly, I was officially writing fiction. Where had these people been all my life? These seekers and readers and writers and wonderers? I was home. I'd found my dream. The first line of my first novel was "Claire sat on her patio, wondering what to paint." Wonder drove my books from the start.

## THE LAST PERSON

Now it was time to put it all to the test. I'd figured out who I was, had publicly claimed it, and was home for the summer, getting ready to move to San Francisco to begin my MFA, when my mother arranged for a meeting with the newly retired CEO of one of the largest advertising agencies in the US. He'd written a book. That was the impetus, but I smelled a rat. Was this her last-ditch effort to push me into a more practical, acceptable way to be a writer? Writing about Keebler Elves? I was steadfast about my decision to get my advanced degree and be around "my people." A place where I finally belonged.

But I was curious. He'd published a book. Maybe he had connections or advice.

We met in his converted gardening shed of a writer's studio. It was covered in the kilim rugs I'd seen in Turkey. He was listening to opera on his reel-to-reel. I felt Mimi's hand in it, and not around a crochet needle.

"Your mother tells me you want to be a novelist," he said, without a modicum of seniority, as if he wanted to be twenty again and I had the key. "Tell me about your writing dreams."

My heart brimmed. I told him that I was writing my first novel. I told him that I was about to move to San Francisco to get my MFA from a wonderful program my creative writing professor had helped me secure.

He listened. Hard. Smoking. Wagner in the background. Serious business.

I remember it like this: "You know, I could get you a great job in advertising with one phone call. You've got the personality. The smile. The handshake. The mind." He paused and smoked and looked out the window into his garden and his prized hybrid geraniums. "But it sounds like you want to write books. Your mother's not going to be happy with me." He leaned forward. He looked like he was going to cry. "Go write books. You don't need your MFA. Just go out there . . . and write."

"That's all I want to do in the world," I said, and I *did* start crying. Finally, someone from my world who understood me. And he didn't even know me. But it seemed that he *did* know me. In the way that counted. Like the painter. Like the journalist. Like the writing professor. Like the film professor. Like the corridor master. Like the theater teacher. Like the Spanish teacher. And maybe even like the "NI" grade school teacher. All the "one person" surprise love.

And he pointed at me with his unfiltered Camel cigarette and said, "If you can escape this demographic, then I'll know you're a genius."

That was my final permission slip.

His mahogany cranesbill geraniums still grow in my Montana garden, and each year, I thank him.

I canceled my MFA that day and committed myself to the writing life, cutting my teeth on odd jobs—whatever paid the bills that wouldn't tempt me away from my dream. I'd be a student of the human creature. I realized that I had been in that line of study all my life. Now it was time to take it seriously. So I wrote. I moved around. I moved my pen most of all—on lunch breaks in delivery trucks, while my infant charges napped, in eaves under staircases, and in closets where I'd call a sawhorse a desk. Not unlike my hiding places.

I wrote novel after novel. I sat at the intersection of heart and craft and mind that is the writing life. I wrote in the wake of death and birth, financial and global crises. I never stopped. And by and by, I fell in love, got married, and moved to the Rocky Mountains—this time in Montana, where people reinvented themselves as a rule—and along came the children. In all of it, the writing never stopped.

**KEEPING THE DREAM**

I did everything I could to pass an unbustable wonder to my children in whatever form possible. Disney had failed me as a child, so I stayed away from those myths and rooted my motherhood in the wilderness. I answered as many of my children's wild whys as I could. I never shamed them for their whys. And Montana served up abundant wonder all around us. My kids received it with true awe in their eyes, noticing the mountain bluebirds' return—something so blue against the last of the winter snow. The magenta fairy slippers rising from the forest floor each spring with their spotted yellow dancing shoes. The mud pies and pine needle upside-down cakes we'd "feed" to their teddy bears. The frog symphonies each night in May that we peeped along with, believing we could conduct them. The dance of the dragonflies in late summer which sometimes made us blush with their blatant, X-rated twitterpation. The hiking up mountains. The skiing down them. The hell-for-leather galloping across wide-open fields on our horses, stopping to let them drink while we skinny-dipped in any number of mountain lakes.

My children understood wonder better than I ever had because their wonder was uninterrupted. Untainted. And never punished. I was the guardian of it. It felt like the most important job of my life. Those early years of their childhood were the most fulfilled I had ever been. I was back in my wonder and now with children, who were thick in it, with no sign of ever letting it go. Not on my watch.

And I wrote about it. I wrote essays and short stories and always had a book in the works. I was learning my craft, and I knew it would take years. Sometimes I had the courage to submit my short-form work to literary journals, knowing the rejections inherent to the publication process. Sometimes I got yeses. Usually nopes. Either way, I worked and worked at my craft. I kept most of it to myself. Focused on wonder. Focused on my motherhood. Focused on my kids' questions. Focused on being their Willie Wonka.

While the courage came and went with submitting my work, I *always* had the courage for my motherhood, my writing, and what nature delivered, and that was the most creative act I could imagine. But the more I worked at my creations on the page, especially my novels, the more I wanted my books out in the world. I had that old longing to build that bridge in a substantial way. And with that longing, angst surfaced again. Angst was longing unfulfilled. I wanted my book babies to be born and shared with the Annies and Pippins and Luisas and Larrys and Frannys. But I lived in Montana, and as much as it lent itself to the writing life, it wasn't a great place to launch a career as a writer.

I started to beg the universe for it: "Please. Please. Let me be published. It's what I'm here to do. I've worked so hard. I've given it my very, very best. I want my books to be read."

But let's be very clear. I also wanted success. I wanted the "Yale" of my craft. I wanted what other writers were getting. I wanted to make good on my dream, and I wanted to do it with force and, yes, grace, but with a certain kind of prowess and acumen. In short: I wanted to be the *staaah* of the family. Only I wanted to stand on bookstore stages and talk about my books and whatever truth I'd tapped into by writing as bravely as I could. I wanted to be Rilke to many young—and old—"poets."

To every sinking sun, I would utter this sad, desperate prayer: "*Please* let me be published to *wide* acclaim." I didn't want to admit it to anyone, but what had once felt like a dream now felt like a divine calling. Yes, an inner one. But something more. Something that lived in the high, thin branches of trees and belonged to little wonder-full, and perhaps wayward, children. Something that wanted more than small literary journals for my words. If it was my calling, then shouldn't I want to go all the way? And if so, where was this destination? And how was I to get there?

## CORRUPTED WONDER

Enter: ego. Being published to "wide acclaim" was the language of Annie, and every member of *A Chorus Line*, and the dancer in *Flashdance*, all at the same time. And I was sick of waiting. True, I was a young mother, but that didn't mean I couldn't have it both ways. I wanted it *now*. Veruca Salt now. It was a dirty secret that I didn't want anyone to know. But it was eating me alive from the inside out. I'd finally sent out my books (the good ones) to literary agents. I'd landed one. A good one. Yet my books weren't getting picked up by publishers. Rejection, rejection, rejection.

The sacred days of writing just for me were buckling under this new, and very shitty, ambition addiction. I wanted commercial success, and I wasn't getting it. The girl at the Blue Mosque had sung "Tomorrow" many times, and my muse seemed like she was under renovation. I was losing steam. My dreams hurt, deeply, and wonder hurt worse.

I wrote in my journal: "Should I just give up? Aren't dreamers owed anything, especially when they feel like they have a profound calling, inner or divine or both? Are there not only no promises, but are dreams actually bad for us? Should I have stayed in the world of the everybody elses? Is this my hell to pay for leaving? Do dreams need to die after all?" I wanted them to live! I wanted to sing my song on the page and have it land in hearts, and yes, take my bow!

There was only one human I could think of who knew what it was to truly sing from his heart in all facets of his life, and that was the cherished musical director of the Trinity Church in Boston. I'd had the extreme honor of singing in that choir after college, and we'd become dear friends over the years. He always had a way of weaving his deepest belief into our conversations: that everything came down to love and fear. And love was greater than fear. I agreed with him and had the high school journal entries to prove it. It's what had bonded us from the moment we met—how we'd made this discovery at an early age and how it had steered our lives. It was our way of checking in with each other, to share where we were along the path of love and fear. I needed to check in. Was I living by this belief when it came to my writing? Was I letting fear eclipse love? Was I practicing fear and *calling* it love? Why should I even write if it was sinking my deepest beliefs?

So during a visit with my sister, I stole away to meet with him at the grand sanctuary on Copley Square that is Trinity. After a hearty hug, that magnificent smile of his turned impish, and I knew to follow him down the aisle and up to the marble altar, so processional, like I was in a rite of passage.

He took a seat at the organ and started spinning out the Bach Fugue in A Minor. I sat, then lay, in my old alto choir pew, staring into the face of the La Farge stained glass Jesus looming over the organ pipes. Just us and the music in that mighty space. I thought of the Blue Mosque and how I'd not seen the interior but had discovered my calling. My calling. Was it even fair to feel that way? Did everyone have a calling? Maybe no one had a calling except to love past our fear. Maybe we weren't meant to achieve great "things." Maybe the best sort of greatness was in loving. I was so good at loving the people I loved. But in that magnificent moment, as if sent through stained glass, I wondered: *Am I good at loving myself?*

The answer was an unequivocal no. I was my own worst enemy, and I was proving it over and over again. And as I stared up at the Jesus, Bach thrumming all around me and in me, rearranging my heartbeat, I realized that my fear had me by the throat, by my own doing. How could self-love stand a chance? But if my way of loving myself had been through writing, couldn't I just leave it at that? Maybe it was time to leave it at that. Writing as self-love, period. I doubted I could.

I felt as restless as I had in those Italy days, yet now the restlessness had curdled in desperation. With the organ piping and pulsing the air of that room where so many prayers had been prayed, so many versions of "Please, please, please, please, please help me to . . . ," my prayer suddenly seemed benign.

When my friend was done playing, he sat silently for a moment like he was watching the last ripple of a thrown stone in a calm mountain lake. "You know," he said with his bellowing baritone. "There are only two things when it comes down to it."

I waited for it, begging it. Knowing it.

I mouthed along with him, "Love. And Fear."

"And love is greater than fear. So that's good news," I added. "I've known that all my life. I've . . . just forgotten."

We whiled away a few hours sitting on that altar, talking about God. Art. Callings. Ambition. But mostly about fear, and how love was its opposing force.

"You know, outside of childbirth, I've only known the confluence of love conquering fear when I'm on a horse. It feels like the perfect moment to share it, especially with you in this wonderous place. Most people wouldn't understand this story."

He leaned in. He loved being a confessor. "Do tell."

"After my father died, I was given a great gift, and I believe it was from him. I'd tried for years to get my horse to swim in the river with me on his back. It looked like a dream! But my horse was terrified of water, and he wouldn't get anywhere near the river. He'd start to rear and turn for home every time he caught a glimpse of it. I tried everything to get him past his fear. Nothing worked. And it got to a point where *I* was afraid of water when I rode him. A rearing horse in the woods isn't a lot of fun. But when I came back to Montana after living in the ICU for a month with my father, helping him die, I went straight to my horse. I had no agenda. I just needed his love before I could rejoin my family and my life. I needed a safe place for my debilitating tear of a world without my father in it. I needed a place where fear felt inert and love was everything. So I got on him bareback, and we headed into the woods. I didn't know where we were going and I didn't care. I just wanted the step-by-step. The breath-by-breath.

No thoughts. No feelings. Just bushwhacking through the woods. And suddenly . . . ." I looked at my friend for ballast, and there were tears in his eyes. ". . . there we were at the river. I didn't know how we'd gotten there, but there we were, stepping, without pause, into it. And swimming. Like we'd done it a thousand times before. Just swimming up and down that river. Fearless. All I did was hold on to his mane and let him take me for a swim." I looked at the Jesus. "It's possible to be in that loving, fearless, placeless place. I just haven't found it like that again. Not even on my horse. And I want to. I need to. But not contingent upon a dear one's dying. That time of my life almost took me down."

"Don't you think that the feeling you experienced that day was *peace?*"

"Yes. That's what it was. Peace."

As we hugged goodbye, he reiterated, "Love and fear. Don't forget again!"

I knew I had to look at my relationship with both. Because peace was something I knew very little about.

## BREATHE, BELIEVE, RECEIVE. IT'S ALL HAPPENING.

Traveling seemed like the answer. It had worked before. And it would be good for our family. The kids were old enough to remember most of it. The school allowed it as long as they kept journals. Duh. We had some money saved. So we went to Belize for a month. Personally, I was asking something perhaps unfair of a place. I wanted it to supply me with my full-blown child's wonder. It seemed like wonder would be the ultimate cure. My regular life was giving me closed doors that I'd been trying to open for too long, bashing myself bloody. I needed a break. But I didn't want to do it the easy, touristy way. I wanted to really dig in, drive around, and see what I could find in the way of wonder. And maybe even peace.

One day, while my family was taking naps back at the bungalow, I did something I'd never done before: I asked for a sign. *If I'm supposed to get published . . . show me a sign.* It seemed important and imminent. Because quitting was a playable card in my hand. Nobody had asked me, or had even wanted me, to be a writer. I wasn't going to quit writing. That was nonnegotiable. But maybe I needed to quit my publishing dream.

I wandered down a thin alleyway and spotted a little hand-painted sign that said ART FOR YOUR HEART, in front of a small doorway. I'd asked for a sign but not an *actual* sign. Was my answer so easily delivered? Write for my heart but not for anyone else's? I stepped in to find out.

No one was there, and there wasn't any art hanging on the walls. Just stacks of bric-a-brac that looked like it was being readied for a garage sale.

As I was about to leave, I looked down and saw a print of a marble Greek goddess with wings, holding her skirts apart, revealing the words "Breathe, believe, receive. It's all happening."

I'd seen a lot of marble women—the bold sister souls I'd tracked all through Greece. Ephesus, Turkey. Italy. These women had lost limbs and noses and heads but were still goddesses just the same. Goddesses who had stood the test of time and never given up.

A man appeared, not through any doorway I could find.

"Is this for sale?" I asked him, holding up the print.

"You can have it," he said.

"I'd like to pay for it," I said.

He shook his head and looked into my eyes. "It's for you."

I didn't have words. The wonder-full world was giving me things. Heart things. I knew to take the print and keep it close to my "heart" that month. And when I got home, I hung it in my office by my desk where I could see it from all angles. For five more years, I looked at it every morning and every night. In the past, I'd prayed. I'd begged. But when I'd asked for a sign, plain and simple, this was my answer. So I spoke those words aloud every morning before I wrote, and I ended my writing time each day by saying them again: "Breathe, believe, receive. It's all happening."

I kept writing. And the words worked in me. Shedding things.

Only now in my writing life, I breathed. I believed. I received. I received the joy of creating and let go of where my writing (and ambition) landed. I received the breath and breathed it back and deemed *that* the ultimate life: doing the work. *That* was all I could control. Whatever this "it" was that was "happening" . . . was a mystery, and the part I could understand was the part where I sat down and wrote. And wrote and wrote. But now . . . surrendered. With love. Not fear. And I was so surprisingly fulfilled.

And here's why: I committed to building the bridge to myself. That's what I had failed to understand in all my wondering and word wandering. I needed to let go of all that fearful *wanting* and fully embrace the love of *creating*. I needed to fully embrace what was behind that creating: the deep longing for truth. My truth. My wonder.

So it makes perfect sense that my sister would send me a new journal she'd picked up at a little bookstore in Cambridge, knowing nothing of my Belize print. Guess what was on the cover. The exact image that hung on my office wall. The goddess. The skirt. The wings. The invitation: "Breathe, believe, receive. It's all happening." I'd had the wrong "it" in mind. The "it" was the writing. And that was "happening" indeed.

## THE MYTH OF SUCCESS

As it so often does when we practice surrender, "it" all happened. The original "it." The one I'd let go of.

Five years of living in that constant act of inner bridge building, and, lo, that girl who wanted to be Annie got her version of "it." I got a book published. It landed on *The New York Times* bestseller list and was published in eight countries. It was an international bestseller too. I got to work with some of the tippy-top people in the industry, a baptism by fire. The "it" was powerful, but I'd been blessed for having gone through the long journey to "arrive." I'd learned that the ultimate power was in the doing. The being. The breathing, believing, receiving. And getting back to work. That's the ultimate "it." And that's the only "it" that a writer, or anybody, can ultimately control.

Turned out that my "it" looked very different than I had imagined it would all those years ago. The "it" was what I brought to my writing desk every day, even though now the publishing world brought that "it" to the hearts and minds of people around the world. And for that "it" I will be eternally grateful. But the only "it" that matters is what we create. And how do we create? Through wonder.

**END OF TIME LINE**
Here is where we land for now. In surrendered, remembered, and perhaps peaceful wonder. In doing this Wonder Time Line, I realized just how much of my wonder had to do with belonging. Dreaming. Busting through the institutional myths that I allowed to define me. Learning that rebelling is still empowering that which you leave. Embracing and creating is where the liberation lives.

No matter where you are in your wonder, it's time to fasten this to your heart: your wonder is all around you. It's in your dreams. The big ones and little ones and dashed ones and yet-to-be-dreamed ones. Wonder is what allows you to co-create with yourself. And to find your truth. That's where it begins and ends if it's going to go anywhere at all. You have to start there. With you. With your questions and love-propelled wonder and your absolute quest for truth. Fear has no power when you live like that. This loving co-creation with yourself is what is behind *everything*. The bridge to yourself. Then, and only then, can you build an outer bridge. If a fellow wanderer in the forest stumbles upon your bridge and stops to walk it to the other side . . . that is gravy. I've been on both sides of that bridge, and I can tell you that it can't be any other way. It *cannot*. Not if it is truth that you seek. Truth is what is behind it all, even your breathing. It's a wordless place. Where your intuition lives. What you knew when you were a baby and just forgot because of all that calculus you had to take. It's about coming home to yourself. Finally and for good.

## your wild why . . .

Now, open up your journal and list the main Wonder Time Line moments from where you left off at seventeen. You can go into adulthood but don't skip too much time. Really look at your wonder moments, year by year. You might even think about the surprise people who popped into your life at just the time you needed them and then were gone. Who were your unsung integral guides?

If you find that your wonder moments are more wounded than intact, list them anyway. List the times when your wonder evaded you. List the times when your wonder lay on a sidewalk, gasping for air. Did you allow it to die? Of course you didn't. You just ignored it. You just lost track. So instead of shaming yourself, consider: What kept you from ultimately letting your wonder die? Was it a person? A place? A moment in your life when you asked for a sign? When you stopped in awe and truly paid attention?

If it's overwhelming, consider making three categories: Wonder Intact. Wonder Wounded. Wonder Found. Maybe you need to start a new list altogether. If so, you can use the scenes from your first seventeen years and put them in whatever category they fit best.

However it works for you, once you have your moments listed, look over your list(s). Hopefully you did the last exercise, which was to write a scene when your wonder was *intact*. Now choose the scene that most captures your wonder *wound* and the end of your wild whys. A defining moment when you started to feel your wonder wound. Was it something someone said or did to you? Was it a moment of shame for how you expressed yourself?

Now write the scene. Again, write it in the present tense so that you do your best to try to relive it. Include as much as you can remember: the setting, the people, the sensory details, the stakes. What did you feel like in your body in that moment? What were your thoughts and emotions? Did you hide from whatever tried so hard to kill your wonder? Or did you confront it? Did you believe that you should let your wonder die? Did you feel that you weren't worthy of your wonder or of wanting it in the first place?

Add in every detail you can remember. Spend some time on this. Look at it with more wonder than anger. There's no need to solve anything. Just for now invite yourself to lovingly look into the genesis of your pain when it comes to wonder.

Now you have a Wonder Intact scene and a Wonder Wounded scene.

If you don't have a Wonder Found list, I encourage you to repeat this exercise and create one using the above directions. You might need to finish this book in order to fully wrap your mind and heart around it. There are plenty of stories and teachings ahead that I hope will do exactly that.

If you write all three scenes—your Wonder Intact scene, your Wonder Wound scene, and your Wonder Found scene— read them together in one sitting, preferably out loud, but only if you are alone. This is for you and you only. These wonder scenes will tell you a story that just might change everything for you. Mine did for me.

*part II*

wonder-challenged

# my wondering:
# why does the wonder wound
# attack the wild why?

We've explored wonder in our foundational years, the origin of the wonder wound, and the fall from our initial Free Child. But in trying to return to our wonder, it's important to look at what challenged it in our adult years. Not what ultimately tried to kill it. That comes in the next section.

In this section I want to explore how we habituate ourselves out of our wonder, leave our playfulness in our childhood scrapbooks, sell out on our curiosity, and *stop* stopping for awe. It begins with the voice in our head. And this voice, commonly known as the Inner Critic, is mean. She's mean because she's scared. And I have learned that the meaner she is, the more scared she is. It's ironic because this is the very voice that tells us we don't have a voice in the first place. Yet this destructive voice *never* feels voiceless. This voice feels cocky and entitled and right. I have never, ever, met someone who doesn't have an Inner Critic.

But we don't see her as scared. We see her as the boss. And we let her run our lives, so often right into the corrosive nature of ambition and the crippling myth of success. I'm not just talking about career success. I'm talking about *life* success. Together, those two "success myths" dancing to the lethal threats of the Inner Critic, hand in hand, will do their best to challenge our wonder and even try to duel it to its demise. They're so good at it that if we allow them to rule, they will make it seem like we are being respectable, responsible, loyal, and societally correct contributors to the human race. It's a lie. A terrified, mean lie. Let's shed it. It's time. We can find a new inner voice. An Inner Champion. She's waiting for us . . . .

## the inner critter

Remember back to 4:00 a.m. and that mean, scared voice ping-ponging in the dark? Well . . . morning happens. And life takes over. And as we run around in our daily world, we forget how cruel we are to ourselves. I think that's why we wake up at 4:00 a.m. We've caught up to ourselves, and our rawness can't hide. It must bleed. And so often it's such a mean bleed.

There's a voice in our head as we go through our days that is constantly scrutinizing us:

*Why can't you be more like* _____?
*You should be doing* _____, *not* _____!
*You need to work harder at* _____!

And if we get close to being successful by society's constructs, too often we get a whopping, often flattening lesson, as if delivered by the Inner Critic itself. As if to say, *You* almost *got there . . . but not quite . . . and you never will! Instead, I will make it so that your ego will never explode and you will always feel less than, because you* are *less than!* This will be followed by a cartoon villain's laugh. So we're back to being ruled by our Inner Critic again, even in our waking hours. It's a cancerous cycle that needs to stop.

The truth is, if we gave ourselves permission to process our fear and our pain throughout our day, we'd likely sleep through the night and avoid a whole host of anxiety along the way. For me, writing helps more than anything else. Writing is my practice, my prayer, my meditation, my way of life, and sometimes my way *to* life. But there are many modes of settling the Inner Critic besides writing.

It all starts with awareness. Tuning in to what goes on in your mind. Whatever it is that your Inner Critic tells you, it's probably on constant repeat, and it's probably very unkind . . . especially when it comes to being in your essential and pure and true nature. It doesn't want that for you. That's its most dangerous ground: when you are in your truth. Which, of course, is the inner place where your wonder lives. And the *outward* manifestation of that pure place is your self-expression. Your Inner Critic *loves* to criticize your self-expression. She tells you things about it. Untrue things. And you believe them and even live your life according to these things. I call these your "refusals." Whether or not you're conscious of them, you quite probably have a raw reel of lambasting phrases that drag and dart through your mind all day long, and you're so used to them that you're not even aware of them. To me, these thoughts are the backlash from the loss of your early wild whys.

Some of the most common refusals I hear from people in the way of self-expression (and sometimes from myself too) are:

"I don't have a voice."

"I'm stuck."

"Why does what I have to say even matter?"

"Someone else already said it better than I ever could."

"Who do I think I am? Nobody *asked* me to express myself."

"When I tell a story, I feel like it's self-indulgent drivel at best."

"What I have to say is not good enough."

"I had a teacher in middle school who told me I wasn't creative. And I believed her."

"My mother and father would never read the poems I wrote when I asked them to. They thought it was cute that I wrote them though. But not important."

"My family didn't value creativity. They thought it was extraneous and weak."

"I was raised to be a stoic. I don't know any other way."

"I was raised with 'silence is golden.' Meaning: 'don't talk!'"

However old you are now, and whatever your personal history is, know this: when it comes to self-expression, *you're* running the show. You. Not anyone else. *You* are generating the thoughts and beliefs and stories that define the way you live your life. Which means that *you* are your Inner Critic. Even if she's a result of certain people and institutions in your life, you still invite this voice into the prime real estate of your heart and mind. You house this voice and give her excellent bedding and her own glamorous bathroom replete with a soaking tub. You feed her your fatted calf. You host this voice, *and* you co-create with this voice. And while it seems highly dangerous when you look at it this way, it's actually good news. Because it means that you have choices. Even when you don't feel like you do. I promise you: you have choices.

I like to call her the Inner Critter because why not be playful with her? The Free Child you're twirling in the meadow knows all about how to play with her. And that's because the Free Child you're twirling in the meadow looks at her like she's a busy little mouse, scurrying around, afraid of its tiny, wee shadow, and *really* afraid of your very huge shadow, especially when it's taking a mighty twirl in a sunny, wide-open meadow. The Free Child doesn't have to play the obsequious sycophant to it. After all, it's just a mouse, no matter how mean it might be.

Why do we have to scream and jump on a chair when said mouse scurries through our kitchen? Must be pretty dangerous, that mouse. We're on a chair screaming, "*Eek!*" but our Free Child is on the floor wanting to invite it to tea. Sweet, scared, mean little mouse to whom we turn over so much power.

Many of us are not even aware of the critical voice that lives inside us, usually viciously so. I was in a long-term abusive relationship with my Inner Critter for years, and sometimes I still am. My Inner Critter poses as an Ivy League tweed-clad professor to whom I've given an inordinate amount of power over the years. I have a habit of assigning that level of power to anyone boasting a "smart" bespectacled academic Joycean opinion, especially about "success."

For years, I allowed that snively old sod to rule the roost in my life. She was a passive-aggressive narcissist with gas-lighting mojo. But she was never, *ever*, allowed in my writing chair. That was holy ground. Fill in the blank with your most sacred space for self-expression. Maybe it's in your mind. Maybe it's in the way you dance alone in your living room. Maybe it's in the way you bake a pie. Speak to a special friend like no other friend. Float on your back in a lake. Sing in the shower. Whatever is sacred space for you to be exactly who you are in full, self-expressed creativity and wonder. The more holy ground you can create, the better. Mind you, the Inner Critter will likely fight you, but you can learn to banish her, holy ground by holy ground.

The inherent problem with our Inner Critter, and why she's so hard to silence, is that we become anesthetized to how she treats us. We become *used* to her. And habits are hard to break. Before I started to rehabituate her, my Inner Critter *liked* living in my mind. Why wouldn't she, with the five-star accommodations I gave her? I mean, my *mind*? Talk about sacred ground. Yet I didn't treat it as such.

Then one day I wrote in my journal, "You wouldn't treat

your worst enemy the way you treat yourself in your own mind." And I realized: "That's who I've become. That's what's in my way. Me." I hadn't even been aware of it until that moment. And the Inner Critter . . . she doesn't like it when you become aware of her.

It was true that I'd managed to keep her out of the free zone that was my writing life. But I wanted people to read what I'd written, and that meant it was time to start getting serious about submitting my work. This was in my late thirties. I didn't realize just how lethal the Inner Critter would be in this realm.

When you submit your writing, you get rejections. It's par for the writerly course no matter who you are or what you write. And slowly, like an inevitable mudslide, my Inner Critter began to seep into my most sacred ground: my writing life. The place I most protect, the place I reserve for my purest self-expression. I was able to keep her out of my writing chair, and "Breathe, believe, receive. It's all happening" helped. But she was there the second I thought about anyone reading my work: *See, you're never going to get published. What a silly idea to be a writer. You should have gone into advertising. You need to make more money! Buck up and be a responsible adult!* It was terrifying to me. I didn't know how my writing life was suddenly penetrable. I didn't know yet how to separate the writing life from the publishing life. It took me years to understand that they must be separate.

With each rejection, my Inner Critter got louder and louder and the blows lower and lower: *Who do you think you are? Someone else already wrote it better than you ever could. Why can't you just get really good at tennis or volunteering or something normal? You'll never get published. Never! You should have obeyed your "supposed to be."*

I hadn't truly begun to metabolize the truth that I know now: Even if no one ever reads what I have to say, I still have my own completely unique form of self-expression just for me. And that's what matters most. *But* if I allow others to read my writing—family or friends—or if I get published and even one person loves and appreciates what I write, then *that* is what matters in the way of making the outward arc complete. And no one can infiltrate that fact, even if it's a voice from my own brain.

When it comes to self-expression, I had to learn this first: Each person's voice is as unique as a snowflake. Or a grain of sand. Or a fingerprint. Or your grandmother's gravy. It took some time, but eventually I realized that if people were going to reject me for my uniqueness, that was on them. No one could take away my voice just by saying that it was somehow wrong or bad or unimportant. Even a tippy-top editor at a tippy-top publishing house in New York City. Even the woman at the grocery store. Even me.

Once I realized my Inner Critter was commandeering my inner sacred space, and once I saw how miserable I was, I declared war. For a while, I tried to exorcise the Inner Critter into the Inner Critter Shitter, deeming her the enemy and treating her thusly. I wrote a whole memoir on this subject titled *This Is Not The Story You Think It Is*. During the time depicted in that book, you see a woman learning to become aware of the mind and how it both serves and sabotages us. In those pages and in that time of my life, I unpacked my relationship with my cruel mind. I didn't know how to play with her yet, so she wasn't the Inner Critter yet. I called her My Evil Twin Sister Sheila. (Not sure where I got that. *All My Children* in the 1980s? Someone at the bottom of a well by nefarious intent?)

Then, a few years into promoting that book, now in my midforties, I had an epiphany: Sheila was *me*. Blaming the people and places that spawned her wasn't helpful because *I* was the one inviting her into that prime real estate of my mind. Declaring war on my Inner Critter meant I was at war with my*self*. And that wasn't working. *I* was the one keeping her alive, feeding her the fat along with the lean. Not a great place from which to lure the muse.

I immediately realized that the muse had been waiting for me to have this epiphany. She'd just been standing there chewing gum, swinging her keys around her forefinger, waiting for me to get a clue. Turns out the muse has really great keys to really great worlds as long as we know how to take care of what goes on in our minds.

And that epiphany led to another: What if Sheila wasn't really evil? What if Sheila was just really freaking scared? That brought on a good, long, wonder-full sigh.

So I gave her a different name. A playful one. I traded Sheila for the Inner Critter, and I started to think of her as a scared little girl who lives inside me with a large megaphone to my heart. If a child came into my room in the middle of the night, raging with fear from a night haunt, would I kick her out? Of course not! I'd hug her, walk her to bed, rub her back, and sing her a lullaby until she fell asleep. I tried it, and it worked! I loved my Inner Critter into submission, as it were.

I learned to daily lullaby my Inner Critter into a long nap so that my muse and I could unlock the world of possibility I so longed to explore. To enter and to *play* before all the ambition took over. Again, like we knew how to do when we were children. We just lose our way a little (or a lot) as we go. I'm not always good at keeping her asleep. She wakes up, and sometimes with a vengeance, especially at 4:00 a.m., but I know how to use the lullaby instead of the cross fire. Most of the time. I know that when she's really, really mean, she's really, really scared. But sometimes I still feel powerless before her. I wonder if I'll ever shake her entirely. Likely not. But to me, it's the most important work of my life to try. And this is the best way I've found so far.

I believe that it takes heart-in-hand, self-aware *guts* to truthfully go into our realm of authentic self-expression. And once we have accepted that the Inner Critter is just a scared child who has been hurt for her self-expression, we can put her down for that nap, even if she's throwing a tantrum. We can start to know what Picasso meant when he said, "If they took away my paints, I'd use pastels. If they took away my pastels, I'd use crayons. If they took away my crayons, I'd use pencils. If they stripped me naked and threw me in prison, I'd spit on my finger and paint on the walls." Or what Michelangelo meant when he said that the sculpture was in the stone and that his job was to release it.

Once we are in that free place of creation, unencumbered by thoughts of rejection or "less than" or "more than," we begin to *hunger* for our voice. That's because when we reach this place, we are in our natural flow. Once we are in that flow, we find ease because we are in our truth. We're no longer in our own way. That's when we know we're in our voice. When we find that flow.

It helps to look at our relationship with conflict because conflict is the Inner Critter's version of "'Come into my parlor,' said the spider to the fly." The Inner Critter knows we are often thrown off, or even frozen, by conflict. Especially the self-versus-self conflict that loves to strike at 4:00 a.m., especially when we know that our work will be scrutinized by others. But if we look at her like a scared child . . . well, then she can't scare us with the inherent challenges of our conflicts. In fact, if she's taking a nap, it gives us room to step into conflict, roll around in it, and even *delight* in the challenge. If we can put our Inner Critter down for that nap, we can even understand that conflict is blessed terrain. She'll tell us to run from it like a burning house. Or, sometimes, to run *to* it because it's our job to put out the fire. Both of them are her scared-of-conflict lies.

Conflict is everywhere. We wouldn't have stories to tell without conflict. Conflict is what makes a story a story. And the conflict doesn't have to be dark and scary. It can be that there are too many choices of ice cream! When we tell our stories or make our points or ask our questions, we must have the courage to isolate the conflict and then to go to the center of that conflict. The heart of it. That's how I like to look at it: find the *heart* of the conflict. It's where all the good questions and good answers live. When we have rolled around in the conflict, what was once scary becomes our guide into the great wilderness of the world we are drawing with our words— whether thought, spoken, or written.

*Then* we can face rejection. Scrutiny. Judgment. Assessment. Analysis. Opinions. Comparison. Other people. Institutions. We have gone bravely into the problem and found our way of expressing it. And we have done it kindly. Not with the scared beratement of the Inner Critter but rather with the kindness of the Inner Champion. But we can't find the Inner Champion if we're too afraid of conflict. In fact, that's the Inner Critter's biggest taunt: *You're not brave enough to go to the conflict*, she tells us, just in much meaner words. And it's simply not true. You *are* brave enough. You just have to start looking at conflict like a great and mighty guide and trust that it will steer you toward some sort of resolve.

Consider that you are in charge of drawing a circle of light and ease around yourself. When you focus on what you can create in that safe circle, then it's only natural to bring in your conflict to see what it has to offer you. You can play with it. See if it has a sense of humor. See if it likes to dance or, when disarmed, is actually full of great ideas. Not so scary after all. If you're in that circle of light and ease, then your conflict can turn easily into the possibility for peace and joy in the moment you're experiencing. Doesn't that sound better than being backed up against a wall because of outside, conflicting forces that we feel we need to fight?

When you're playing with the heart of conflict, then you are living in *creation* mode. Which means you're in your wonder. Ask yourself: *How can I take this conflict and use it to find my way to resolution?* This is the way to your soul's language. The essence of your self-expression. The question "What can I create?"—which focuses on the possibility, not the problem—is the most powerful question I know. Whether subconsciously or not, you're asking this question constantly when you think things like, *What do I make for dinner? Coffee or tea? Go right or left?* These questions and these choices are all about creating your life. And yet "What can I create?" is also the question you're most likely to forget or to not proactively tend.

Creation mode comes in all things. I like to focus on writing because most of us create some sort of writing daily in one way or another. And when we put our writing out there, whether in an email, on social media, or even in a book, we set ourselves up to receive feedback. If, in these moments, we let the Inner Critter reign, focusing on the product being worthy of a Pulitzer Prize, then we'll never create anything at all. This is why, when it comes to our creative self-expression, it's essential to drop society's definition of A-plus good and F-minus bad and the most corrosive of all: *perfect.* This is truly the best advice I can give. This is where creativity can enter into your world. This is where wonder can do its wonderful work.

Let's choose to live in the realm of playfulness. Especially when we're dealing with life's biggest challenges. When my friend and client had fourth-stage uterine cancer, she referred to it as the Mangy Wolf. I never heard her vilify her Mangy Wolf. She said it had things to teach her. The Inner Critter does too. Once you become aware of her, how she treats you, and what she's scared of, you can even start to show her compassion.

Imagine taking your Inner Critter's scared hand and having the courage to show her what you've created in a truly curious and awed, wonder-full way. If it feels safe enough, you can invite her into your sacred ground kindly. She might rear her head and start criticizing your creation. But remember, she's just scared. You can teach her how to be in loving dialogue with you about the things you create. She might say, *Wow! You wrote a poem! That took courage and third-eye-wide-open aperture. Good for you!* Now you're training your Inner Critter to be your Inner Champion.

However you express yourself, from your thoughts to your words to your actions to the written word, you have an opportunity to be free. If you can remember that your Inner Critter has been a mean voice inside you that is just a scared child, you can have more compassion for her. She would rather be let off the hook. She'd rather be part of your stunning essence: the Free Child that is in your loving arms, twirling in the meadow with bluebirds and butterflies flitting about your heads.

## your wild why . . .

Keep your journal with you for one whole day and record every time your Inner Critter attacks. Write the attacks in your journal verbatim. Then, for each attack, write down answers to these questions: Are you in a dialogue with your Inner Critter, either in your head or verbally? Or is it a physical response? (Heart palpitations, sweating, holding your breath, tightening your jaw, etc.) Maybe it's both. Write it all down.

At the end of each attack, and each written account of each attack, ask yourself: *How do I feel?* I bet it's not great. So then ask, *Can I put her down for a nap? So that I can create? So that I can live my life and find my wonder? My voice? My delight?*

You can even hum her a lullaby. Literally picture her like a scared child who is finally letting go and settling into slumber.

At the end of the day, look over your list. Now it's time to connect the dots: Where were you emotionally each time she attacked? Were you lonely? Exhausted? Ashamed? Scared? Sad? Angry? Write an emotion that is true for each attack. You might be surprised at what you find.

Going forward in your life, start practicing an Inner Champion's voice. Maybe the Inner Champion is your protector too. Maybe the Inner Champion addresses the Inner Critter directly and speaks kindly, but firmly, to her fear. Maybe the Inner Champion is the one who puts the Inner Critter down for a nap so that you can get on with your life, free from her attacks and free from her fear. It takes a while to cultivate this Inner Champion, and I go into it more fully in Part IV, thanks to the artist and wonderer, Frida Kahlo.

# a storyless life is a wonder-challenged life

Once (upon a time) I was walking in the woods of Montana with a friend who is more full of wonder than almost anyone I know. I was, as usual, picking his brain about the subject. He's one of those rare adult kindreds who has never lost his wonder either. It's just that I'm usually much more wonder-taxed than he.

I had worked myself into an emphatic rant: "People throw around this word, 'awesome,' and I can't hear a drop of actual *awe* in it! Then, in almost the same breath, they tell me that they're not creative! We're *all* creative! Every act of living is creative. Every step we take, every choice we make, every word that comes out of our mouths—it's all an act of creation! It's a *lie* that we're not creative. How could we have forgotten what the child in us knew so well? We are by nature creative because we are by nature full of *wonder*. Have we forgotten our *wonder*? Wonder is what's *behind* creativity! You know? I think if we say that we're not creative, or if we fear our creativity . . . it means that what we've really lost is our wonder!"

He stopped on the trail then and smiled at me. My friend likes it when I get riled up. He runs on the steady, grounded side. "'Creativity' is a big word for most people. And 'wonder' is even bigger. I think you're onto something. Since people use the term 'awesome' all the time, maybe that's the word to start with."

"Agreed! We know what to do with our curiosity! But we don't stop and *stand* in our curiosity. Instead, we start clicking away to find the cyber answer. I hate that about our society. If Montana has taught me one thing, it's how to stand in my curiosity in a true place of awe."

I could tell that he took my word "hate" to heart. He doesn't like to dwell in the negative. His smile widened and his eyes electrified in that mountain-man way of his that might cause him to rip off his clothes and dive into a glacial lake in February. "Do you think you could build a fire that would burn for sixty seconds, in five minutes, using only what's in these woods, with one match, and only one entry point to ignite the fire?" he asked.

"Of course," I said. This guy is never far from using the woods to teach a lesson. I was game. Especially if it would teach me about wonder.

He smiled even wider. "Let's each of us do it. I'll time us. We'll build our fire structures here, but you can go anywhere you want to gather your materials. When four minutes have gone by, I'll make a sound like a raven. That means we have one more minute."

Of course. A raven. That's so him.

"Okay," I said, forgetting about wonder and awe and the state of our society. Instead, I felt the challenge put its full weight on me, giving me a good shove. I marked where we were in the forest, thinking, *I'm clever, and I know my way around the woods. I know my way around fires. I'm going to build the best fire he's ever seen. I'm powerful. Watch me.*

*Mine will be just as good as yours, Mr. Mountain Man. Mine might even be* better *than yours. Mine could keep a cabin in the woods warm in thirty-below temps for days. Mine could rotisserie-cook a wild boar that I've just caught, along with the black truffles it was rooting out from the belly of a ponderosa root system. I'll invite my literary hero, Jim Harrison, and my culinary hero, Anthony Bourdain, to reincarnate and come over for dinner in my little cabin, with my perfect fire, for a thirteen-course dinner, and I'll tempt them with Brouilly and Barolo and Brunello and Bandol. And so of course they will show up because they're both writers and have a penchant for B wines. And they'll use my high school nickname, Lulu — that's how much they'll love me and my fire and my cabin in the woods and my wild boar and black truffles and wine.*

I darted my eyes across the terrain, thinking, *What burns, what burns, what burns?*

I ran to the first birch tree I could find and peeled some bark off an old fallen branch. Then I saw some dry bear grass and picked a few clumps, and then some dry sticks, pine needles, a few larger sticks, and a small fir cone.

An almost-raven cawed through the forest. *One more minute.*

I dashed back and constructed my fire structure: first grass, then pine needles, then bark, then the cone, and then I arranged the sticks in a little tepee — small sticks and then the larger sticks. *This will burn for sure!*

I looked around.

My friend was sitting on a log with some dried grass bundled near his feet. "Time," he said. Then he came over to my fire structure, crouched down, and passed me a strike-anywhere match and matchbox.

Carefully, I held the match as close to the grass at the bottom of the tepee as possible, lit it, and gently pushed the flame into the grass. The grass ignited and flared and licked a pine needle, the flame running to its end, curling it, and then fading into char and smoke. It didn't touch the bark. Nor the cone. Nor the little sticks. And no way the larger ones. No fire. Not even for two seconds, never mind sixty.

I shrugged and didn't exactly look him in the eye. "I make a fire in my woodstove every day all winter. Just so you know. And a lot of the time with just one match."

It was his turn. He went over to his log and knelt by the little nest of dried grass. Then he struck a match and held the flame to what looked like a small piece of sap. And we watched as it ignited and lit the grass — and became a fire. And burned. For a lot longer than sixty seconds. And I thought, *That fire really could have been something. If he'd wanted it to be.* I wanted to go over to my little tepee and borrow its sticks to feed his fire.

I could feel him looking at me, smiling, wanting me to learn something about wonder from his exercise. I swallowed hard and said, "It was only supposed to be a sixty-second fire."

He smiled. "That's all. Just a sixty-second fire."

"I know, I know. You don't have to shove my face in it. I'm an overachiever by nature. And I'm sure I get in my own way all the time because of it. I'm not sure why I always think I have to be so perfect and prove so much. My ambition gets in my way. A lot. Even when I drop its sword, I seem to pick it up again as if it's the only way. Which makes me so ashamed. I know there's always another way. It hurts to hold the sword."

"Just a little ball of sap holds so much power. You know?" He smiled so bright that his holy showed.

I sat on the forest floor and gazed into what remained of his little smoking fire. "So, do you think perfectionism and achievement-based thinking get in the way of our wonder and our ability to stop in awe? Has our competitive society totally ruined our wonder? Or, should I say, has our *participation* in society totally ruined our wonder? Is our creativity only as good as inventing the next i-whatever? Do we even know how to stop and stand in awe? Do we all just need to walk in the woods more often? And look for sap?"

He sat there on his log, smiling at me. Finally he said, "Or just look for nothing. There's an Apache proverb that says that wisdom sits in places."

Then it occurred to me: "You didn't even get off your log, did you?"

He shook his head slowly and kindly.

I felt a little sick inside at how poorly I had played his game and how dense I had been to his wonder-*full* lesson, getting so wrapped up in the challenge. "I ran all over the place. When I had everything I needed right here. Didn't I?"

He smiled and nodded, again slowly and kindly. "But I bet you didn't know about how sap burns, did you?"

"No I didn't. But if I had stopped and just looked and wondered, I bet it would have occurred to me. I mean, I've seen how sap flares when it burns. I was just thinking more . . . big picture. You know, big bonfire. In front of my Wonder Cabin in the woods." I rolled my eyes. "There may have been literary celebrities involved. And really good wine. So maybe my cabin wasn't much of a Wonder Cabin. Maybe it was a *greed* cabin. I want a true *Wonder* Cabin."

We watched the last of his little fire's smoke.

"You'll find it. If you stop long enough." His smile even stopped for a moment.

I said, "You know, I think you just managed to so accurately model what true creativity is and is not. I went running all over the place with a plan, with a fierce commitment to being successful, good, very good, if not perfect . . . to build not just a little dinky fire but a bonfire! I totally lost track of the simple, wonder-full, piece of it. I lost track of what's behind a fire, didn't I? Something as small as a little nugget of sap. Which is everywhere in the woods. True creativity begins with sitting still in wonder. And awe. Curiosity is key. But it's awe that I think we need to practice more in our lives."

He smiled as if to say, *You know what they say about curiosity and cats* . . . .

"Something so little and obvious."

He smiled some more and said, "And it was just supposed to be a sixty-second fire."

"So you're saying that your fire burned because of your ability to stop and be right where you are and create something small and simple instead of racing and chasing and muscling the situation in order to win the Bigfoot Award. Aren't you? Wonder can be very small. It probably *should* be very small. Something you can access right where you are. And be in awe of."

He nodded and played with his long gray beard as if he were awe itself. "Sometimes you have to learn to sit still, to see where power lives. I sat a long time before I finally learned that sap is the best friend to fire."

"I love that about you. You know how to stop and take it all in and not make it hard. You know how to make it easy." I thought about my moment on the stump and the mushrooms in the trees.

"I know that it *is* easy. You just have to stop. And wonder. *Then* you can create. *Then* it comes with ease. And then what you create can turn into something *huge* if you want it to. Not that huge is best." He smiled. "But start . . . right where you are."

That one hit a janky nerve. "Damn, it's so true. I make everything so difficult. I'm always braced against life. Ready for things to be hard. Like I'm going to have to fight a mountain lion. Always having to prove myself. What a wonder-buster."

I looked at him sitting on that log with the wind in his beard and the sunshine in his eyes. And I said, "I bet that's why people are so convinced they're not creative. They think they have to get an A-plus. Kids don't care. They just want to play. They don't walk around saying, 'I'm not creative. I don't have a voice. I'm stuck.'"

He smiled again, and I could see exactly what he must have looked like when he was a little boy. "You don't always have to build a really big fire, Laura," he said. "You just need to know how things burn. That's all."

I added: "And that takes wonder. And that is the definition of 'awesome.'"

Then a real raven cackle-laughed above us.

We looked at each other and then upward, cackle-laughing back.

There's a lot to digest about this story in the Montana woods. It's full of teachings about awe. But I also shared it with you because it shows how storytelling can bring us back to our true, fundamental self-expression fueled by the "sap" of wonder.

Maybe you learned something about yourself from this little scene in the woods—about your ambition, or your wonder, or creativity, or intuition, or wilderness, or life in general. This little scene from my life taught me more than anything in recent history about how our creativity works and what gets in its way. (Again: awe + curiosity = wonder. And wonder + creativity = self-expression. Ambition + perfectionism = wonderlessness.)

Maybe you learned something about me in this story—about how I was not full of wonder in that fire-building challenge. Rather, I was full of want. Greed. I was focused on the endgame. Not the process. It's all about delighting in the process. Think of a small child in the act of creation. She is quite likely full of delight. And it's coursing through her whole body in every little finger gesture and in the way she moves her mouth. Pure wonder. Wonderlessness cannot beget true creativity. It just can't. It might beget a product of some sort, but with any level of soul? I doubt it. Wonder is the sap to the fire. And don't we want the fire?

Here's a worthwhile question: What is the sap to the fire of your creativity?

Not long ago, I wouldn't have had an answer to this question. Maybe you're struggling with it now.

So let's reframe it. What if the engine of our creativity and our self-expression is story? If wonder is what's behind creativity, made of curiosity and awe, then what better manifestation of it all than story? We live our lives in stories. Stories are how we relate to one another.

If you've caught yourself saying, "I don't have a voice," or, "I'm stuck," or, "I'm not creative," then take a moment to consider the power of *storytelling* as a place to start feeling more confident about how you express yourself. Stories are familiar to all of us. You're in the scene of a story right now, wherever you are in the world, reading this book, thinking and being in this space of yours. Maybe you've underlined some things in this chapter. Maybe you've gazed out a window to contemplate or imagine, based on words that you've read in this book. Maybe it's in your lap next to the dog. You might choose later to share this scene. Or not. But why not start with the wisdom and magic of the story to find and communicate your words, your curiosity, your awe, your wonder, and your consequent acts?

I am a student of the human being and always have been. Maybe you are too. I've noticed that our society has tried very hard to take our true stories out of us. Sure, we have myriad opportunities to share tiny story snippets on social media—a photo, a video, a few choice words, a link to something we care about. But what about the sorts of stories that are told around a campfire late into the night? The long ones?

The circuitous ones? The surprise ones? The ones that run as vertically as they do horizontally? That make us belly-laugh and ugly-cry? What's happened to those stories? I think that we've decided as a collective culture that those sorts of stories are a time suck. Or maybe too dangerous in their potential misinterpretation. Or just too plain exposing. So we abandon the "What happened?" altogether, and instead we begin and end with the message.

Try paying attention to how people tell stories. How dedicated to the "What happened?" are they? Or, instead, how adamant are they about the point they are trying to make? Which do you learn more from? Also pay attention to how *you* tell a story. Are you making room for the "What happened?" in your life? If not, why? A storyless life is a wonder-challenged life.

Maybe this bit of teaching will help you in your examination of your relationship to storytelling: Consider what it would have been like if I'd started this chapter off with the line "Wonder is the sap to the fire." What if I *desperately* wanted you to learn what *I* learned from that scene but didn't give you the *actual* scene in the woods with my friend and our fire attempts and our discussion? What if I gained all sorts of wisdom from it and started spewing that wisdom on the first page of this chapter, bursting with clear and hard-won philosophy? Or, heaven forbid, what if I gave you the dreaded "ten easy steps" to finding your wonder and your creative self-expression? What if I never even let you into that scene at all and just *told* you that I had a really profound afternoon in the woods of Montana with this mountain dude I know and that I learned all this stuff that changed my life and now I'm so *wise*.

I'd lose you, wouldn't I? Because you'd just have to *believe* that I'm some sort of authority on this supposed wisdom that I'm spewing. But let's face it: you don't know me from Eve. Not really. I don't have letters after my name that start with a P. I haven't been on *Super Soul Sunday*. What do I know? Why should you trust me? And especially, since I'm keeping my experience in the woods with my friend to myself, how can you possibly see into my world? If I just *tell* you all the high-brow things I learned from that scene, how can you relate to it?

How can you *learn* from me if I don't let you into that moment? You might even be frustrated. Or feel inferior. Maybe you'd even close the book. And yet, this is happening all around us every day. Too many of us are engaging in just spewing what we think about things, shoving lessons down people's throats without showing the stories behind what we know. You may have heard the old adage, "Show, don't tell." The *show* is the story. The *tell* refuses to let you into the story. We relate and learn from the *show*. The *tell* is what "I'm not creative" is made of. The *tell* is the manifestation of the wonder wound. The *tell* is, quite often, hiding.

Sadly, though, it's the *telling* that society prizes. Not the showing. And yet, *showing* is the story that illuminates the human experience. That's what's on the line. I'm not talking about novels or movies. I'm talking about real life. Sitting at the dinner table and swapping stories about your day with people you love. Running into a friend who asks how you are. And *not* skipping to the point but stretching the "What happened?" We're all living in stories all the time, so why don't we honor that, trust it, live by it, learn by it?

In a time line it's fine to *tell*. In my Wonder Time Line, sometimes I *told* for the purpose of summation or learning, both for mine and yours. And sometimes I *showed* when I knew that it would help us better imagine the lesson and learn along with my experience. In those cases, I purposely took my time. I wanted to invite us into a vital teaching moment. I hope that if you haven't already, you'll take the time to write

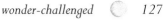

out your own Wonder Time Line in that way too—not rushed but luxuriating in story, especially the hard ones.

In true story sharing, your goal should be to activate your listener's imagination. Which means you have to activate your own imagination. That is where the wonder-full stories live. What I just showed you in my sixty-second-fire story was a "word movie." Hopefully, you could see the woods in your mind's eye as I took you through my experience with my friend. You could see me peeling the birch bark, imagine the bonfire I was setting out to make in my mind, hear my friend's raven call, smell the lit matches, see my fire fizzle and his burn. Hear our dialogue. See his bright eyes and his big smile. Feel my self-judgment but also my heart opening to a lesson learned but only analyzed at the end.

I can tell you this with almost no doubt in my mind: If I hadn't let you into the story and if I had only *told* you about what happened without any concrete details of that scene, your imagination would not have been activated. You would not have been able to see it in your mind's eye. If I'd just *told* you about my experience, you wouldn't have felt empathy or connection. You need your imagination to be somehow activated in order to wonder, *How are we the same?* Empathy happens when we engage with the question *What can I learn about myself through a story that is very different from my normal life?* And when you are asking questions like that, you are wonder-full! You are in your wild why, not your wonder wound!

I work with so many people whose lives have taken major twists and turns and who want to capture their story in a book, whether in a memoir or in a fictionalized version of their story. But nine times out of ten they want to *report* all about it rather than let the reader in to what they know. In other words, into the *story*. They want to *tell* all about what happened or *that* it happened. They don't know how to get out of the way and show the "word movie" of it instead.

The scene. As I said in the first pages of this book: We live our life in stories. Find the scene, and you find your voice. It speaks *for* you. And remember, ten people can experience the same scene, and each of those ten people will have a different account of it. No one lives your life but you.

Even if we're writing a dissertation on wisdom, we're still in a library with cold coffee and a dead fly on the windowsill, looking over the quad where ruddy econ majors are playing lacrosse and wan philosophy majors are quarreling with their egos in hammocks. We're always in a scene.

The scene is the infrastructure that holds the possibility for wisdom. And there is no wisdom without wonder. There is no intentional fire that burns without a good dose of wonder. Creativity doesn't build the fire. Wonder does. And that's why we're so scared of the word "creativity." We think we have to start with creativity. But that's not it at all. It's *wonder* that builds the fire. And *then*, yes, creativity. But wonder is where it all begins. Wonder is my friend's log in the woods before he made his fire. Wonder is what made him sit down on it and ask himself, kindly and simply and with delight: *What do I have, right here, that can give me everything I need in this moment?* Wonder is what granted him the permission to have his creativity come with ease. And his fire to burn from a piece of sap, some dry grass, and a match. And wonder is what had him know that in the middle of the woods, if he truly needed it, he could build a bonfire, not by taking half the forest with him but by finding that one small piece of power upon which everything else is built. And how did he learn all of this? By sitting on a log in awe. Waiting for the lessons that he knew were all around him. Wonder has us live from the inside out. Not the other way around.

Wonder can't happen without the log and the forest floor and the person sitting on it. A man's mind might be in the clouds, thinking about how this challenge is going to teach his friend something about wonder, thinking about where he can find a ball of sap and some dried grass to show her that she doesn't have to be so overactivated in the creativity department. To show her that her lust for creativity and hellfire way of proving to herself and everyone around her that creativity doesn't scare her, that she's a master creator, that she could kill someone with her creativity . . . and maybe herself too . . . isn't going to create anything in the end. He can sit there on that log and wonder if she is going to realize that everything she needs is right in front of her. That it doesn't have to be so difficult, this birthing of life, moment by moment. But a mind in the clouds, full of wonder, doesn't build fires. In other words: this man sees me. What does it take for us to see ourselves?

Wonder ignites the creativity that finds the sap and grass, and it strikes the match and makes it burn. And it turns it into heart language, whether spoken, written, or thought. My friend is heavy on wonder, and it results in creative ease. Flow. Fires that burn for their simplicity. And, yes, function.

But none of this is going to sink into your mind and heart if you can't imagine it for yourself. And how do you inspire someone to imagine? Tell them a story. Give them the scene. Let their mind go wild with it so that they can connect with you and learn. Once you activate their imagination, it just might inspire them to go out into the world in wonder and to stop for awe. Imagine if your voice did that. It will if you allow it.

## your wild why . . .

If you're feeling wonder-challenged or voiceless in your life, try sharing stories. Long ones. Deep ones. Life-changing ones. It might feel like unsafe ground. You've likely been trained into "the long and short of it." The *telling* of it, not the *showing* of it. If this is the case, create some guidelines and boundaries for yourself.

First, choose a story that you want to explore with another person. Choose one in which you learned something. Or one that challenged you. One in which you came out new. A story that really lit your heart on fire. One that had you truly stand in awe of what you beheld. It's helpful if you've got questions that you'd like to parse with the other person.

Second, write it in your journal, in scene. Try to capture every important detail. Try reading it aloud afterward in a place where no one can see or hear you.

After that, it's time to take your story on the road. Be sure to choose someone safe to practice your story sharing with. Someone who likes stories, likes questions, likes to parse things. And someone who will be honest and kind about it with you.

Set up clear boundaries, and venture in with a seeking spirit.

Here's some sample language for you: "I'd like to share a story that I think you'd be interested in, and it takes a while. Half an hour or so. Maybe more. Do you have time for it? I'd love to unpack it with you afterward. It's full of hidden gems that I think we both could learn from if we put our heads together."

Your boundaries might freak them out, and they might suddenly say that they forgot they have a dentist appointment. Fine. They weren't going to be safe in the first place, and the reason is none of your business. Find someone who is. Someone who will sit down with you and who promises to listen. Those people are out there, though they are rarer and rarer.

Then, as you share your story, check in with your feelings. Are you worrying the whole time that you're boring the other person? Are you afraid you've lost them altogether? Do you feel shame? Do you wish you were funnier, or deeper, or just different? Do you wish you could share a story the way *fill in the blank* does? (I've met Phil Intheblank. He's boring.) Or do you feel exhilaration? Do you feel relief and even freedom in knowing that they're making good on their promise to listen, no matter how "good" your story is? Is it nice being listened to? Having someone bear witness? *Loving* witness, even? Is it new for you?

Finally, if they *don't* make good on their promise to listen, or if they start to fidget, or if their eyes are darting all over the room, or if they're looking at their cell phone, just stop. It's highly unlikely that they'll say, "Wait, are you finished with your story? Seems like you clipped it off too soon. I want to hear the end!" Instead, they'll want to tie it up in a bow and say that they've got errands to run. You've dodged a bullet, and as my friend from Texas says, "A dodged bullet is a dodged bullet, whether it misses you by a mile or an inch. Take it as a good thing."

But if you get to the end of your story and you feel that they've really listened, and if it feels safe, then revel in the gift you have just given by sharing your story and by trusting them. Maybe you'll say, "I'd like to dig into this story. What did it mean for you?" Whatever you say, start an analysis time. You can ask them how much more time they have if you want to have exceptional boundaries. I recommend it, especially if your wonder wound includes "I talk too much."

Thank them when you're done. You might be surprised when they thank you back.

You might even find that the two of you sit there together, feeling true awe about your story and the giving and receiving of it.

# keeping your voice to yourself for a while

As you know by now, one of the greatest enemies of my wonder has been a long-lived and crippling addiction to ambition, even in the innocent woods of Montana, as you've just seen in the prior chapter. It likely started with the "*you are going to be the staaah of the family*" messaging.

Again, being told that you're special is not necessarily helpful nor a gift. Sometimes it can be a plague. Because where I come from, choosing to be a writer wasn't the kind of star quality people were hoping for. I was never going to figure out how to live the writing life within the institutions of my origins. I may have left those institutions, but without knowing it, I ended up addicting myself to a new one: the institution of the traditional New York publishing world.

My Inner Critter craves my ambition addiction like a vampire craves blood. It goes all the way back to *Annie*, *A Chorus Line*, *Flashdance*, and maybe even Cinderella's castle. But not *Willie Wonka & the Chocolate Factory*. Willie Wonka didn't really want much, except to find one pure child. He acted like he was an ambition addict. But he wasn't. It was

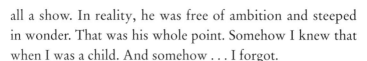

all a show. In reality, he was free of ambition and steeped in wonder. That was his whole point. Somehow I knew that when I was a child. And somehow . . . I forgot.

This is the story of what broke my ambition addiction wide open, setting the stage for ultimate release and healing later when I found "Breathe, believe, receive. It's all happening." Or, should I say, when it found me.

I was in my early thirties, a young mother, a mostly unpublished novel writer, and my wonder wound was a festering mess. I wanted to be widely published so badly it hurt. Everywhere. That's when I received the best homework assignment of my life. It is my true pleasure to share it with you wherever you are in your relationship with ambition, dreams, and wonder. Here goes:

It's a simple summer day in the early 2000s. I am a young mother of a four-year-old boy and an eight-year-old daughter. She is at that age when every time the phone rings, it could be Santa Claus. Even in August. For me, this call turns out to be just that.

I'm on the toilet when the phone rings, and my daughter barrels into the bathroom, holding the phone out in front of her. "Mom, it's Terry someone on the phone." Her braids sway to the timing of her post-toddler purpose.

*Terry?* It couldn't possibly be *the* Terry!

I shriek-whisper, "Can you tell her I'll call her back in a few minutes?" Why do angels descend when we're, uh . . . indisposed?

My daughter offers an incredulous eye roll.

So, pants down to my ankles, I take the phone. "Hello?" I say, without a lot of, well, *vim.*

"Hello, Laura. It's Terry Tempest Williams, and I only have a few minutes. But I'm so enthused by what you sent me, and I want to give you a homework assignment I gave myself years ago."

One of my utmost literary heroes. And me on the can, without a pen, paper, laptop, nothin'.

My daughter stands at the door. "Who *is* it?"

I swat her away. I hate doing that, but this is a big deal.

Backstory: A month prior, I'd heard Terry speak about wilderness conservation after her book *Red* came out. This wasn't really an author event. More a night of awareness about open space and protecting it, so the ambition addiction was at bay. We were going to be focusing on keeping wilderness wild, not getting one of my novels published. And frankly, I was relieved to not have that desperate, cloying feeling of, *Oh my God, there's one of my literary icons who has actually come to my valley and I have* got *to get her attention somehow . . . and her* help *. . . and her love . . . and* acceptance *. . . and, and, and . . . Aw, heck. Leave 'er alone. My lack of platform and publishing success is my fault. It's my fault for leaving the land of movers and shakers and publishing-world parties and little black dresses. It's my fault for being afraid to* really *hammer the pavement and send my work out to the degree that an author has to. My fault for not being mature enough to look at it like a numbers game in the end. My fault for thinking I have a calling and hence deserve some sort of divine outcome. And then discovering . . . that I am not special. Plus, she doesn't care about writers tonight. She cares about trees.*

So I just sat in the audience with the friend who had basically dragged me to the event. She knew I was feeling deflated in the realm of my dreams. And my wonder too.

With her usual eloquence, Terry answered all the smart questions about trees and watersheds and subspecies and aquifers and things that in 2004 I didn't really know that much about, even though I'd lived in Montana for ten years. I'd been having babies and writing books and was just learning my flora and fauna. But part of why I was there was because when

I read Terry's work, I saw myself in her words. She was the writer sister who felt truly kindred—she just didn't know it. Yet. The longing to connect with her started rumbling inside me. How could I make her know it? How could I let her know that I carried her books around with me like security blankets? She represented all of what I wanted to be in the world as a writer. She showed up as exactly herself, and her readers loved her for that perhaps most of all.

But something old and mean barked at me: *She would never be your writer sister. You're afraid to show up as exactly yourself. If you did, your readers would all say, "You talk too much. You ask too many questions. You cry too easily. You're too sensitive. In fact, while we're on the subject: You want too much. You are too much. There's nothing eloquent about you or your writing."*

Wow. *Really* mean. So *really* scared. I wasn't aware of the Inner Critter yet, so I just sat there feeling bad about myself and my writing and my life, staring up at her in her ivory-embroidered cape, trying not to indulge my longing.

When the Q and A was over and people were lining up on the stage to meet her, I just wanted to get back in my car and cry to Joni Mitchell's *Blue* album. It had become the soundtrack to my life.

"You need to go up there and meet her," my friend cajoled with that smile of hers—a smile that could save an entire wetland.

"Uh . . . she has enough people who want a piece of her," I said. "I'm going to just leave her alone. I've learned that writers can't really help writers get published anyway. I need someone who can help me find an agent. Plus, I write fiction. She writes memoir."

"Go buy her book. I'll get us a glass of wine and you get in line. You need to know that woman." If my friend didn't look just like Joni Mitchell, maybe I would have said no. But for some reason, in that moment, I did what she said. Even though I felt like an asshole.

My Inner Critter bellowed, *Whatever you do, don't talk too much. And don't cry!* I didn't tell her where to put it. I agreed with her.

I bought *Red* and stood in line, watching people fold into Terry's arms as she wrapped them in her cape, many of them crying, her sage words no doubt changing their lives forever.

I started to feel nervous. Really nervous. Like . . . what do you say to someone so beloved that she scares you with her dignity? *She's probably friends with Maya Angelou*, I thought.

So I did what any other normal person would do in that situation. I started practicing being myself. Like that ever works. I'd done the same thing when I met the then CEO of Condé Nast and his wife (then editor-in-chief of *The New Yorker*) at a dude ranch in Wyoming, about eight years prior, at a sunrise pancake campfire. It hadn't gone so well. Long and short of it: with a desperation disguised as they're-on-my-turf-now clubbiness, I intruded on their family breakfast in a secluded (to protect them from people like me) gazebo and asked if I could send him my first novel. He kindly agreed as he fished out one of his business cards from his vest pocket, while I had the debutante's grace of leaning over to his wife, slapping her on the knee, and saying, "At least I don't write short stories, or I'd be bugging *you!*"

She got up, justifiably, took her children, and left. I mean . . . fuck me. I'd been such an idiot around people who had power in the world of publishing. *Such* a powerless idiot. Was I going to be an idiot now? Before the picture-of-grace-eternal Terry Tempest Williams? I did *not* trust myself. And that's *not* a good feeling.

What did I even really have to say for myself, when it came down to it? That I'd written a bunch of novels? That a few were good? That the rest were exercises in learning?

That I hadn't tried all that hard to get an agent? That fear of rejection felt incapacitating sometimes? That I'd had a few short pieces published in obscure literary journals across the country? Nothing to write home about.

I looked around for my friend, but she had likely gotten into a conversation about selective logging, a bit the way a big sister does when she pushes her little sister down the driveway on a bike without training wheels . . . and then lets go.

I was on my own. And I really wanted that glass of wine. But I was next.

"Hi, Terry," I said, putting out my hand and looking her in the eye, as I'd been trained to do from childhood. But this wasn't a prep school interview, nor the advertising job I'd never had since I'd instead made the absurd choice to become a writer and move to the middle of "nowhere." *Should I ask her for writerly advice?* It felt wrong to ask anything of this woman who gave so much. *Just state your name and thank her. Ask her to sign her book.* "Hi. I'm Laura Munson. I want to thank you for . . . ."

I paused.

She smiled.

The world stopped.

I was looking into the eyes of an angel. Trying to ask for nothing. But I wanted everything.

I wanted to scream, *Please, please, please take away all of my pain! Pain from years of feeling so alone in this pursuit. Pain from failing at what I was sure was my calling.* I wanted to look into her wide, wise eyes and beg, *Can you give me my big break? I've done the work. I've paid my dues. I've sat at the intersection of heart and mind and craft that is the* true *writing life for a long time. I'm ready. Can it please be time? Can you connect me with someone who might* get *my writing and want to be its steward?*

*And I do care about trees and birds and wandering rights. I do. But right now . . . could you please . . . just give me a tiny hug? Just a tiny one? Maybe wrap me in your cape a little? And tell me that everything's going to be okay? Writer sister to writer sister?*

But how can you ask any of that of an angel? She was saving watersheds and old-growth forests. So *what* about my dinky little writing "calling"?

I held my breath.

And then she leaned into me and gently pulled me to her. "Laura Munson? The *writer*?"

I had never felt more seen. Or more surprised.

I nodded my head and squeaked out a tiny "Yes." Then I started to shake. And then I started to cry. My Inner Critter was rolling on the floor, snort-laughing, but I wasn't going to let her ruin this moment.

"I read your piece in *Northern Lights*. It was lovely."

I couldn't speak. She'd actually *read* my little essay? The very first thing I'd gotten published—about studying wonder through watching my baby girl absorb a fiery Montana summer sunset. An essay called *Taps*. And she'd remembered my *name*?

Whereupon she took the copy of *Red* from under my arm and said, and I'll never forget these words as long as I live, "Oh sister in words. What can I do? How can I help?"

I tried to collect myself as she signed my book, including not just her email but her *street* address and phone number. Instead of anything remotely significant or writerly, this is what came out of my mouth: "I swear I'm not a stalker. My kids wear David Duncan's kids' hand-me-downs." As if this affiliation with a dear mutual writer friend would somehow prove me safe. That's when I coined the phrase "assing out." First the editor-in-chief of *The New Yorker*. And now Terry Tempest Williams.

Terry smiled at me and pulled me into her cape. She didn't seem to care that I'd just assed out. She simply and graciously said, "Send me something you've written."

I couldn't speak. I didn't want to get snot in her hair. Or saliva. Or spiritually scum her with decades of writerly woe.

"Thank you," I managed to say.

The next day I sent her a book of personal essays I'd written about going from city girl to country girl. I told her that I likely wouldn't try to publish it, as fiction was my true love. But since she wrote creative nonfiction, I figured she'd be more interested in that genre. The truth was: it scared me too much to let her see my novels. Instead, I included a cover letter explaining the essence of the essays and which ones I wanted to get published. But I also felt compelled to share about my self-doubt and fear of judgment. My self-inflicted Inner Critter whippings and the resulting scars, even though I hid them well. I shared how confused I was about the publishing world. How afraid I was to submit my work to agents. How hard rejection was for me. I longed for some sage advice the way I'd longed for my sister at age five. I didn't quote my fourth-grade journal to her. I saved her from complete self-pity. It was a desperate letter from a desperate young mother and semi-seasoned writer. I hadn't isolated and identified the wonder wound yet. I was too far in it to see clearly.

Back to the phone call on the toilet. And the homework. No pen. No paper.

"I want you to take the next year and write your story," she said. "The first part of this book. The pre-Montana part. And I want you to stop trying to get published. Don't even think about it. Write only for you. For one year."

"Really? But it's so uninteresting. I mean . . . being a WASP? In a fancy suburb of Chicago? Boarding school? My inner melancholy that I can't seem to shake? I really don't want to stare all that stuff down, Terry. It's not very interesting, anyway, if anyone was to ever read it. I'm a totally unsympathetic character."

"Write it, just for you."

Just for me? That hadn't been a respectable option.

But maybe she sensed the haunt of my fourth-grade journal. Maybe she had a similar haunt. She seemed like the type to write in a journal in fourth grade. And keep it. Maybe she felt *bad about all of it* too.

Then she told me a story about how her friend had encouraged her to turn one of her most famous books into nonfiction. How she'd written it many times as fiction. How she'd had to learn that her story was . . . enough.

I won't mince Terry's eloquent words here, but what she shared with me was enough to make me stop the madness of trying to get published. To put it totally out of my mind. For one year. To take a deep and much-needed breath from my longing and the limits of it and to start writing my story. Nonfiction. With absolutely no intention of getting published.

What a complete *relief* that year was. I wrote with an innocence and a purity that I'd lost along the way. I loved every minute of it.

I can't say that book was any good. It remains in my office closet. It's called *Break Me In, Montana*. It tells many stories that were just for me, and my words flowed. They were all mine. They felt good. Writing had always felt good, but the fear of rejection and judgment hadn't. Somehow fiction felt like much safer ground for me. I wasn't beholden to the facts. I could create a world and the characters in it. Or maybe I'd been too scared to write, as Terry says, "past the embarrassment of exposure." Being the main character in a book did *not* feel safe. If I could learn how to feel safe in my words, real or imagined, maybe I could learn how to surrender the fear, too, no matter what genre.

It took a sister in words a decade ahead of me to give me the permission I came to give myself after a year of living that way. If she hadn't given me that homework assignment, I wouldn't have had the courage to later write the book that put me on the map: *This Is Not The Story You Think It Is.* A memoir. Nor would I have the courage to write this book and expose my wonder wound.

Terry Tempest Williams and her assignment healed my fiction. I no longer needed to parse my childhood fears and sadness and shame and guilt and loneliness in made-up characters. If I wanted to be the main character, I could be, whether or not I was a sympathetic one.

During that yearlong assignment, I basked in the fact that the book was for me and only me. The content was highly personal. I bled too profusely in it for public consumption, and I meant to bleed that hard. Needed to bleed that hard. Somehow, Terry knew.

After that year, I put *Break Me In, Montana* in my closet, thanked it, and started a novel. A fresh, new novel about entirely made up characters, none of them remotely resembling myself or the people or places in my life. That novel got me my agent. Spending that year not caring about other people's opinions of my writing (that is to say, my *voice*), and letting my craft teach me what my mind and heart so longed to know and swallow whole, changed everything. My novel felt pure, and my intentions for getting it into the world felt pure too. I didn't feel desperate any longer. I felt like an author who wrote something that would bridge to people out there, and profoundly so. Terry's homework assignment changed *everything*, but, perhaps most of all, it created a steady confidence in me, not just in my writing but in the root of my self-expression. It was the antidote to my fourth-grade journal wound.

We pass it on, this thing called grace. Because it's in this sort of freely given love and wisdom that we find what it is that we have to say and heal from whatever has kept us from giving ourselves the permission to do so in the first place.

When you have the opportunity, please pass it on.

## your wild why . . .

Think of one of your greatest heroes. Imagine that you have a chance to meet your hero and have a few minutes to ask them for advice. What questions would you ask? Here are some preliminary questions to ask yourself to help you come up with your list:

*What is a central problem that I need help solving?*

*What support would I ask my hero for if I had the opportunity and the courage?*

*What's blocked in my life that my hero might be able to unblock?* (Think tangibly here: networking, think-tanking, problem/solution.)

*When it comes to getting out of my own way, what might my hero see for me that I can't see?* (Think psychologically here: take a break from your goal and focus on another that is more doable, etc.) You can even ask your hero this exact question! That is: "What can you see that I can't see? How am I in my own way? Your honesty will help me!"

Now write a list of the exact questions you'd like to ask your hero. For instance, if you are in a *should I stay or should I go* conflict (with a job, a relationship, a geographical move, etc.), you might ask your hero to share a story of their own similar conflict and how they resolved it. You might then take their method and tailor it to your own resolution.

Here are some examples:

"When you're stuck, how do you find your flow again?"

"Do you have blind spots? If so, how do you see them?"

"How do I find the courage to go deeply into my conflicts and find the wisdom and resolution?"

Now, answer your questions as if you are your hero. What might your hero say to you in response to your questions? Answer *as if*. You likely know a lot about your hero. Try to channel them. Step into their shoes.

If you have no idea what your hero would say to you, then read up on them. (Find interviews, Q and As, podcasts, personal essays, etc.) Study what conflicts they've faced and how they handled them. And then do your best at creating their answers to your questions.

Now that you've asked and answered some key questions, think, *What homework assignment might my hero give to me that could possibly solve my problem and even change everything?*

In doing your homework assignment, consider the answers you created, in your hero's words, to your questions. They will serve as a good guide.

Now, give that assignment to yourself. And commit to it. Maybe for a year. Maybe for a week. Whatever is possible yet practical. Truly commit to it.

To set yourself up for completion, be sure to create parameters that are in keeping with who you really are: your responsibilities, your habits, your personality, your energy level, etc.

Write a statement of commitment to set your intentions and to make a pact with yourself (I.e., "I commit to _____.") Keep it short. It should be something that you can memorize. Put it somewhere that is easily accessible. Read it often, as a reminder of your personal pact. In my case, given Terry's homework, I wrote: "I commit to writing nonfiction for one year without trying to get published."

Live by it, with delight and wonder that you are taking this potent stand for yourself! You have taken control over your wonder challenges. Deep bows to you.

Of course if you have an opportunity to meet this hero in real life, why not go for it? Or why not try writing them a letter? Or reaching out to them on social media? If you don't hear from them, don't take it personally. They're probably busy or didn't even get your note at all. At least you tried. And no one can take away your answers to these questions, the homework assignment, and your commitment to it. Those are all yours.

# the day that curiosity
# and awe shook hands

I have a tall stack of books on my bedside table, and I daily attempt to read a few paragraphs in pursuit of discovering new wisdom, or a character of some astonishment, or a fresh angle into the human heart. And yet, all too often, I find myself gravitating to the top left shelf of my bookcase where the Jim Harrison lives and pulling down a dog-eared, underlined, bath-bloated, old, roughed-up book friend.

I know of only one writer who can compose a novel in which the first hundred pages mostly discuss his protagonist's penis. And then, woven into the elegance of words like "pecker," "noodle," "wanker," and "worm," he threads NPR, bluebirds, a beloved dead dog, and cherry farming, and he describes a cell phone's worth thusly: "It's a prime weapon against our essential loneliness." Harrison.

I love Harrison because he's midwestern and Montanan, and his love for these places is all over his writing. I love him because you can feel his pain in his humor and his humor in his pain. And sometimes the mixture of those two things makes him downright bawdy. But I forgive him for it because he's willing to be honest about who he truly is. And that truth is part poet, part philosopher, part word sorcerer . . . and hard-pressed to call himself much more than a sewer rat. I love him because he's obsessed with his craft, and you can tell on the page when a writer isn't. I love him because he writes things like this: "I'm sort of neutral in terms of religion, but ever since I was a kid I've thought moving water to be the best thing God made."

People often ask me what I like to read. Although I published a memoir, memoir is not the genre of my heart. That affection belongs to fiction, and within the genre, Harrison is my favorite. I try to read the other books in my stack, full of literary gems new and old. I try to widen my literary garden path, but I can't see for all the Russell Chatham–bedecked blossoms lining my top left bookshelf.

Harrison published dozens of books: fiction, nonfiction, and poetry. I own all of them. One of his poems hangs in a framed lithograph over my office desk. I have a file on my computer called "Jimmy" that has as many unsent letters as books he published. He had a ranch in a town I frequent in Montana and, as locals like to talk about where people live and where people hang out, I've had to take my hand out of that candy jar more than once. He did *not* need me camping out at the end of his road with dozens of books to sign and dozens of letters to deliver and dozens of bottles of Domaine Tempier Bandol or Barolo or Château Lafite Rothschild to drink, a '49 Latour, a '61 Lafite, a '47 Meursault—not that I knew what his favorite wine was or anything. Or what kind of cigarettes he smoked. Or what D. H. Lawrence quote was taped on his writing desk. It's not like I've been paying attention. Or anything.

Guts come from despair and desperation sometimes. And that's how I finally found the courage to send Jim a letter. A big book deal for one of my novels had fallen through, and my family was sick of hearing me talk about it. I drew inward. My wonder was on fumes. Maybe my dream of becoming a published novelist was never going to come true. I wanted to write to someone who understood this *obsession* that had ruled my life—and Jim was my man. I'd read somewhere that he'd described his own writing as a "dirty secret." I'd always likened my writing to the feeling of getting away with something. Like a kid faking sick to get out of going to school. Maybe a bit gentler. But, yes, a dirty secret just the same.

So, I let it spill. I told him all about my many years of learning my craft. I told him about the Terry Tempest Williams assignment. I told him how it had healed my fiction and about my great agent and how close we'd gotten with two novels. I told him about my recent book-deal debacle. Then I went further because it felt cathartic to rat out the powers that be, and I suspected that he'd have some sort of epigrammatic Harrison-esque reaction because of the sheer insanity of it. I told him about almost making it through two major publishers with two different novels, working on the sly with in-house editors, one of them *his*, only to be accepted by the editors but rejected by the marketing team. *Twice.* I wanted to know how a writer is supposed to deal with the fact that they can write but that business is business. I wanted to hear that there was still something pure out there in the world of publishing. I knew/hoped he'd be able to give me a scathing comment next to a sacred one when it came to publishing a book. But what I really hoped for was a dissertation on how art and money shouldn't have anything to do with one another.

I sent the letter snail mail, via his publisher, and figured that Jim would never get it. It took about all the courage I had in the way of reaching out to my top literary hero. I might even get a nasty note that would exhume the fourth-grade wonder wound. Who knew? But if Terry had shown up the way she had, maybe Jim would too. I had learned by now that elders, whether inherited or found, were essential to a person's life. But you had to ask.

At the end of the letter, I'd had a flash of extra courage and mentioned that I was taking my family on a camping trip to Arizona (near the small town he called home during the winter), and that I loved birds, like he did, and would gladly welcome some local suggestions about where to go bird-watching. I admitted that I was keen on maybe even seeing the famous elegant trogon. I quoted the snow geese line from his poem "Counting Birds." Then I showed off by telling him that every spring I drive over to Freezeout Lake to see the three hundred thousand migrating snow geese rise off the water at dawn, cross the highway, and feed on the spent grain in the wheat fields. And then back again at sunset. Ten thousand tundra swans. Thousands of northern pintails. Then a coda: "My son would do anything to see an elegant trogon bird." That line was so loaded it wasn't even worth its words. I was the only one in the family who really cared about birds. My son was more interested in the binoculars.

And then at the very end of the letter, I took a deep breath and typed, "P.S. If you're around, I'd love to meet you for a drink while we're in town." Rejection for my authentic self-expression had gotten me in trouble all my life. Tears leaked down my cheeks because I was so afraid that this epic elder of mine would reject me too.

I was shocked to hear back from Jim in an email the next week. I don't know how publishers can take six months to reject you but somehow get their authors' fan mail to them within days. I mentally tore the virtual letter open like a Wonka golden ticket. *My* golden ticket.

He told me where to go bird-watching: the Buenos Aires National Wildlife Refuge.

But the gold was in his own postscript: "Usually, I can be found at 4:00 at the Wagon Wheel bar, trying to hydrate." *Oh. My. God!* My whole body shook. Was this an *acceptance* letter? From Jim Harrison? Seemed like it was!

A few weeks later, my little family rolled into the Buenos Aires National Wildlife Refuge at the southern part of the state along the Mexican border. I was talking nonstop about all the raptors we were going to see and how this was the premier destination for bird-watching aficionados, according to my literary hero. "I'll just bet that we'll even find an elegant trogon!"

My husband and daughter were tolerating me, knowing that I was still rocked by my recent publishing gut-wrench, but my eight-year-old son was all innocence. I'd so far kept him screenless and video game–less, and he liked it that way. "Yeah, Mom! We are definitely going to find the trelegant whatever bird!"

But as we drove into this "refuge," I went nonverbal. Bars on the windows of its vacant Visitor Center. DANGER signs plastered over bird migration maps. Graphic graffiti all over the building walls. My healing gut told me to look up instead. I'd never seen so many raptors in my life, riding warm thermals in the expanse of Arizona sky. "Let's find a campsite." No one objected.

It turned into a major adventure, off-roading in our rented camper, a vehicle covered in images of the American dream and not meant to go over deeply rutted roads dead-ending at will, with thorny pinion trees scratching slashes through Lady Liberty and the all-American kids at the Grand Canyon that we named Heinous, Odious, and Misbegotten. We finally found ourselves lost in the wide-open, sun-caked desert, more raptors in one place than I'd ever seen.

While my husband and daughter stayed at the campsite to play a few hands of gin, my son and I hiked to the side of a bald ridge with our binoculars and camping chairs. With every raptor, my son shouted like he was watching fireworks. "Look at that one, Mom! It's huge! I bet that wingspan is like ... pterodactyl wide!"

I smiled, watching him handle his binoculars, steady and stealth, aiming them at birds but also at the grass, his hand, a bug.

"Can you believe it?" I said straight to his eight-year-old wonder. "Amazing what you see when you look up! So many hawks. That's a red-tailed, but that's I think a Cooper's? And look! A golden eagle. Oh wow! And I think that's a great horned *owl*! In broad daylight!" I followed it until I lost it to the lower plateau. "Listen. Can you hear it?"

He listened with one ear to the sky. "No."

"Exactly! Because it's an owl! You'll never hear an owl."

He smiled at my trick question. I took out my bird book and flipped to the owl section to show him a diagram of their feather structure.

As if to punish me for having my head in a book in this wildly spacious moment, he said, "Mom! Look! There's an elegant trogon! Aww ... you missed it!"

I suspected that he was giving the "look up" advocate a taste of her own medicine. Or maybe he believed he'd seen this elusive bird. Either way, I wasn't about to mess with his wonder, so I held back from spewing data at him—the elegant trogon hangs out along flowing streams and in the branches of sycamores, not in an open sky like this, full of thermal-riding raptors. "That's incredible! You saw an elegant trogon! Good for you! You've always been a good looker." That's a high compliment in our family.

He cleaned his binoculars with his shirt, looking very pleased with himself. "Mom. This is so fun! Those guys are missing all the fun!"

I thought of my husband, wonder-challenged at work these days and not so kind on the home front. My daughter, forced into the wonderless muck of tweendom against her better sixth sense, also wobbly in the kindness department.

"Remember this," I said to my son. "The world tries to take this away. Don't you dare let it."

"I won't. I promise."

He was utterly serious. As if his life depended on it. And it did. His binoculars went back to his watchful eyes.

After a night of gin rummy and camper-challenged sleep, we woke at dawn to the sound of helicopters all around us. I looked through the window and beheld a scene that broke my wonder and bashed my hope.

Armed men jumped out of helicopters, like hawks on gophers, scooping up entire families hiding in the scrubby grass. Cold, terrified mothers gripped their children to their chests, and fathers stood tall, armed only with their bargaining power and last hope for a Hail Mary show of empathy. Instead, they were pulled from the field and pushed into the aircrafts.

I traced the deep fear lines around their eyes like maps of what they'd left to where they'd hoped to go. What had our camper stood for to them, I wondered, with its Statue of Liberty and happy kids posing in front of the Grand Canyon? The promise of an American dream Christmas card life? I was sorry, deeply sorry, that our camper hadn't delivered.

"What's Border Patrol?" asked my daughter, looking out her bunk window, just as there was a rapid knock on our door. My maternal instincts scanned the camper for a place to hide a Mexican family. But it was an armed guard.

"You'd be smart to get out of here. Now," he said, gripping his machine gun. Funny. I hadn't thought of the immigrants as dangerous. Just the Border Patrol. Maybe I'd lived among raptors for too long.

We packed up quickly, wordlessly. In my case reluctantly. Even the kids were mute. As we left the refuge, we saw a fleet of helicopters moving in like the worst kind of human raptors. I did my best to explain to our kids about dashed, albeit illegal, dreams. "Dreams are legal. But sometimes living them . . . isn't." I felt compelled to add, "That doesn't mean that you should stop dreaming, though, no matter *what* your dreams are. You can always trust a dream if it comes from your deepest wonder. Do not lose your wonder! Promise me!"

They looked scared. They didn't answer. They knew it was a command.

My husband shot me a *take it easy* look. So I resorted to the moral-mother trope: "I've learned that you can usually find a way, a legal way, if you want your dream badly enough."

Now we all were quiet. It was that scary. And we felt that lucky.

As we drove through the Arizona morning, raptors took over again, and the road opened to our next adventure, hopefully more bird-forward. I thought about Jim. Had he tried to put me through some sort of test? Did a drink with Harrison need to be hard-won? Did he doubt that I'd spend a night at the refuge when I saw what shape the Visitor Center was in? Did he know that if we went for it anyway there would likely be lessons to learn?

Regardless of the ordeal, if it was a test, I'd passed. And if there was a lesson in it for me (forget my children), it was: you have to fight for your dreams, even if you know that they might be deeply dashed. My little publishing-world heart-break seemed small against the maps of those mothers' eyes.

At four o'clock, we pulled into Patagonia, Arizona, the Wagon Wheel bar in my sights. *Hydration time.*

I convinced my husband to park the crude Americana camper around the corner, and I told him, "If Jim invites me to his house to have one of his epic dinners with his wife, I've never seen you or the kids before." It was sort of a joke, and sort of . . . not.

He knew that this was my big moment. This was the "it" party I'd left behind when we'd moved to Montana for his job.

For years, I'd been up to my ears in diapers and carpool and T-ball and piano recitals and everything mother. My publishing dream had taken hit after hit. My writing time was more and more limited, given my increasing motherhood duties. I loved being a mother with all my heart. But I also needed a break. My one hour of spring break. Just for me. As a writer. Nobody gives a writer what she needs. She has to take it for herself. I think it's that way with any dream. The backlash: people call you *selfish*. You can't worry about it. You have to stand in your passion and make it happen. And moments like this came along *never* in the life I'd chosen in a remote town in Montana, USA.

I walked into the Wagon Wheel alone and weak in the knees. Every person in the bar turned their head.

Did I look like such an outsider? Didn't the Montanan in me show?

I went straight to the bar with as much confidence as I could muster, scanning the room for my literary hero. Plus, after the morning we'd had, I wanted a drink.

"I'll take a beer, please," I said to the bartender. "Whatever's on tap." I don't really drink beer, but this didn't seem like the kind of place where you'd want to ask for a wine list.

I sat down on the stool and tried not to be obvious. *I bet he has his own private back-corner booth*, I thought. Or his own bar stool. Like Hunter S. Thompson at the Woody Creek Tavern near Aspen. I'd sat on that stool. And Richard Hugo's haunt in Missoula: Charlie B's. I'd "pilgrimaged" there many times. His brokenhearted poem "Degrees of Gray in Philipsburg" is one of my very favorites. What was up with me and old male writers who frequented dive bars and taverns? Who cared. Everyone has some sort of porn, and this was apparently mine.

My wonder did flip-flops. What would he be like? What would I say to him? What would I do with my precious time with my hero? Hopefully I wouldn't totally ass out. I sipped my beer and thought about why I loved Harrison's writing. Maybe because I'd discovered it in my early twenties when my boyfriend gave me *Dalva*. It was the first time I so related with a character on the page, and the way an author put words together, that I deeply believed I had novels in me.

Or maybe it was because he liked to write about delicious gout-giving food being cooked in a cabin somewhere in the woods, and great French wine being consumed by people who use words that I've never heard of and then in the next breath say a hearty "fuck," causing me to simultaneously grab for the dictionary and chuckle naughtily. There's no one who can have me craving a steak and jotting down notes for edifying things I need to look up like Harrison.

Harrison had been compared to Hemingway and Faulkner, but Harrison was still alive. A living legend. And I was quite possibly about to have a beer with him. All because of a letter and some guts. And more than a modicum of wonder.

Suddenly, outside the bar window, I saw a short, leathery man, the wind sending his white fray of hair skyward. It was Jim.

He opened the door.

Half the bar stood up.

*Oh shit. They're all here to see him! I'm nothing special!*

Just as I was trying to sort out what to do, what to say, he came up to the bar and, in his midwestern burr, uttered the most magical words I've heard outside of "ten fingers, ten toes" and "book deal": "Where's the writer? From Montana?"

My heart almost fell out of my mouth. "Here I . . . here I am . . . mister . . . Jim," I said, raising my hand like a kid at Bozo's Circus who wants to be picked for the Grand Prize Game.

He looked at me, and the rest of the bar sat down, unchosen.

*Oh my God oh my God!* Outside of my experiences with mothering, I had never in my life been more filled with curiosity and awe.

The bartender came over.

"I'll have a beer and a shot of vodka. Cuz that's how we do it in Montana." He winked at me with his good eye. "My other eye's a fake," he said.

I tried to act surprised. Of course, I knew the whole story. I knew what he liked for breakfast.

"Uh, I'll have a shot of vodka too," I said quickly, smiling at Jim in a beer-and-vodka clubby way. Really? We weren't having a shot of *whiskey*? Or tequila? *Vodka* and beer? When in Rome, with Caesar himself . . . .

It was at that very moment that my husband walked in with the kids. *Why?*

I shot them a *don't you dare* look and, as directed, they marched right past me, my son doing a little wag of his rear end, my daughter rolling her eyes, and took seats a few bar stools down from us. My husband ordered a beer, Cokes for the kids, and a bag of potato chips. And they marched past us again and went straight to the pool table. Couldn't they have found some *other* place? The camper was packed with food and drinks and books and games. I tried not to keep a mother's eye on them and focused on Jim. *This sort of dream just doesn't happen. Ever. Not to me.*

"They don't let you smoke inside," he said, patting the pack of American Spirits in the pocket of his white Carhartt T-shirt. And I followed him to the back patio, where we sat at a plastic table under a string of Miller Lite flags, like prayer flags, and talked.

Truth be told, I can't remember much of what we talked about after that. I think he said that Orson Welles, Fellini, and John Huston, all of whom he knew in his screenwriting days, used to fake heart attacks at restaurants to get out of paying the bill. I think we talked about claustrophobia in airplanes. I think we talked about antianxiety meds. I remember he said, "You're up in Whitefish, huh. You're almost Canadian."

And I retorted, "You're down here in Patagonia. You're almost Mexican."

Then he said with a good-eye wink, "I'd rather be almost Mexican than almost Canadian."

I paused. It was clearly a test. And I wanted to pass. So I said, "We went to the Buenos Aires National Wildlife Refuge." I paused again. "I've never seen such raptors. I felt like I was in Africa." Another pause. "Border Patrol is pretty rough down there."

He widened his good eye, smiled, and took a drag off his cigarette. "Did you stay the night?"

I nodded.

He took another drag of his cigarette. "Get any writing out of it?"

"Yeah. Mostly about raptors."

He looked into me, not at me, with his good eye.

And I added, "Fuck publishers."

He laughed. It was full of a lot more than laughter.

*I passed . . . .*

"And now we're going to try to find an elegant trogon. At Patagonia Lake," I added as a small but worthy coda.

"You and everyone else," he said. "They're like the snipe. You'll never see one."

*I flunked.*

Just then, my kids came bounding out of the bar and onto the deck, plopping down in the other two chairs at our table. My son had an open bag of chips in his hand. It was the only moment, since becoming a mother, that I did *not* want my kids, or anyone else, at that table. Where the hell was my husband? *Just a few more minutes with my literary hero? Please?*

Jim lit up, pointing at my son and at the bag of chips. "Can I have one?" he asked.

"Sure," my son chirped, like we were at the end-of-season parent T-ball picnic. "Mom, we're *starving*."

*Really? Your father can't freaking feed you dinner tonight! Ugh! The camper is literally around the corner!*

Nope. Dream over. Upstaged. And just when I was about to ask Jim about his process in writing the female character Dalva. And his writing practice. Legal pad, right? And his favorite pen. The Uniball. Vision Elite. Dark blue. Right? Using "yrs.," as his sign-off: What did it mean? "Years" or "yours" or both? And why the period-and-comma combo? To mess with people? Like me? Who worshipped him? And what about dealing with publishing-world rejection? That's the salve I needed most, and I couldn't imagine anyone on earth who could give it to me in a way that I'd take it. But the attention was on the bag of potato chips.

I tried to segue. "I read an article you wrote in *The New York Times*. About the little Italian restaurant here in Patagonia. The one owned by the couple from Sicily. I'm getting sick of camping food. Any chance you'd like to join us for dinner there, our treat? We love little family-run holes-in-the-wall." I put that in for good measure. I had read all about his favorite holes-in-the-wall from France to the Upper Peninsula of Michigan to Livingston, Montana, and beyond.

He took another drag. "That place closed years ago."

"Well, is there another little hole-in-the-wall local gem?"

My kids sat there looking at him with wide eyes and open souls, their eyebrows going into various contortions as they sized him up. Mommy's literary hero looked kinda scary. Like that Shel Silverstein guy on the back of that green book that makes her cry.

He pulled a drag off his cigarette and looked at me, his good eye floating with something like cataracts, and his fake one fixed on something that had likely activated his third eye since his childhood accident.

"Well . . . ," he said.

Wait for it.

"*Basically* . . . yer fucked."

Then he smiled and leaned in, like he prided himself on testing the reverberations of the f-bomb on small children.

So many tests. Now the side of me that had scanned the camper for hiding places internally begged him, *Please, please, please don't tell my son that he's not going to find an elegant trogon . . . .*

He took a drag off his cigarette and smashed it in the ashtray as if it were holding his high road and turning his tests to ash. Still, it was like he couldn't stop. "If you want to work for it, you could go to my favorite Mexican restaurant." He lit another cigarette and, I swear, looked me straight in my muse. *Not* my motherhood.

My mind tried to understand. *Maybe this is what a true mentor does. Dares.* Maybe his ultimate test was to see if I would choose wonder over fear.

"Where's your notebook?" he said, like he was on a mission now and the road was open and clear.

"My notebook?" I fished around in my purse. Shit. How had I come to meet Jim Harrison without my *notebook*?

"You're a *writer*? And you don't carry a *notebook*?" he said, but he was smiling.

Quickly, I produced my checkbook and tore the drab manila-colored back flap off it. I had been picking my cuticles, and when I passed him the paper, I saw that it had a drop of blood on it. He didn't seem to notice, or maybe he just expected a little blood to come along with a blank piece of paper from a desperate writer. Especially if they don't have their notebook.

I did have a pen though. *The* pen, and he took it and smiled. "Good pen."

Then he wrote out directions to a tiny restaurant across the border in Nogales, an hour away.

"You want to order the *cecina*." He wrote that down too.

Then he turned over the piece of paper and drew a map of the San Rafael Valley. "You should do this drive tomorrow. It's *stunning*." He made that last word stretch for miles.

He passed me the bloodied piece of paper, and I took it as if it were a lost sea scroll. (I still have it on my writing desk, in a frame.)

My son leaned into Harrison like now he was the test giver. "We're here to see an elegant trogon. Are there elegant trogons there?"

*Please* don't *take away our elegant trogon*, I thought.

My husband emerged then from the bar and came to the table with his arm outstretched. "Nice to meet you, Jim." Polite but underwhelmed. Something to check off his list, having listened to me yammer on about Harrison since we'd met in college. "I loved your piece in *Esquire* about the chicken thighs. We've never gone back to breasts."

Potato chips. Chicken. What else? I stared into the beer flags.

"How did you two meet?" Jim asked us, but mostly me.

"In college," I said flatly, really wanting my family to leave. Wanting to ask Jim about writing his novels, or the Zen reader he loved, *Nine-Headed Dragon River*, which had lived on my bedside table for years. I wanted to talk about the D. H. Lawrence quote that lived on his writing wall and on mine because of it:

> I am part of the sun as my eye is part of me. That I am part of the earth my feet know perfectly, and my blood is part of the sea. . . . There is nothing of me that is alone and absolute except my mind, and we shall find that the mind has no existence by itself, it is only the glitter of the sun on the surface of the waters.

The mind had no existence? Maybe a good long talk about that alone would heal my publishing wounds. I wanted to talk into the wee hours all about fiction, about writing, about the writerly life—all of it. I wanted to recite the very first poem I ever wrote in seventh grade. I wanted to tell him I won a writing award for it. He'd care, right? Even though no one besides my English teacher really had back then. Not the way that I wanted them to. I knew it was a good poem when I wrote it. I knew that it was beyond my years. I knew that I should heed the call of it somehow. And I knew that he'd had that same beyond-his-years moment when he was a youngling too. And my poem was about a man with a bad eye. Which I suppose was his third eye. Which I suppose was his intuition. Which I suppose was mine too. I ran it in my mind while I stared at the beer flags:

> The withering man with the idiot's eyes lives under a shelter of rock.
> He lives a life full of sorrows and lies and digs for shells by the dock.
> The sea is his friend and the waves talk to him. There is nothing that they haven't told.
> The tree gives him shade as he climbs on a limb, and watches the world grow old.

Good God, was Jim the withering man? Was the limb the call of wonder itself? The thin limbs of my childhood tree house flashed in my mind. I could feel the wind as I held them hard, soaring above my suburban backyard. Watching. Maybe I'd decided in those thin limbs to have my writing be my thin limb. It wasn't fair to ask Jim to tell me what I already knew, even if I felt a child's desperation in that moment: *Answer my questions. I have so many. Just please don't hurt me for asking them.*

It felt like my whole life had come to this moment. And I couldn't think of one thing to say that wasn't somehow loaded, giving Jim the complete jurisdiction to heal my wonder wound. And that wasn't fair. And that wasn't even possible. So I kept quiet and stared now past the beer flags and into the bald hills. Of all the things that Jim Harrison would ask: how I met my husband. Which was really a question of how we fell in love.

I looked at my husband then. He always had something to say in these moments. But he was silent too. Probably because he knew I didn't want to talk about a frat party in the late 1980s with my literary hero. But likely having something to do with the fact that he'd been wondering the same thing, about how we fell in love.

So I offered a small, "At college. At a party."

Jim looked at my husband then, smiling, smoking. "And *you* . . . got *her.*"

My head jolted to attention. People didn't really talk about me like a big gift you'd be lucky to receive. My grandmother had. And then my husband. But that fascination had faded lately. I studied my husband's eye-map, like I'd studied the eye-maps of the Mexican mothers, holding their children from imminent dream-disruption and even mortal danger.

My husband nodded at Jim and then looked back at me, but not altogether fondly.

Jim cocked his head at that. Then he looked at me. Had he seen something I hadn't been willing to see? Was my husband's malaise going to turn into a full-blown midlife crisis? Considering his recent distance and emotional neglect, maybe it was.

But that line of thinking felt entirely subtext-empty. I was sitting with my literary hero! Interpersonal-relationship issues could wait. Plus, Jim was saying, directly to my husband's face, that I was a good catch. As if that's what he got for interrupting his wife's writerly dream and talking about chicken. Like Jim was taking my side. I tried to live without sides.

My heart swelled nonetheless. I hadn't gotten that sort of treatment in a long time. Not from my husband. Not from publishers. Not from my tween. All bets were on Jim. I didn't realize how badly I needed the exact support he was offering. *Whatever you do . . . just* don't *take away my son's elegant trogon.*

I knew we were done with our visit. I asked Jim for a photo and he agreed. Of course my eyes are closed in it, and his face is completely in shadow. Another ego-explosion-less writer moment to add to the list.

Some fans came out to introduce themselves to Jim then, and my kids were hungry and my husband was over it, so I told Jim goodbye and he looked up and said, "If you can ever get a novel into print, I'll blurb it."

*Oh. My. God.*

I took that bit of wonder, and I blew it up as big as my fizzling-out ego, and I said to Jim and to my family, "We're going to Mexico for dinner."

Jim smiled. "The *cecina*. Don't forget."

*A-plus!*

My husband and kids knew not to complain. They knew I was on a pilgrimage. They knew it was important to reward guts in the people you love. Even if you don't quite understand what they love and why they love it. They also knew that they hadn't had a chance to cheer for me. My dream of being a published book author hadn't come true yet. They felt my pain. This was their attempt at administering my hero-directed salve. To put aside their own struggles and champion me. It felt so good.

With an inner purpose I hadn't felt outside my motherhood in months, maybe years, I followed those directions like a treasure map through the dark. My husband dutifully drove the camper across the border and into a sketchy border town—all to eat the dried-beef dish that Harrison had raved about at a hole-in-the-wall full of locals and not one gringo except for us. It was heaven. A lot of people take their kids to a Taylor Swift concert. I took mine to a wilderness refuge where a lot more than raptors were trying to find refuge, a one-pony bar in a one-pony town, and then a hole-in-the-wall restaurant on the other side of the US-Mexico border, thanks to Jim Harrison.

My takeaway was this: Jim believed in my wonder over my fear. And maybe he even believed in my ability to intuit powerful experiences over cautionary tales. I felt feral at the Buenos Aires National Wildlife Refuge. I felt feral eating *cecina* in that little hole-in-the-wall restaurant in Nogales. I felt feral at the Wagon Wheel, drinking beer and vodka with my literary hero. I felt feral when I wrote and sent that letter. Somehow I'd tapped into something finally worth sending to Jim that wasn't full of pleading and pain: "I'm going camping with my husband and small children. Where can I see some mighty birds? Maybe do some writing?"

I believe that Jim saw something of himself in that letter. Something painful and maybe something poetic. But definitely kindred. He responded as if to say, similar to Terry: *Stop trying so hard to get the attention of the powers that be. Live the writing life that you have to live. Live in that borderless, edgy, internal place that is the only place you are formed for. Watch birds. Love your kids but do not give them your last longing. Save that for the page. Spend time with writers who can't not write and who understand that you can't not write either. Maybe your dreams will come true. Maybe they won't. Live like it doesn't matter. Because it doesn't.*

Sometimes I still hear him saying to my then husband: "And *you* got *her*." To me, that was Jim's way of saying, *I know what she's made of. She's not going to stop. Hope you're prepared for the ride.* I'm not sure if it was a warning or a call to action. But I am sure that he saw something in me that he recognized. And sent us off for one of the best dinners of our lives as medicine he knew we'd need.

It boils down to a simple trajectory that I spent so much time thinking was impossible: I wrote the letter I'd been circling around for years. I got a dream response with a few challenges. I took them. I also know this: it was one heck of a letter. I'd been writing it since the moment I left my non-feral life in the suburbs of Chicago and honored my longing to find my truth, never knowing that it would land in the writing life. I'd finally wandered enough in my wonder to write a letter I could send. I'd finally lived in my truth long enough to trust my self-expression. My truth had said it was time. I had listened.

It's with that truth that I live my life. Or try to. When my truth tells me to do something, I listen now. I wonder how many lost opportunities there have been because I doubted or was too afraid to abide by what my gut knew. My truth has been my guide in the field of self-expression. My truth has taught me that it's not ultimately about the words. It's about what's behind them, in between them, and what's left in their wake.

Jim Harrison died before my first novel got published, so I had no way to take him up on his offer to blurb it. But he did approve two excerpts from his poems for me to publish at the beginning and end of *This Is Not The Story You Think It Is.* And he did sign off the letter, "Love, Jim." He's thanked in my novel, *Willa's Grove.* Of course he is.

This is all to say that I am proof: if you can conjure the courage to write, and even send, that letter to the person, famous or not, who has inspired you most . . . you never know what gifts might ensue. You might end up having one of the best dinners of your life. You might end up not seeing a bird . . . that you and your child will never forget.

The experiences I had with Terry and Jim led me to take my wonder-challenged self and imagine a future in which I could live in the truth of my creative self-expression, without the excessive addiction to ambition, without the exterior world defining who I was, without needing to prove myself in this life I'd stubbornly chosen, even if I didn't look successful on paper. Having the courage to reach past my hero worship taught me to stop giving away my power to those I admired. And to see that they are as human as I am.

What I also learned in my divine appointments with Terry and Jim (for that is what I believe them to be) was that I had let my wonder go in the face of believing in the lies of ambition and the myth of success. I wasn't playing in the woods of my wonder, holding on to the thin branches or charming birds. I was splaying myself supplicant on the altar of ambition.

It was time to let . . . that . . . shit . . . go.

## your wild why . . .

No matter how afraid you are, write a letter to the hero you long to write to. Even if you don't send it. Go to your truth. Express your truth. Your longing and your wondering and your dreaming. Do not put that other person on a pedestal. They might be farther along in the freedom of their truth and self-expression than you are, and that's okay. Sometimes we have to look at ourselves in the mirror of someone we can't imagine becoming in order to know that we can be anything we want to be. If we are honest enough.

Consider sending it. Don't expect a response. The writing and sending are enough. If something more happens, follow the magic. Ignore the steel bars and graffiti and DANGER signs. Welcome the wonder.

# success and failure are myths

If you have a dream, and I know you do somewhere inside you, there's a story that goes along with it. That story lives in your mind and heart. It's not always a pleasing story. It's often quite destructive. That's because a lot of what holds dream stories together is based on the dual notion of success and failure. That is, by society's constructs. It took me a long time and a world of ongoing pain, likely created by my wonder wound, before I realized that success and failure, by society's constructs, are myths. If I had learned this as a teenager, I never would have lost my connection to my Free Child.

My dream story had a success component and a failure component. My success was defined by becoming a well-published and well-read author. My failure was defined by the horror of not achieving this dream. And while my dream eventually came true, the road to "success" was a tortured one. For years, I was completely defined by a lie: my self-worth on this planet was defined by my success. This lie almost took me down and my wonder along with it.

So, when I finally *did* get published to wide acclaim, and had become seasoned in this new reality, I realized that I'd been living in a tortured myth since my early teens. I owed my young self an apology—and a promise.

I decided to write myself a letter. It was as if I was promising myself that I would not need to write such a cautionary tale again in another two decades.

Here's what I wrote:

May 27, 2018

Dear Unpublished Laura (age twenty-one to forty-three)

I have a lot to tell you. I have news from the front lines, and it's going to change the way you live.

No, the enemy troops are not marching toward you. No, you are not in a house that will soon be burning. No, you don't go hungry, and no, you don't die. You live. That's what I'm here to tell you. You live. And the soldiers go home. And the bombed-out trenches bloom over with tall grasses and lupine, and the beetles and ladybugs come back, and there are rainbow-covered picnics in places where dying, bloody bodies once lay.

Are you sitting down with your tea? Do you have slippers on? I know how you forget to put on slippers and how your feet are cold but you don't bother to cover them because it requires a trip up to your bedroom, and you have just one more sentence to write. I know you sometimes forget breakfast. And sometimes lunch too. And how you don't go outside for that walk even though it's a sunny day and the valley where you live gets an average of one hundred days of sunshine a year, and your dogs are waiting on the front porch, and all of you could use the exercise. But you don't get up from that chair. I see you. I know you. You sit there all day . . . and write. And yearn to be published to wide acclaim.

So, here's the thing. You will "make it." But it won't look anything like you think it will. There is no war, and there's also no party. The soldiers in the trenches lying there bleeding and dying . . . are *you*. The woman standing in the little black dress against the wall in a New York City brownstone, talking to her agent, her editor, and a big-time book reviewer . . . is you. You will find out soon enough that the "war" you concocted doesn't have winners and losers, and the "party" doesn't have an elite guest list. You'll also find that none of it is actually real. And that will blow your mind and bust your story into smithereens. It takes a while though.

Here's what the other side looks like. (We're not calling it Success. You'll find out why.) You will write something in 2008 and send it to your agent—yes, you will have an agent. You have an agent, and a viable novel, because you were smart and you took on an assignment from a famous author named Terry, and you finally wrote a pure novel. After that, you got serious about the business side of publishing. In other words, you realized that a magic fairy wasn't going to come down and champion your vast genius and wave a wand and *poof! You have an agent.* You ignored your wonder wound and your Inner Critter, and you wrote the requisite query letters to agents, and you got the dreaded rejections. And, yes, it got you down. Of course it did.

But listen to me when I tell you: none of it ends up making any sense, so stop believing that there's a recipe. You're doing the work. You're learning your craft. The business side of it will defy rules and ask you to play with it instead. So when the time comes, why not try! Playfulness is almost always the right choice. Remember when you used to hide in leaf piles? That little girl remembers. Whatever you do, don't forget her.

Anyway, your "success" story goes like this:

You will be in a hot tub in Santa Monica in 2002, drinking mojitos, and you will tell a woman filmmaker that you're a novelist, and she will ask what your book is about, and you will tell her, even though you've never been any good at the elevator pitch. But this will be more like a third-mojito hot-tub rant, and she will say, "Sounds like it would make a great movie. Send it to me."

And you will think, *Huh. Maybe that's the way to go. I'll get a movie deal first, and then that will attract agents and publishers.* But you won't know the first thing about literary rights, so you will call a Hollywood-connected friend who will tell you to call a friend who is a screenwriter. "But be warned," she will tell you, "she never answers her phone."

But you will call anyway. Because suddenly you will be championing your book, and why is that? Because someone else has deemed it a great story. Someone *else.* Hmm . . . .

The phone will ring and the woman on the other end will pick up. "Mom? Are you okay?" she will say.

And you will stutter. "Uh . . . this is, uh . . . Laura Munson? I'm a writer." And you will tell her that your mutual friend told you to call, and she will say, "That's so weird. I never answer the phone, but my parents have a place in Montana and I recognized the area code so I picked up."

You will tell her about the hot tub and your half-drunk pitch, and she will say, "You know who you need to talk to . . . ." An hour later, you will be calling her friend, a new literary agent in New York City who used to work at ICM and knows all about the film business and literary rights. Which is all you've got your mind on. You're not even thinking about it as a book anymore. This woman won't have started her new job as a book agent yet, and she will be sitting on the steps of her brownstone when you call because she has no cell service in her apartment. On that call she will be cutting in and out so that you will only hear about every third word. Plus, there's a landscaping crew at your house building a rock garden, and your kids are playing on the trampoline. It all requires more than half an eye on it. You are not in pitch mode.

"You shouldn't try for a movie deal first," she will tell you. "You should try to get the book deal first. What's it about?"

Again, you will go into the story, in sort of a hot-tub way, until it will dawn on you that you are actually talking to an agent about your *book*! A friend of a friend of a friend, no less. A new agent looking for clients. You will realize you'd better put on your A game. Only you don't really have an A game for this book. You just finished it, and you haven't sent it to anyone yet, and you're just minding your own business trying to learn about literary rights and the movie industry. Aren't you?

You will shake yourself awake. *You're frigging pitching your book to a New York agent at a major boutique blue-chip agency! Get it together!*

Which is exactly what you will do.

And she will say, "Why don't you send it to me."

And you will say, "You mean just thirty pages, or a query letter, or what?"

"The whole thing," you think you hear her say, even though she's cutting in and out, and a boulder breaks free from the Bobcat and tumbles down the garden path toward the house, and the kids are trying backflips against your one-at-a-time rule.

"The whole *thing*?" you say. "You mean, for potential *representation*?"

"Yeah," you think you hear her say. Even though you're pretty sure she just said, "Nah."

So this is what you will do. The old-fashioned way. You will get the book printed out at the local copy shop (which has been taking pity on you for years), and you will buy a box that fits just right. You will take the book to the post office like you've done with other books so many times before, only never to mail it to an agent who actually *wants* to read your work. Always cold and unconnected with the publishing powers that be. That's what you get, after all, from moving away from the city and planting yourself in this Rocky Mountain high heaven.

When you get to the post office, you stand in line, and you see Madge, the postal service worker at the counter, who is also a writer, and she will do what she always does when you send out your manuscripts, even if there's a line out the door. Which there is. She will lay her hands on the bundled pages and pray with an uplifted voice, "Lord Jesus, may this book find its way by your will," and then pop it in the mailbag, smiling at you while you try to smile back at her in the most grateful and pathetic way. Because you'd frankly like Jesus to get involved — maybe shoot you a little miracle for this one. You're just not sure how to ask anymore. I mean, you've prayed and even begged for your publishing dream, and instead you've been given so much in every other department: Healthy, happy children. A healthy, happy marriage. A large chunk of land and a handcrafted home, all in one of the most pristine corners of the lower forty-eight. Praying for publication at this point feels . . . greedy.

So you will not tell Madge about your calling, nor your dream, nor your decades-old prayer: "Please let me be published to wide acclaim." But you do appreciate hers. It's so entirely pure.

You will try to forget about the whole thing as you go through your daily motherly ablutions, but it will gnaw at you. And then one day a few weeks later the phone will ring while you're planting bulbs in the new rock garden, and it will be the agent. She loves your novel and she wants to sign you. Right there kneeling in the dirt. Or maybe she said, "It sucks." You won't be able to tell because her cell phone is still cutting in and out. (You'll learn, by the way, that every important call in your career from now on will have bad cell phone service and your ego will never, not once, ever, get to explode. Even when you get published to wide acclaim. In fact, you'll come to find out that every single time your ego activates, that's the exact time you'll catch every other word so that you're constantly feeling sort of deaf, sort of dumb, and sort of blind. Get used to it.)

Five years will pass and you'll be in your early forties now. During those years your agent will send out the hot-tub novel, and then another novel that you will write after that one, to big-time New York editors. You will have done your damnedest to give those editors the right ammo—taking out a couple hundred pages from both manuscripts, rewriting new material, and, in one case, even bringing in a secondary protagonist. Both of those novels will *almost* go all the way. Almost. But in the end . . . *nope.* You're a no-name from Montana, and even though the editors love the books, Marketing and Publicity doesn't want to back you. You have no platform. *Huh? Isn't it supposed to be about the writing? And what's this thing called "platform" anyway?*

*Twice* this happens to you. Pick an expletive of your liking. I'm pretty sure it's gonna start with an *f.* (What you also don't know is that when you finally do get a novel published, it will be March 2, 2020. You're supposed to be on a book tour for two months. You've been all over New York City, Boston, Chicago, and Minneapolis, and you're on your way to the West Coast. And then on March 13, the world will shut down due to an illness called COVID, and you will have to cancel your thirty-eight remaining events and go home like everybody else. #thewritersegonevergetstoexplode.)

Long before COVID, however, and after both of those novels almost get published . . . you will go through a rough patch in your marriage in which your husband will tell you he doesn't love you anymore. And that's *lots* of fun for you, but you will write your way through it because that's how you process life. Plus you're experimenting with a new way of thinking and being, in which you don't define your happiness by things outside of your control. It's a positively free way to live your life. In fact, it makes you feel the way you did when you were little, holding on to the thin branches in the wind above your tree house. You haven't felt that way in a long time. So you write and live and write and live for six months.

At the end of those six months, the marriage comes up for air, and you've never been more emotionally free in your life. Even if the marriage had been over, you still would have found this new way to live. It's absolutely life-changing. The blood sport of needing to be published starts to lift a bit, given this way of living. But the publishing story is the hardest one to crack because it's so wrapped up in your ambition, identity, and, you will later come to understand, your earliest wound.

You tell your agent, "I just went through a rough patch in my marriage. And I wrote a book. I think it's good. It's full of wisdom that people could really benefit from no matter what's going on in their lives. It's a philosophy I've been working with, and I think it's new news to people that you don't have to suffer emotionally because of the things people say and do to you."

And she will say something to the tune of, "It sounds great, Laura. But I'm not sending it out. No one knows who you are."

You make a diminutive case for yourself: "But . . . I've been published . . . in literary journals."

"Yes. But I can't keep sending your stuff out until you develop some kind of platform."

"What am I supposed to do?" Yes, you will be whining to your agent, but you can't help yourself. The internet is still in its infancy. "Platform" is a powerless concept, especially in Montana.

"A lot of people read Modern Love in the Sunday Styles section of *The New York Times*," she will suggest.

Your agent knows and you know that this is one of the hardest nuts to crack, the Modern Love column, but you will tell her you'll try. And she will tell you you're one of her most talented clients but that she's not sending out your work until you have a platform. Period.

You will get off the phone and sob and scream at the mice in the walls and the coffee stains on your desk and the knife twisting in your heart. You've just spent decades devoting almost everything to this craft. And you're good. And that's not *enough*!

You will drop your head to your desk (but not in the oven, Sylvia) and weep and weep. This will be one of the worst (and best) moments of your life. You can't fight in the revolution. You can't even go to the after-party. This was *not* how it was supposed to go. Your Inner Critter will do her victory lap: *This is the end. Face it. Cut your losses. Your dreams aren't going to come true. It's time to take up tennis and golf like everybody else.* (Pickleball isn't a thing yet.) While you're sobbing, that line from *Flashdance* will flare up in you until it smolders into this sick statement, which you utter to the mice in the walls: "'If you lose your dream . . . you're dead.' Maybe I'll just die now instead."

Which you would never do. Because you have children. Children that are your everything that is not your books. You owe them their happy, wonder-full childhood! But right now, with them both in school, you sob and sob about the death of one of your oldest dreams. Your calling. You will never be published to wide acclaim. All of your work has been for naught.

But you are not one to give into defeat. Especially when it circles in close. That's when you historically take action. Only, historically, the action you take is to hide. That won't work right now. You have to be completely seen, if only by yourself. Being seen by yourself is the only thing that exists in this moment. And the way you see yourself is with a pen in one hand and a piece of paper in the other. So you will grab the closest thing to write on—a depressing little fluorescent-yellow Post-it Note—and a Uniball Vision Elite navy blue ink pen, and you will write what you will later refer to as your Writer's Statement. The moment that changes everything. "I write to shine a light on a dim or otherwise pitch-black corner to provide relief for myself and others."

And you will ask, out loud, and not of the Inner Critter but more likely of the same entity that you've been begging to get you published to wide acclaim: "Relief? From what?"

And it will answer this time: *From this beautiful and heartbreaking thing called life.*

"For *myself*?"

*You write for yourself. And you write for others.*

"I'm writing from a place of *service*?"

*Yeah. You know that. You're writing out of service to all the Annies out there. You always have been.*

And you reel with this new concept because the book you've just written isn't a novel. It's a memoir. And 'tis true, you will realize right then and there, it could help a lot of people. What you've written is actually a book about dealing with rejection. You've been dealing with rejection from the first time you charmed a mourning dove. And told someone about it. And they didn't believe you. Your journals were your safe place, and then the books became your safe place. But your journals are just for you. These books are for . . . I want to say that they're for others. But they're for you as much as they're for others—and that's okay.

And that's when you learn the most important thing about self-expression: we can't bridge to others unless we've bridged to ourselves. And sometimes it's *through* the writing that we build that self-bridge. You've been learning how to bridge to yourself in this way by writing novels all these years. Now you've written a memoir to bridge to yourself while you've gone through this crisis. But it's got a huge service piece. This will be the first book you've written that is truly of service to others, not just to yourself.

With this fierce, new purpose, you decide to write a personal essay for Modern Love. Your agent is right: the memoir would make a terrific personal essay. Yes, you've been rejected four times from this column, but golly. *You'd* want to read that essay, and why can't that be the case for thousands of readers out there just like you? You have one hour until you have to pick the kids up from school. So you bang it out. You don't even edit it. And you email it to the editor. And you don't even pitch it. You write, "See what you think of this one."

And they take it. The next day. They *take* it. It's a simple email that will forever be: before and after.

This is a B.A.D., as your teenager says. Big . . . Ass . . . Deal.

Let me tell you, little rebel boot-straps-puller-upper twenty-one-year-old Laura, let me tell you what happens next. You're old enough to be able to handle it. Ready?

Okay. You know those words that you fling into the ocean and the sinking sun every time you're standing on a western-facing beach? Those sometimes-spoken, sometimes-thought words that come out like a beggar's prayer? "Please help me be published to wide acclaim"? Even though you're kind of embarrassed by them, this is a time for total transparency after all.

Well, it happens. And shit gets real.

The message in your Modern Love essay will tap into a global zeitgeist. Your essay that you dashed off in an hour will crash *The New York Times* website comments section, and it will finally get you that book deal you always dreamed of—with one of the hottest editors in New York, no less. And with her steerage and the A-list marketing and publicity team that signed on to be its champion (Platform = Power to the People, in my case), the hardback will land on *The New York Times* bestseller list. The book will get published and read all over the world. All of the morning television shows will call you and try to get you on. Even the Oprah show will call. You will feel like you've arrived.

When this happens all over again a year later with the paperback, and as it rolls out in eight countries, you will finally achieve what you've always wanted: Wide acclaim! Whoo-hoo! Mission freaking accomplished! Tip your cocktail waitress. Don't drive home alone. Mic drop.

But then something unexpected will happen.

Your "success" and acclaim—it will start to feel dangerous. Even cancerous. Or just a bit sickening. Or just plain wrong. Like you've done something bad and you got busted and you're about to get expelled from boarding school. Or like the bully from college is going to corner you and say, "Just who do you think you are, deactivating from our sorority?" Or like your fourth-grade journal is correct: You *have* talked too much. You *have* felt too much. You *should* feel bad about it. Or like one of the older women in any given room is going to shake her head and say that you've embarrassed yourself by being so vulnerable on the page and sharing such a personal story. Or a publishing-world doyenne is going to say that there's been some mistake and you weren't supposed to get published after all.

Your *New York Times* ranking won't last long, so that will prove something to you. Like it really was a mistake. And everybody knows it. Plus, it's not a *novel* or anything. It didn't win a *Pulitzer*. So what if the Book of the Month Club named it one of the best books of 2010? Who's in *that* club, anyway? Your mother's bridge group? You're a failure, really.

And your ego will never, ever get to explode because there are dampeners all along the way to preclude it from doing so.

Take this one, for instance: You will spend your publication day puking in a Midtown Manhattan hotel bathroom because you chose to celebrate with your family in Mexico the week prior and you ate a very funky *taco al pastor*. Or this one: You will turn down *The Oprah Winfrey Show*, not once, but twice. Not because you don't love Oprah! Of course you love Oprah! Who doesn't love Oprah??? But the producer will try to get you, and your family, on the show. You have rules, and exposing your family is a deal-breaker. You tell them that *is* the story you think it is, but what writer turns down *The*

*Oprah Winfrey Show*? Twice??? I guess a mother-bear writer.

Or this one: You will go on *Good Morning America*, and while they're doing your hair and makeup, the stylist with the mascara wand will say to the stylist with the straightening iron, "Anybody interesting on today?" And he will say back, so close that you smell his breath, "Not that I care about." And, frankly, you will agree.

In truth, responding to the nonstop interview questions, the global media circuit, the seemingly unstoppable interest in this story . . . all feels like opening up your veins and bleeding to the entire world. Even if it's a regulated bleed, it still feels like you're doing something wrong. Like you're about to get into big trouble. Like you've asked a big and verboten wild why. It's not the party you imagined it would be. It feels more like the war. And you'll want to hide.

But you will keep on writing, so that's the good news. Even if it's your grown-up way of hiding. At least you know now why you write! It's for you. And it's also for your readers. That part feels pure and good.

But now there's a business side to it. A public persona. And for a while, you will be lost in it. You will not know what to do. You are expected to now build a *brand* around this book. To become a social media goddess. But you are not twenty-four. You are forty-five. You are expected to have invincible talking points and to be mediagenic (which means "young and beautiful"). You are expected to be wise, which you apparently know how to be because of all the messages you've gotten saying that your book changed people's lives, so all is not lost! But you feel overwhelmed by all the people and places trying to pull you away from your family. Your nerves are firing this way and that and you feel like you can't get a handle on them. You've simply got to get control. But you're not sure you can. This is not sustainable. *This is business,* you will tell yourself. *Practice what you preach! You are not a victim! You have choices in this department, emotionally speaking!*

So you come up with a mantra one morning in a hotel room somewhere. It comes to you unbidden, and those are the ones to pay attention to: "I give myself permission to be exactly who I am and have it be easy."

This will be a mantra that you will utter every day and that you will attempt to live by. Sometimes you will succeed, and sometimes you will fail, but you will realize something that will rock your world. And it's this:

There is no such thing as success. It's a lie. An illusion. A myth. Success itself is a wonder-kill. A dreamy interpretation of events that feels mostly like total shit because the true self behind the ego knows what's behind it *all*. And that true self wants her wonder back.

It happens in a limo, with your publishing team, on your way to a Barnes & Noble reading in New York City. You will look out the window and see your teenage self, walking down Fifth Avenue, going on and on about one day finally being the *staaah* of the family. Your poor boyfriend is doing his best to pretend to pay attention. And you see that your younger self is setting up a life of self-torture. And you have an epiphany: the limo-you feels no different from that teen-you, except that she's got the prize in her hand, and it feels like . . . well. It feels like nothing, really. Just like the character in *A Chorus Line*! You wrote a book and it got published. People read it. But *you* feel no different at all. And you want to shout out the window at the teen-you: *Success and failure are myths! The only thing that is real is doing the work. And that's good news because it's the only thing we can control!* Instead, you will turn to your publicist and say, "Thank God none of this happened when I wanted it so badly. Because I know the woman that I am. And the writer that I am. And I will be this book's perfect messenger. I'm so grateful for what you have done. It's helping people."

It will be in that limo that you realize that you must thank all the ups and downs you've gone through to arrive at this severe truth. And also where you discover that you have to reinterpret what it is to experience being a published author. You can no longer live by ambition because it's ambition that has been trying to kill the wonder that has driven your dream. You can have ambition and wonder and dreams all together, of course you can. But you must be careful to preserve the wonder most of all. There is levity in wonder. Playfulness. Hope. Possibility. And, yes, curiosity and awe. That's what was on the line in all the believing that there would be a *there* there once you got published to wide acclaim. But there's not a there there. Gertrude Stein was right. On the other side of wide acclaim, instead, is expectation. The need to keep up. The push to keep doing more. The departure from wonder's soul.

The levity will come back in a playful wallop. You'll be lying in bed on a Saturday morning, at home, before your kids are up. You'll feel like you're being pinched, your shoulders up by your ears, tight and braced. You will recognize what this is because of all the work you've done with horses and body awareness, and you know to pay attention when your shoulders are up like that. It means you're terribly fraught with something that is usually a giant dose of fear.

The worrying will have to do with a reading in Connecticut at a private club where 150 women will have prepaid seventy-five dollars, which will include a signed copy of your book and lunch. You will be worrying that they'll be disappointed that they spent all that money just to see you. You will be worrying about the ten pounds you've gained and what to wear, knowing that no matter what you wear, it will be wrong. You will be seized by the idea that there is no way to avoid letting these women down.

Lying there in bed, you will start to smile. Then laugh. Because you realize that event has *already happened*! Almost a year prior! The event went off beautifully. The women there loved you. So you are lying there worrying about something that's not only ancient history but also a smashing success. *Literally.* You will realize in that moment how you hold those speaking engagements *in* you. Hoarding them like you will need them for later should the end of the world come, a.k.a. the end of your career, where you will need ammo, fuel, cover, proof.

You will decide that you need to scan through them one by one and remember what there is to remember, without judgment—to simply forgive yourself for whatever imperfect moments might have happened. Yeah, you probably shouldn't have worn a long-sleeve shirt and a long skirt if it was going to be ninety-four degrees with 100 percent humidity and the reading was outside under a tent. Yeah, you will find one of your books on top of the toilet in the powder room after you finish the event. Oh well. Put it all to rest. Even if it takes you all morning. And it nearly does.

But then, for the first time in a long time, you will breathe a fresh, free, unencumbered sigh of relief.

So, take a deep breath. That's the story. That's what happens. You will become the *staaah* of the family. And you will realize, finally, after having tormented yourself for so many years, unpublished or published, that you don't need to prove anything to anyone. You don't need to be anybody's star. It doesn't solve anything. It doesn't *heal* anything. It doesn't *erase* anything. It doesn't change anything about how you feel or how you fear or how you live or how you express yourself.

What you will learn from all of this, dear Laura, is that only one thing matters, outside of your motherhood. Your writing. Get back to work on what you know and trust best. That's where your wonder is safe and held.

Trust that you can and will write in wonder, no matter what.

I am sorry that I couldn't save you earlier. But I guess this is the way we had to do it. This is how we become an *us* again.

I promise you: I won't let us get there again. But I want you to promise me this: you will keep our Free Child in our arms. That is your job.

With deep love (and only minimal self-loathing these days),

—Published Laura

## your wild why . . .

Using your sense of wonder, isolate your wildest dream in one line and write it down. (Mine: "I want to be published to wide acclaim.") Now take your wildest dream and write a letter to yourself as if it has already happened, using my letter to myself as a model. Allow yourself to make it a long letter. Let your imagination go wild! Go deeply into your wild whys! What would this dream really look like if it came true? How would you thrive and prosper? How might you get in your own way? How might you make it come true despite its challenges? Really let yourself go into the possibility of your dreams, keeping the Inner Critter out of it as much as possible.

Here's the catch: Be sure, in your dreaming, that you do not kill your wonder. Your ability to be in curiosity and awe about your dreams. When you're finished, and it might take a while, maybe even a few days, find a safe, quiet, private place, and read your letter aloud to yourself, kindly, as if you are its Inner Champion.

When you see your courage, thank yourself. When you see your fear, wrap your arms around yourself and say, "That's okay. You're just scared. I will keep you safe." Write this letter as if no one will ever read it. Of course, if you want to share it with others, do so. But be sure that the people you share it with are safe. And be sure to stay away from sharing it with others (especially unsafe others) in order to be seen or heard or understood. This exercise is designed to be as pure and true and unencumbered as possible for you, and if you're writing it to share with others to be *seen* versus trying to help yourself and/or others, it will likely inform your self-honesty. It might also keep you from dreaming big. And, yes, it matters to dream big. And to be honest with what your dream could be in its full potential. This is a great opportunity for creative, truly awe-some self-expression!

Now write a one-line Wonder Statement of intention about this dream. (You can use my Writer's Statement as an example: "I write to shine a light on a dim or otherwise pitch-black corner to provide relief for myself and others.")

Maybe it starts with: "I wonder to shine a light on . . . ."

Now you have a wildly wonderous *how* to ignite and preserve your wonder. You let yourself dream. Now let yourself live *into* your dream.

# the sacred wail

The Dark Night of the Soul went black. It was my forty-seventh birthday and I was lying in bed, in the dark, alone. My dreams of a forever family were dashed. My motherhood felt in peril. My marriage was over. My world as I knew it seemed to be ending—bank accounts drained, house in foreclosure, no health insurance. Just because you're a best-selling author with a speaking career doesn't mean you're rolling in the dough, especially in the face of overhauling what was once a united financial life of two. The shame had steamrolled in and wouldn't budge. It seemed to have one mission: to flatten me.

My kids were at their father's house, the most counterintuitive thing I could imagine as a mother. I was brand-new to it and helpless in its throes. Dividing time with my own kids? Having them in a different, strange house? A new bedroom with none of their things or smells or memories in it? *What?* But I had no choice. It was the new rule. I still wasn't sure how the state of Montana had encroached on my motherhood, but it had. On top of that, the dog had just died of cancer, so mine was the only beating heart in the house. And that heart hurt.

The loneliness was swallowing me, but I couldn't think of who to reach out to, especially in the middle of the night. I'd been in hiding. When I wasn't parenting of course. But when I was on my own, I couldn't even trust what would come out of my mouth—that is if I had the guts to open it at all. I'd pulled away from my friends and family. They didn't need my drama, never mind my truth. (The last thing I needed to hear was some version of "You talk too much.") My readers expected another book, and I hadn't delivered. I hadn't published a novel yet, and that had always been the big dream. Instead, I'd been asked ad nauseum about my personal life, and even though I knew my memoir's message about how to find emotional liberation was helping people, I was just plain over it. I wanted to be left alone to live my little life and to write fiction. To not be the main character in a book so that nobody could ask me to relive a painful time in my life, or ask snarky questions, or tell me their sad stories and expect me to have salve for them. I needed my own salve. Badly. I didn't feel emotionally free. At all.

I slid out of bed and onto my knees, the way my grandmothers prayed every night all their lives. Only they were in their nightgowns, with soft clasped hands, believing that their prayers were being heard and likely even answered. I was naked and prayerless.

I opened my mouth, wanting to make one sound I could trust. One soul-sound to know that my soul was, at least, still whole. But no sound came out. What does the soul sound like when it's trying not to die? *Wailing* came to mind. Nothing came out of my mouth.

Almost five decades on this planet, and I still didn't know how to let myself properly wail. And I don't mean cry, weep, or sob. Those came easily to me and all too often. No, I needed that keening, primordial wail that is twin to our first breath—when we are more soul than flesh. I wondered if I'd even let it out at birth. It felt stuck at the bottom of my being. Maybe they kept babies quiet in my suburban hospital.

I rocked and gasped and coughed, trying to let it out. My heart flipped like a hooked fish. My eyes throbbed with blood pressure. And this wasn't the first time. This was ongoing. These nights were soundless and soul-stealing. I felt powerless before them, and they leaked into my days. I could not continue this misery and be any kind of good version of myself for my kids or for me. Luckily, these Dark Nights of the Soul attacked on the nights when my children weren't at home. Another reason to want my chicks in my nest.

But these were different from the 4:00 a.m. haunt. These were the sorts of nights that don't let you fall asleep at all. They require that you stay acutely awake for all of it. I had no idea how to make them stop, and I needed them to. They were all white-hot panic brought on by white-hot fear from having the rug ripped out from underneath what I believed to be a stable and good marriage. But that was over, and there were no promises that I could land in any sort of secure, peopled place. And even if I landed with any grace at all, I wasn't sure if I would land there still whole. In other words: alive. Whatever held me by this grip wanted blood.

It was no longer dearth. It was death.

Or was it birth? Did I need to be born into the rest of my life? And if so, I suspected that it could only happen alone.

I knelt there by my bed and scanned my relationship with this stuck and sacred wail. This birth needed to start there.

Was it a word? A sound? Whatever it was felt heavy with rejection, judgment, pain. Something old but not quite as old as birth. The word no came to me. Then the word why. Was my wail made of all my unexpressed nos and whys? Those dangerous words had made me a "bad" girl. I never wanted to be a "bad" girl. What words made me a *good* girl, I wondered?

Maybe those were the words that would set my wail free. I knelt there and tried to find the good words. Nothing came.

Instead I felt no and why grumbling in my gut. I tried to give them voice. To will my way back to those leaf piles. Those closet pillow forts. Those thin, high branches, holding on in the wind. I tried to feel the butterflies flitting in my rib cage, wanting to tickle my throat and fly out through my mouth and take me with them into our day. What sound would I make if I were that little Free Child being born into that free day? Could my wail be made of wonder instead of pain? I opened my mouth.

No sound came out.

But the whys started to stir, and I was quick to welcome them. *You are safe to come out now,* I told them. They seemed to believe me because they began to crawl up my larynx. *Why is the sky blue? Is God real? Why do people die? How do we live knowing that everyone we love is going to die? How do we live knowing that we're going to die? How do I practice love and not fear? How do I find peace? What makes a rainbow?*

I closed my eyes as if doing so would force my mouth to produce words. Then I opened my mouth. A hot and long whispered "Why?" came out.

It didn't feel wild though. Not at all. It felt scared.

I sat back on my thighs and dropped my head to the comforter. Where was my wail, potent and unabashed? Had I given it away when I signed the divorce papers, when I'd agreed to the parenting schedule? Had I not uttered "Why?" enough? And "No! Hell no!"?

I thought back to the years when I got big, tall, and smart. That's when I learned that I could fight for, and *with*, my whys and my nos. And win. I wasn't a physical warrior, though I could have been. My words were my sword. And "why" and "no" can be so lethal to those who resist them. A person who can express herself, especially in the field of resistance, and regardless of her shame, has a strong chance of word-winning. At least on the outside. Inside is another matter. It was my insides that needed to erupt.

Had the trauma of my current life activated the trauma of my early childhood? It made sense, and in the same order: Expression. Rejection. Punishment. Betrayal. Shame. Erasure. God, had my life been so bleak? On the outside, it felt so blessed. I could never, ever complain and have anyone call me a sympathetic character. I had enough of the things people called "lucky." Successful. Enviable. *I should just shut up. Too emotional. Too . . . .*

No. Not that. Not at almost fifty years old.

On this Dark Night of the Soul, I knelt naked by my bed, trying to understand how I'd let this vital part of my self-expression shut down. And that's when I heard the 4:00 a.m. voice, hot in my ear: *Pick up your sword. The one from your twenties. You are not done with it.* But then I realized—it was not the mean, scared 4:00 a.m. voice. It was the kind one.

"My sword?" I asked. "But I'm sick of fighting."

*I'm not asking you to fight. I'm asking you to protect.*

I imagined a sword there on my bedroom rug. I imagined picking it up and pointing it at every damning person or institution of my life that tried to take away my wonder and replace it with shame. And suddenly, my body started to contract and ache, like the pains that open the cervix to let a baby pass through the birth canal and into the world. I bore down and pushed, holding the darkness at bay with that inner sword—Gandalf's "You shall not pass!"

Now I stood, wielding my sword, knowing I was exhausted but more wide awake in the way I'd wanted to be for years. My whole body reminded me that I'd done this before with my firstborn—a twelve-hour Pitocin-induced natural childbirth, one unrelenting contraction. Fear had no place. My job was only to birth. To use the pain. I'd birthed my daughter, but what about myself? Had I failed to birth myself? My *true* self? The self behind the words? The self behind the shame? My . . . voice? Had I worked so hard to not be this or that or *them* that I had expressed my way out of the words that brought me back to *myself*? Was it not a fast-lane exit but a circle?

The answer was unmistakably clear: I needed to come back to my own birth to finally live my own life on my own terms. The time was now.

My ears rang with a high-pitched but silent scream. My mouth filled with a bitter rush of spit. "*Puuuuuuush*," I heard myself say.

But this pushing wasn't downward.

It was upward.

And then it emerged—a haunted, whole-toned sound out of my open throat. Primordial yet pink. The wail. My wail.

I wailed past the "Speak when you are spoken to" and the "Don't you dare talk back to me" and the "You are so sensitive" and the "You are so dramatic" and the "Don't talk so much" and the "You should know better than this" and the "What's wrong with you?" and the "When are you going to stop this nonsense and be like everybody else?" I wailed as voice became life. In that moment, I gave birth to my own unshakable voice for no one else but me. And there would be no turning back.

As I wailed, I felt a warm rush of knowing, afterbirth maybe—a knowing that at the very root of me, deeper than my shame, was the belief that what my wail was made of . . . mattered. Because it was made of truth. Truth was what was wailing. Truth was always what wanted its way out of me. It lived in my writing. But what about in the way I treated myself? I'd given away what I'd fought for in my twenties. I'd given up the fight in the name of motherhood, and family, and trying to write books to help people, but I'd failed in holding the sword of self-protection. Self-preservation. Self-kindness. Self-love.

The child who had been willing to be punished for her truth had grown into a martyr. Some people say martyrs are made. Maybe this is so. It doesn't matter. There I was, finally finding my wail.

*Don't put the sword down yet. I want you to look at how you got here. Your shame isn't convinced that it can't still flatten you.*

"Wasn't the wail enough?"

*No. Now you have to use it wisely.*

Standing there with my sword in hand, I could see it: for the last few years, I hadn't been okay. I'd been in deep, shame-darkened pain where the truth couldn't shine. I'm not saying I wasn't speaking my truth in my books and speeches, or, most important, in my mothering. I'm just saying that I never felt *good* about it. I couldn't stand out of *judgment* of it. And truth has a really hard time busting through the armor of self-judgment and feeling good on the other side.

The thought of my journals came to me then. All of my journals in a box in my office closet. All the way back to fourth grade. I had never, ever, gone back to read *any* of my journals. I'd been *scared* of them. But in that moment, I needed to surround myself with proof of my utter essence in the only place I knew to trust it, whether it felt safe or not. So I threw on a bathrobe and went to my office closet and pulled out the boxes, and I spread out journal after journal on the floor around me. And I sat down and started to read my words.

These were not words of a complainer nor a judger nor a good nor bad girl. These were the words of a seeker. A lover. A *wonderer*.

There it was! It was *wonder* that had gotten me into trouble. Wonder felt dangerous to other people. It created friction where people wanted the neutral, the uncharged, the inert. It raised questions that were likely to upset the norm. It illuminated the line others were walking to be as filament-thin as it was. My wonder did not make me wrong. It made me *powerful*. And that power could be isolating and alienating because when the world got tired of being asked too many questions, it outwardly deemed wonder *dramatic*. And *impractical*. And *foolish*. And even *rude*. Also, *untoward, uncouth, inconvenient, too much.* Inwardly, however, the world thought wonder was dangerous in its all-too-transparent nature. People didn't want to look into water that clear.

It was all there in my journals. Wonder had led me to be alone. Punished and alone. From the beginning. I didn't feel sorry for myself. I felt rage. Sacred rage. A deep longing to protect that child and preserve what was left of her wonder. To hold her and love her and never let her go. All she wanted was to understand.

As I read on, what I saw was a little girl, turned teen, turned young woman, turned wife, mother, career person, midlifer, who had believed in the power of words over the power of shame. Wondering words. I read the wondering words of a being who fastened herself to the power of words, despite the shame and against the odds, as she slogged through the punishments into an almost obscene need to express the truth that funneled through her. In choirs and plays and speeches and writing and lay reading and singing and praying and reading to her children. And then in speaking her words to groups of thousands at a time—all along the way, pulled toward every stage, soapbox, lectern, podium that called her. Had she been called so fiercely because she was trying to prove that she was loveable?

Did it matter if she was or wasn't? Because trying to answer a question like that just brought in the shame. And it was one thing to have it in my bedroom, but to let it into the place where I write? No way.

Now I held up my fourth-grade journal as if it were my sword. And for the first time in my life, I looked at that girl/woman in those journals as brave. Very, very brave. And it felt so very, very good.

I stayed up all night reading my own words from fourth grade until present day. In doing this, I saw something that I hadn't ever really understood: my writing was full of truth, yes. Well-written, deeply felt truth. Truth that would land in any heart, no matter how cold or shut down or resistant. But the truth was also so eclipsed by shame that I'm surprised I didn't end up on serious drugs, recreational or otherwise.

That night, I found the key to it all: 1975. Fourth grade. I wrote:

> I am in trouble again and I don't know why. Everyone's mad at me and all I said was "Why are there always bad guys in movies?" They all screamed at me to be quiet and I got sent up to my room. They're all still downstairs watching TV and I want to be downstairs. Why is everyone so mad at me for asking? Do they like bad guys? Aren't they afraid too? They act like they're not afraid. Is that why they're so mad at me? Am I not supposed to be afraid? Or if I'm afraid, am I not supposed to say anything? I'm never watching *Kojak* again. I hate them. I can't stop crying. I'm sorry! I'm SORRY! I talk too much. I ask too many questions. I cry too easily. I laugh too loud. I'm too sensitive. (I'm not sure what that means.) And I feel bad about all of it.

It dawned on me that if my journals were this riddled with shame, then maybe my unpublished books were too. All along, my self-expression had been nonnegotiable, but I'd let shame rule me. An organ for an organ. *I'll give you my truth, but you are the gatekeeper, oh Shame.* Maybe it was time to go back and read not just my journals but also all my books. See which ones were shame-steamrollered and which ones weren't.

I lay back on the floor, flooded by self-empathy and self-compassion. And again I heard the kind voice:

*Go now. You are love. Go be love.*

My Inner Champion believed in my love force. My wonder.

In that moment, lying there on the floor of my office where I'd written my books, nearly fifty years old, I asked not *why?* Instead, I spoke aloud to that little pink patent-leather journal with the word "Private" on it, and to all the journals, and said, "I love you." And I smiled, tears warm on my cheeks, spilling into my ears. "You are wonder-*full.*"

As long as we have wonder, we will have truth: thought, spoken, written. So hold your words tight. Protect them with your sword. And when the time is right, drop your sword and pick up your Free Child. Whisper in her ear: "I am proud of you. Especially when you ask why and admit your truth. I accept you for exactly who you are."

## your wild why . . .

Go back to any journal you have and read it like a study of your heart. If you don't have a journal, find an old letter. If you don't have an old letter, see if you can find something in a memory box or scrapbook that you wrote. Maybe it's a poem in a school literary magazine that's on some dusty shelf. If you're striking out, think of a trusted friend or family member who might have an old letter that you wrote to them years ago, squirreled away somewhere, and ask them to send it to you.

Now, read the words from your younger self and acknowledge the courage it took to put those words—any words—to the page. If you see that you could have been more *true*, more shameless and brave, then rewrite the journal entry or letter. Go deep. Be kind to yourself. You are building an Inner Champion instead of an inner shame steamroller. It's time for that steamroller to leave. It's time for your words to be exactly what they must be. And for you to love yourself for them.

# the truth bridge

There's a point in every book that I call the Hinge. The Hinge is the moment upon which everything before it and after it hangs. I like to think of it like a hinge because hinges are constructed for movement. One way or the other or a little of both. Like life.

In poetry, this point is called a "turn," where the physical becomes the metaphysical. One of my students told me that the way I describe the Hinge also fits for ballroom dancing, where it's called the "volta." This chapter, then, is the Hinge, the turn, the volta of this book. I like to think of the "plot" of our path on this planet as one with culminations and confluences. I like to live expecting them. Recognizing them when they come. Not necessarily forcing them. Just believing that I'm firmly on a path, making choice after choice, and hopefully good ones. And then I like to watch as if I'm in a movie. Or, better, the author of my own story. Because I am. And you are too.

So if you think in this way (it's made such a difference in my way of looking at what it is to be truly and mindfully alive), ask yourself: *What is my next big confluence? How would I like it to go? What threads am I carrying along with me, braiding together as I go? Have they become a full braid now, fortified as a unit? And if so, what am I going to do with that confluence?*

In thinking about my next Hinge moment, I like to think of it like a bridge that I'm building with every step. When I think of a bridge, it puts my mind at rest and to work simultaneously. Intention by intention. Wonder by wonder. And for the reason of connection. Maybe someone will meet me on the other side if my bridge finds its connecting point. Or maybe not. It's the bridge *building* that matters. Curiosity has me search for the next piece of the bridge. Awe has me sit on the bridge and see how far I've come and how far I have yet to go. But sitting on the bridge and beholding it all in wonder is where I want to be at the end of the day.

So far, to invite you into this place of wonder, I've given you concrete stories, teachings, examples, and writing prompts. Now let's take a moment to be more philosophical.

I keep this poem very close to me. It was written by Jim Harrison, and it's the best example of what it is to live in this bridge-building wonder that I have ever read.

> Most of my life was spent
> building a bridge out over the sea
> though the sea was too wide.
> I'm proud of the bridge
> hanging in the pure sea air. Machado
> came for a visit and we sat on the
> end of the bridge, which was his idea
>
> Now that I'm old the work goes slowly.
> Ever nearer death, I like it out here
> high above the sea bundled
> up for the arctic storms of late fall,
> the resounding crash and moan of the sea,

the hundred-foot depth of the green troughs.
Sometimes the sea roars and howls like
the animal it is, a continent wide and alive.
What beauty in this the darkest music
over which you can hear the lightest music of human
behavior, the tender connection between men and galaxies.

So I sit on the edge, wagging my feet above
the abyss. Tonight the moon will be in my lap.
This is my job, to study the universe
from my bridge. I have the sky, the sea, the faint
green streak of Canadian forest on the far shore.
(Jim Harrison, "Bridge," from Dead Man's Float)

If every moment of your life was about connecting with yourself in hopes that it would somehow connect meaningfully with the world, what would that look like? Would you be willing or able to express what you really want to express in every situation that you face? What if that act were easy? How would that change your life? How would that change who you are? And I don't just mean by writing or speaking. I mean by thinking. Acting. Being. All of it is self-expression. The way is clear to me, and it begins with a question: Are you being true, or are you being untrue? And whatever is your answer, the next question is: Why?

The kind of self-expression that builds bridges is, at its essence, truth. And truth is wonder's voice. Truth is everything when it comes to the bridges in your life. Even if you're telling a made-up story, it's still based on the truth of the human experience. Throw action into it, and now you're a bridge builder. The truth needs a place, a structure, in order to go from one mind to another mind. From one heart to another heart.

Some people are so sure of the truth they know that they spend their lives building truth bridges in the widest part of the wildest waters where there is no land in sight. But, like Jim in his poem, the sage bridge builder knows that the big bridge will never be entirely built—the waters too ultimately ending in death, or consciousness, or the consciousness of death, or fear, or fear of the consciousness of death . . . or whatever makes it impossible to have world peace. And keeps trying anyway.

Along the way, some bridge builders come to find that the smaller truth bridges across the tiniest gurgling creeks, made out of a few old logs, are the ones to build. Maybe some-one, on a Sunday walk in the woods, will come across it from the other side and stand on it and find something new there, on that small bridge of truth. Something they can use for all their lives, all their walks, or just this one.

Some try for the bigger truth bridges across the bay, where you can still see to the other side, or from island to island, where you can imagine an archipelago as one whole landmass before it went into fracture. Those are the suspension bridge builders and the stone skippers. Some of them are excellent swimmers too.

But what everyone knows who wants to express anything that's worth a damn, or doesn't know and that's what stops them, is this: you can't build any sort of truth bridge if you haven't built the truth bridge to yourself.

And here's the most confounded thing of it all: part of how we build that bridge of truth to ourselves is by simultaneously building the outer bridge in *order* to build the inner one. They build each other.

Some spend their whole life solely building the bridge to the other side. Some spend their whole life solely building the bridge to themselves. You will find both of these sorts of people perpetually on land, standing with their heads slumped to the ground they cannot seem to leave. Why? They have lost their wonder. You can't find the truth it takes to build a sturdy bridge without wonder. Period. Are you a believer yet? I hope so. I so hope so.

The truth tellers. The thinkers. The speakers. The communicators. The spinners of stories. The writers. The word wanderers. The wonderers . . . . We stand on the banks and we stretch one hand out to the waters (of otherness) and the other hand back to the forest (of selfness). And we bend our heads to the heavens. We ask to be stretched all the way, as far as our bodies will allow. That's because along the way we realize that we *are* the bridge.

And if the bridge is made of our truth, then what makes it passable is empathy. We have to be the bridge and we have to be the empathy. We can't control it if others stand on opposite shores with no interest in coming together in wonder, to see that we are the same, even in our differences. But we can build the bridge.

This, however, is my warning. In this act of radical empathy, with all of your steadfast reaching to both sides, it's critical that you don't break in two. That is the risk. So daily, moment by moment sometimes, I think of Harrison out on that bridgeless bridge, dangling his legs over the edge of it, studying the universe, knowing that it's his "job." I ask you only because I ask myself: What is yours?

## your wild why . . .

Think of the bridges you build in your life as a way to connect with the world. What are the main ways that you outwardly build bridges in your life? With family? Friends? In your career? List as many as you can. Maybe there's one main bridge. Maybe there are twelve. Be honest. This is for you, after all.

Now ask yourself: *Do I actively try to build bridges inwardly to myself?* If you're not sure, begin with these questions: *Do I value self-connection, or am I more focused on outward connections? Connections with people, places, events, institutions, groups, etc.?*

There's no right or wrong answer here. This is about self-awareness—and self-awareness is a critical bridge to build to yourself! What do you actively do to inwardly build bridges to yourself? To your essence? List them. Maybe it's one thing or maybe there are many.

Now let's think about your inner Free Child that you hopefully still have in your arms. If you've let her go, pick her up again. She's not going to give up on that twirl. Even if it feels dizzying. Allow yourself to be dizzy. Off-center. Wobbly. To even be a whirling dervish in a sublime trance. This is the perfect way to tap into your bridge building. She wants this inner bridge so dearly, and she wants you to call on her for her knowing. Like the famous Brazilian writer, Machado, who stopped by Harrison's bridge. She knows so *much* about you. The real you. Imagine sitting out on your bridge with her, dangling your feet over a wide sea. Imagine that you will keep her safe, and, in return, she will share her wisdom. Maybe this is the only place where you'll truly listen to her, out on this wild why of a bridge. And if your bridge could ultimately be built, you still need this exact moment with her. She holds your answers. So ask. Now's the time to ask. Remember, she's closer to your wild why than you likely are. Pick her brain.

In your journal, start with these questions. You can always add to them:

What does she want?

What's in the way of getting what she wants?

Is she in the way of getting what she wants?

What does she fear?

What's her central conflict?

What would it take for her to find resolve for her conflict? That's where she needs you!

To that end, after you ask your questions of her, you could flip it and spend some time trying to mother her. Hopefully at this point in the book you are open. And I bet mothering her would come naturally to you. Consider:

What lessons do you want to share with her?

What warnings do you have for her?

What advice do you have for her in the realm of safety?

What advice do you have for her in the realm of daring?

Now imagine standing on the shores of a small stream with no bridge. You are on one side. Your Free Child is on the other. Times are dark and turbulent, and you've lost your grip on her. But there she is, waving at you, wanting you to scoop her up in your arms and keep her safe. She wants to be one with you. That's when you're both strongest. But she's too small to build a bridge. She needs you and your big, grown-up body and big, grown-up mind. What would it take for you to start building that bridge to her? What would it be made of? I'm not talking about actual building material. Think more metaphysically. What would make your bridge to your inner Free Child sturdy?

Wonder?

Empathy?

Wisdom?

Practice?

Courage?

Compassion?

Deep breaths?

Humming?

Singing?

Laughing?

Dancing?

Running through the stream to fetch her on the other side?

Pick the one that she's calling for with all her heart. And meet her there, even if your heart is less enthusiastic.

And then ask her: Once you're whole, what will you do with your moment? Will you play in the stream? Or do you have other plans? Do you have work that you know you need to do together? Can you play first?

Ask her. She knows what to do with your wholeness.

After she's told you . . . go do at least one of the things she asks of you. Right now.

*part III*

wonder-lost

# my wondering:
# can wonder really die?

In all the thinking and living I've done to find an answer to this question, I've decided that it's impossible to truly kill wonder. Just like you can't kill your intuition. To me, intuition is wonder's stunt double. Our intuition might play tricks on us. It might make us feel like a prophet at times. Or a clairvoyant. It might make us fall to our knees in surprise humility and laugh so hard that our stomach objects. As we enter into this next section, I invite you to activate your intuition. Even if you feel it's already activated, try to tune into it as sharply as possible in these pages.

We think we lose our intuition, just like we think we lose our wonder. But we don't. It's there waiting for us, just like our Free Child. And the Free Child wants us to finally be ready to meet it all.

What is intuition? To me, intuition is our central knowing. While our wonder holds our central questions and our pure awe, our intuition is the motherboard to it all. Our intuition doesn't have questions as much as it has knowing, but we can't access our intuition if our wonder is shut down.

I believe that there is a place in our bodies that stock-piles our wisdom and our wonder. You've heard of the "sixth sense" or "gut instinct." The child in you knows this place well. If wonder is behind creativity and self-expression, there is one more layer to go, and that is to wonder what is behind wonder itself. And, to me, that's truth, but it acts as intuition. Deep knowing.

If you can't feel that child in your arms, if you can't allow yourself to be in that dizzying twirl, here's a trick: Look up. Look up. Look for birds. Follow them across the sky. Watch as they go from tree to tree. Pause there. Breathe there. This is a no-brainer for your Free Child. She is constantly watching the sky. She knows how to *play* with the sky. Play. Please. Can we all play for a change? Our intuition wants to wake up, and it likes to play.

When we stop and pay attention to what's going on around us in the natural world, when we remember to tune into it instead of blocking it out in the name of hurrying from one thing to the next, so busy busy busy, we are in a "sin of omission." We are depriving ourselves of the vital nature of our existence. How are we to thrive if we are constantly busy? Nose to the grindstone, eyes on the screen, ten inches in front of us, myopic, forgetting that we cannot be separated from the whole of creation and all it has to teach us.

Can you right now stop what you're doing, take a break from reading this book, and look into the sky? Can you find one bird and watch it for a while? One cloud? The way the sun is casting rays along the horizon? The way light moves around a room? Can you watch one bird for fifteen minutes? One ant? And, no, not to post a photo of it on social media but to simply and wholly know it and let it give itself to you? To let it be fuel for how you are living this remarkable thing called life? Can you let it be all the fuel you need for this one moment? Let it ignite your wonder and set it on fire? If you can, then you are closer to your intuition than you might know. Your intuition is always looking at the sky. Your intuition and your awe are kin.

Like wonder, our intuition was intact when we were children, but we grow up and we stop looking at birds. Stop believing we can charm them into our hands. We close our third eye. Science proves that we have a gut sense with its very own nervous system in addition to the central nervous system ruled by the brain. Only the *gut* nervous system doesn't think. It only *feels*. With every cell in the body.

I am going to share a gut-epiphanic moment that I experienced in the way of intuition. As you read, I invite you to tune into your sixth sense. If you don't feel connected with your intuition, can you remember a time when you *did* feel connected to it? That's a good place to begin.

Tapping into our intuition is a lot like praying. Whether you believe in God or not, when hard stuff happens, *really* hard stuff, most of us say a prayer to our go-to powers that be. Intuition is like that too. We call upon our intuition when the shit is going down but then forget to pay attention to it when we're coasting along in life. We abandon our intuition all too often.

For me, there's one place I can count on consistently when it comes to finding my intuition, and that's when I'm writing. When I lose track of hours and wake up from what feels like a meditative waking trance. When I'm in my flow. In my ease. Not bracing against or resisting but allowing. I think of it like writing is just a byproduct of being in my third eye/ sixth sense/gut instinct. Like I'm keeping my mind busy so that the real stuff can happen. Writing is the opposite of the intuition suck that can be social media or internet rabbit-holing. Writing brings me into a flow state I can trust. It's there, and in the wilderness, that I find what I already know. The answerlessness of my wild whys. The holy moment of wonder.

For me, writing then is the closest I can come to co-creating with the creator. Sounds lofty. So what. Why play small? How does that serve you? It doesn't, so Cut. It. Out. What do you love to do that puts you into an instinctive trance? Reading? Gardening? A good conversation with a soul-friend? Walking in the woods?

I hope that you can walk with me in this story of my own intuitive waking. It's a hard story for me, but in the end, I felt glorious because of my waking. I hope you'll walk away with this fact: You. Get. To. Be. *Glorious*!

## activate your intuition

It's 2011 and I have just spent three weeks in Italy with my fifteen-year-old daughter and a dear friend who has taken us on a lavish trip, the gift of a lifetime, to places that make me want to write romance novels, or mysteries with titles like *Lust by Limoncello* or *Murder, Michelangelo, Mussolini, and Me*. We've gone back to my beloved Florence, where I lived in 1986 and 1987, cooked with my Italian host family, eaten in their backyard overlooking the braided hills of Tuscany, and toured the Duomo and Santa Croce with a private guide who answered every question like it was warm chocolate in her mouth. The entire vacation was in honor of my lifelong dream of becoming a published author coming true. We've laughed and learned and lollygagged, and now it's the last few days—my turn to treat our hostess to a dream night at the opera. I've spent hours planning it just right.

We are in the tiny hill town and artist colony of Pietrasanta. We spend the afternoon swimming in the Mediterranean. We tour Puccini's home in Torre del Lago. That evening, we go to the outdoor auditorium, built as scaffolding to the stars—La Scala's summer home. We take our front-row seats for *La bohème*—the first opera I saw as a young, dreamy woman (standing room in the back) at the Vienna Opera House, and now it's my daughter's turn. At one point during the performance, the moonlight and orchestra pit providing a back-glow, I see that all three of us are weeping through wide smiles.

Back at the little hotel I've booked, I soak it all in. I'm proud to be gifting this night to my friend who has given me so much. This has been the most incredible vacation of my life, and tomorrow it will be over. We have one more stop before going home: London. My memoir has just been published there, and I'm going on the telly. On my birthday. I'm a seasoned warrior in the world of book promotion and big media by now, and I imagine the appearance will be fun for me and educational for my daughter. But for now, I'm sitting on the rug in post-opera bliss, with the ceiling-to-floor windows open to the tiny dark street below, the uneven stones wet with moonlight, my daughter lying in the small bed, recapping our trip in her journal.

Perhaps because this trip is all about my having achieved my dream, I do something I rarely do. I allow myself to take it all in: The glory of getting a book published in eight countries. The years of promotion—media, interviews, television appearances, public spotlight, coast-to-coast book signings, all of the things I'd dreamed of, but never in my wildest dreams starring me as the main character going through a marital crisis, and in my first published book. That was never the plan.

Still, in keeping with my Writer's Statement—"I write to shine a light on a dim or otherwise pitch-black corner to provide relief for myself and others"—it makes sense that it would happen this way. I remind myself of the single most powerful letter from a reader of my memoir: "I am a blind woman from Tel Aviv, Israel. I've never been married, nor have I had children, but I listened to your book over the weekend and it helped me get over the greatest loss of my life, and that was the death of my seeing-eye dog to cancer. I wanted you to know." For this one moment, on this golden night in Italy, I allow myself to feel proud.

Buoyed by this incredible trip, I decide to make a list. I need to really look at the time line that has been my life, especially over the past few years, just to fan it out in front of me and believe it actually happened. I've been living in a constant state of overwhelm for some time, and I need to see my life for what it's been. I need to spell it out, this last crazy chapter of my life, while I have some perspective. After my marital rollercoaster, I've been on a journey of publishing success, invited to be a spokesperson for a message that many need to hear, and yet I am without any formal training to be this messenger. I've been grilled on television, radio, podcasts, and in magazines, newspapers, lectures, conferences, and corporate retreats about my message of emotional liberation. That you can find inner freedom and calm no matter what's going on in your life simply by tuning into your thought patterns and becoming aware of how they both serve and sabotage you. Unlike any other so far, this chapter of my life has been brimful of dreams coming true and dreams falling apart. As far as I know, the marriage, at least, is not at risk. We're in recovery mode. So far, so steady.

I open my journal and make a list. Just to stare it all down once and for all, this sudden and stymying global exposure that I brought upon myself. Do I regret it? Am I glad for all that's happened? I've protected my husband and children at all costs. But me? I need to look and see what's true to make sense of it.

### Time Line of My Twenty-Five-Year "Overnight" Success:

**1988–2008:** Dedicated my life to writing, moved to Montana with my husband, built a house on land, created a family, found my voice, and set it free.

Wrote a lot of unpublished books. Most of them novels. Some of them are good. Got a great agent. Submitted a handful of them. Almost got them in print. Twice. Shut down b/c of zero platform but "no shortage of talent." Glad for good therapists along the way.

2008: Went through a marital crisis. Wrote my way through it in a book called *This Is Not The Story You Think It Is: A Season of Unlikely Happiness.*

2009: The darn thing gets published on the wings of a shorter version of it, which I wrote for the Modern Love column in *The New York Times.* That short essay goes viral and ends up being the #2 most-read Modern Love essay *to date.* After twenty-one years of writing novels, I write a memoir—and *that's* what gets published. To wide acclaim.

2009–2011: Trains, planes, and automobiles, city after city, book signings, lectures, motivational speeches, interview after interview for print, radio, and TV all over creation—crawling the vertical of Manhattan in limos, doing two out of three of the major network morning shows, saved (and slayed) by hair and makeup, navigating my way through cornfields in Ohio in a rental car with wrong TV-station directions, a live interview in fifteen minutes, and no GPS, knocking on farmhouse doors, "Do you know where the NBC affiliate station is?" Getting there with five minutes to spare, applying lipstick in the rearview mirror of the rental car. In a phrase: Thank God for the color black. (Nod to Madam Secretary Albright, who gave me this advice in a shared limo.) Along the way, I've changed clothes in airport bathrooms, in gas station bathrooms, and once in a custodial closet. Ah, the glamorous, ego-exploding life of an author.

**2011:** Marriage seems to have survived the book. He gets fan mail thanking him for being willing to be a book character who's going through a crisis. I had his blessing, and people say they can feel my gratitude toward him in its pages. I tell people constantly, "The entry point is a marital crisis, but it's not about marriage. It's about taking care of yourself no matter what's going on in your life." I never would have sent it to my agent if he hadn't given it the green flag.

Regardless, people are hungry for redemptive stories, and mine struck a chord and, yes, sometimes hit a raw nerve. Turns out, not everyone wants to know that they don't have to be an emotional victim— that they have choices around the things that people say and do to them. They want to stay stuck. My editor tells me that means you've written something powerful—when it pisses a few people off. Mission accomplished. Book helped people. Time for this chapter to end so I can get back to writing fiction.

I sit on the floor in Italy and let the thoughts bump around in my mind. The more I sort through the last few years, the more my Italy-infused euphoria feels tinged by impending doom. Maybe it's that I need to breathe free of all my career responsibilities. So I do. I take the deepest, mustiest, most ancient-Italy breath. But in this borrowed, middle place between things . . . there is something blocking me. It wants me to be brutally honest: yes, my marriage has survived, but I've been watching my husband sink into personal woe. It seems the happier I get, the more he's adrift. Emotionally unavailable. Unhappy. Not the guy I fell in love with. But people go through stages. I signed up for better and worse, short of abuse, of course. My book has gotten us out of financial gravity. It's helped a lot of people. And I've had my little Italy victory lap. Now it's time for our family unit to thrive back home in Montana. The kids need us to. But it's been so long since I've seen my husband truly fulfilled by his life. I'm worried.

I've justified it with "Dad's troubles at work." But it's getting old. For all of us.

I look out over the *La bohème*–blessed streets and sigh. Set aside my journal. I'm sick of this marital roller coaster. I just want to be *happy* again. Really *happy*. Not just up for air. We *were* happy. We moved from coast to coast, city to city, courting each other and life, adventuring together and loving each other. We landed in Montana because he scored a dream job running a microbrewery in a ski town. Suddenly, that meant I could write full time. We could have babies, and I could be a stay-at-home mom! He wanted that for me too. He was proud that he could give that to me. It was heaven. We built a gorgeous farmhouse. We had fabulous parties and wove ourselves into our sweet little mountain community. We took wonderful vacations. We visited our extended families of origin as often as possible. My husband and I were a united force. We still *are* a united force. We are an "us." Aren't we? In the brutal honesty of Italy air, I think of the couples I know who have divorced. The thought of it is unconscionable to me. I brush it away.

We have the rest of our summer ahead of us. We'll live it like we've always lived it! We'll take family hikes in Glacier National Park. We'll pick huckleberries and make jam. We'll go out on our boat on any number of mountain lakes. We'll have picnics on the shores. We'll go to my son's baseball games. We'll be a family, just like we have been for years. Laughing. Learning. Playing. Wondering.

I'll write more books, novels with different entry points, not starring us. My husband will get somewhere he can be proud of in his business. He'll have a spark in his eyes again like he did in his brewery days. Everything is going to be okay. The kids are going to make it through their adolescences just fine. We'll go gracefully into our empty nest and travel the world just like we always said. I repeat: *everything is going to be okay.*

But something tells me it isn't.

My daughter is still journaling, so I power up my computer to check my email. There's something from my husband. I smile but cringe, too, because these days I'm never sure where he's going to be in every sense.

I double-click on the email. I see words that I can't decipher at first. They're new words for him. "Compassion" is one. "Grace" is the other. He can't stand it when I talk about grace. He can't stand it when I *say* grace before a meal.

Uh-oh.

The immature side of me pictures two prostitutes, one on either side of him. Compassion and Grace. Ha ha. I keep reading.

The next words come in drumbeats, like the beginning of a dark and dangerous ceremony. I see letters. I think they spell words. I know I need to understand them: He loves me? But he's not *in* love with me? What does that mean? I don't recognize him in these words.

My heart starts pounding.

I read the rest of the email as fast as I can, tumbling over words. Getting to the plot. Guessing the ending.

There it is: when we get back, he will have moved out. He says the marriage is over.

Whether or not I agree with him, this is an emergency. I am far away from home, my son, my family of origin, my house, my comfort. *Use your philosophy, Laura. Practice what you preach.* But I feel totally helpless, except for what I can control . . . right now. And I'm not sure exactly what that is. I look over at my daughter, so innocent. I want to brush her hair and sing bedtime songs and suspend us in this Italy amber.

Then it hits. I get that white-hot hit nerve feeling from my toes to my hair and I absolutely . . . freeze. I am not breathing. Or moving. What . . . so . . . ever. I stay frozen until I have to breathe. And even then I hold my breath longer than I should. Until the only thing left to do is gasp.

I gasp.

I shut my laptop, put on some shoes, grab my journal and a pen, and head for the door.

My daughter yawns. "Where are you going, Mama?"

"I'm just going downstairs to the café to write in my journal. I don't want to keep you up. The next few days are going to require a lot of energy, and I want to be in the right headspace for it. It's exhausting doing television."

She rolls over and gives a Cindy Lou Who coo. As innocent as it gets. How dare he take away her innocence!

Downstairs in the hotel café, I order a glass of wine and find a corner table. My pen is my guide, and I let it go where it wants. And it doesn't go into the past. It doesn't go all CPR. It's pragmatic. It makes a list. Tonight is strange that way. I'm not a list maker. But here is what it writes:

My truth:
I want someone who loves me.
I want someone who wants to be with me.
I want someone to sing with.
Dance with, laugh with, read with, travel with, learn from. Cook with. Garden with.
I want someone who is advanced spiritually and intellectually.

Someone artistic and witty.
Someone who cares about how they present them-
selves and is careful with their words.
Who is kind. Truly kind.
Not selfish. Innately giving.
I want someone who inspires me in ways I am afraid
to be inspired.
Who has my back and who would want to talk
with me about hard things, be clear and emotionally
responsible.
Who isn't passive-aggressive.
And someone who thinks football is a ridiculous
game of war.

I look up, breathless. Take a sip of wine. This is a surprise.
This is new. In all my journal ruminations throughout my life,
I can't remember ever writing what *I* want in a relationship.
I've written what I don't have, or have tried to work through
what I do have when it's been less than optimal. But never
what I want in a partner.

In this Italy-kissed moment, it feels revolutionary to write
what I want, free from the confines of my life. What I want in a
relationship. As the woman I have grown to be. Not as a wife.
Nor a mother. And this list is as far away from what I have in
my marriage as I currently am from Whitefish, Montana: an
ocean, most of a continent, and the Rocky Mountains.

For one solitary moment, I feel like I am standing on the
most rock-hard ground I can imagine. I am standing on the
*pietra santa* of my own creation. The holy stone of my own
desires, or dare I say . . . manifestation. My own "could be."
If my marriage to this man is over, there are new horizons!
New ideas to wake to and live into each day. New ways to love
and be loved, new people to share my life with who celebrate
and hold dear the things that I have come to celebrate and

hold dear. Who live in light and love and revel in the holy and sacred mysteries of life. Who live in Possibility and Yes and Abundance and Intention and Truth and all the things I have grown to value and live by.

Suddenly I see a world of those people holding their hands out to me, and I am ready to walk toward them. And maybe even a man. Maybe a man who would write a list like the one I have just produced on this little moonlit post-opera night in Pietrasanta.

It becomes crystal clear: I deserve to be loved for who I am, exactly as I am. I deserve to be met. To have my love received whole. I have so much love to give. Over and over and over again it is rejected by him. *I* am rejected. *No more!*

This feeling is . . . absolutely . . . freeing. It's like Michelangelo is speaking to my intuition: *The sculpture is inside the stone. Your job is to free it.* I can see it all so clearly: I am free! The holy stone! The white-hot nerve flashes stop poltergeisting through my body. This might be the greatest day of my life as a woman!

This feeling lasts for about two more seconds, and then the future comes crashing in.

I close my journal. What is about to happen? This is horrible timing! I want to throw up. Couldn't he wait a few more years? Get the kids through high school? We're happy enough, aren't we? Can't we see how he feels once he gets his business afloat? There's just too much to mess with. People's marriages endure a lot worse. We still laugh together. I still catch him looking lovingly at me across the room. We still lie naked together and find our way to each other.

I decide not to respond to his email. I have to get my daughter and myself to London, and I need to focus on our hearts, still intact, before they are sure to soon shatter.

A sleepless night and a bird-early flight later, and I am in a limo with my daughter. Little Brown, my publisher in the

UK, has sent it to bring us to the television studio, and it is raining. We have umbrellas. I hate umbrellas. For some reason that's all I can manage to think about, knowing that my life is about to become a serious shit show. Hopefully it won't go down on air . . . because I feel like a beast is trying to crawl out of what's left of my stomach lining, like in the movie *Alien*. She's gonna blow. *Please, God. Not now.*

My clothes smell like musk and overripe lemons from three weeks in Italy. Luckily, I'm wearing a black knit dress with distracting embroidered flowers. I'm told they have hair and makeup waiting, so I have my hair back in a ponytail. My daughter, with blow-dried hair and a fresh summer dress, looks like *she's* the one going on TV.

We pull into a loading zone and there are people everywhere with cameras. Flashing. Shouting. Everything goes into slow motion. I think about Princess Diana. I think about the Brits and their nasty-bit tabloid lust. I can't imagine who all these people are or that they could be here for me and my book. *Oh my God—did he go public? Does everybody know?* It's not rational, but I'm not rational. I've been so careful to keep my children's lives private. I grab the umbrella, open it in front of me, and say, "Stay close behind me and we'll push through. Hold on to my purse strap!"

My daughter obeys, which as a teenager means she's legitimately scared, and we push through the crowd of photographers to a service elevator filled with shortish men in straw fedoras. I've learned: the famous men are always short. I whisper it to her to try to break the mood, but she doesn't smile. I feel like I'm taking her virginity. I should never have brought her with me.

The people in the elevator pretend to ignore us, and we pretend to ignore them.

I hate elevators. I'm a claustrophobe. I always take the stairs if I can. But the thought hasn't even crossed my mind.

I've never *been* so happy to take an elevator. As we ascend, I feel relief.

"That was crazy," I finally say, aware of my Americanness.

"Indeed," one of them says. He looks like Justin Timberlake.

"I'm glad I have no idea who you are," I say. "Or I might be intimidated."

He smiles. "It's better that you don't." (Later, we find out that he won the equivalent of *American Idol* in the UK and he's a huge celebrity.)

The elevator doors open and we are greeted by a woman with a clipboard who's probably the only person in the building who knows who I am. I introduce my daughter. We are escorted to hair and makeup. My daughter thinks I'm cool as I take my chair, looking into the mirror with the lightbulbs all around it. I can tell in the way she stands close behind me and looks at my face in the mirror and scans me as if I'm new to her. Pride rises up despite the chaos of emotions coursing through me. I'm not just her mother. I'm modeling what it is to not be completely defined by my role in our family. I'm showing her that it's important to have passion for things outside of motherhood. Maybe this wasn't a bad idea after all. She's about to have her whole world reordered, and she's seeing her mother thrive in adversity. She just doesn't know it yet. I wonder if she'll look back on this day and respect me even more. I wonder if I'll ever tell her I knew while I was in the television studio in London. My head is full of wondering about too many things, and it's time to focus. Live television interviews require total third-eye-wide-open aperture. Intuition fully activated.

While the makeup artist says, "Look up, love. Look down, love," I feel like kissing his cheek. This is going to be a positive experience. I've been clear with the producer and my publicist: the UK media has relentlessly spun my story as a recipe for how to stay married. Which is the absolute last thing it's about. One of the magazines ran a piece with an image of a wife handcuffing her husband to the kitchen table. Not exactly the message I was going for. As such, I've been clear: No touting me as a relationship guru. No asking about the nasty bits. I've done countless interviews in every form of media. "I know what the audience wants," I've declared too many times to count. They're tired of the nasty bits. They want the message. They want to know that they can find emotional liberation in a time of great pain. And that's what I'm going to deliver. So please, no "How the American woman kept her husband!" Let's instead have an enlightening conversation!

They've agreed. Pinky sworn.

As we follow the producer to the studio, I catch something out of the corner of my eye on a TV screen. It's my face. It's me on the telly. At first I get a rush of excitement to show my daughter this rare experience, but then I see more.

Right under my face are the words "How I kept my husband."

I want to scream, *What the fuck?!*

Instead, I walk down the thin hallway. It's always a thin hallway. The ceiling always a bit suspect. Like it might fall in. Symbolic. Fame's a sham, apparently like my marriage.

*Shoulders back, Munson.* Just like my father taught me. Good farm stock.

We keep walking, and there are the cameras. This is the "Lights, camera, action" I've gotten used to, and which I'd dreamed about since I was a little girl. Now that I've experienced a lot of it, I've learned that the fame part sucks. What matters to me is the *service* part.

But *shit!* This feels different. I'm not in the US. I'm in the gossipy UK. And I smell bad. And I'm Italy *relaxed*. I've got Michelangelo on the brain. And I see *red*.

As I walk toward the hosts, who are already seated on the couch, waiting for me, for a moment I want to let it all out: *The marriage is over! And the message is the same! Better even! It was never a recipe to stay married! It's a philosophy for how to find emotional freedom in this fucked-up thing called life!*

I'm seriously considering doing it. Think of the superhuman courage it would model to my daughter right here on London TV. Fuck the whole thing. I'm goin' down to their level. I love the UK and my UK publisher, but I'm so over the UK media. I'm going to sit there and say, *Well, here's the deal. The marriage is over. So can you just get the fuck over yourselves? It's not about staying together. It never was. The marriage is officially over, okay? So can you throw down your darts and your tabloid sensationalism and just get the message that you can be responsible for your own emotional well-being no matter what is going on in your life?! Whether married or not married, the message is the same! It's probably going to be more powerful in divorce! So there!*

*I swear, I'm gonna do it.*

*In five . . . four . . . three . . . two . . . .*

I throw my shoulders back, take in a deep breath, and walk to the couch, the sequin British-flag throw pillow beckoning me. The neatly dressed married couple with hearty but cheeky smiles. The live image of the river Thames behind us. Raining. I wish I had my umbrella. As a shield, or maybe a weapon.

"So, tell us, Laura, how is it that you stayed married despite your husband's . . . codswallop." At least that's what I think I hear. I think of Compassion. And Grace.

And I look at the couple. Then I look at my daughter standing in the shadows. My publicist. My lovely editor. My people.

And I don't spill it. I'm a mother.

After it's over, my daughter and I have a brilliant lovely lunch with my brilliant lovely publishing team at a brilliant lovely little pub. And now I just want to go home.

Actually . . . scratch that. I *don't* want to go home. I

want to disappear into the pages of a book and have a stealthy British novelist write me into a Greek sunset.

Lunch is followed by my big birthday splurge: high tea at Brown's Hotel. On the outside, I am high tea-happy, but on the inside I'm writhing in worry. *Where is my son? How am I going to keep my kids safe? How am I going to keep our house? How am I going to make a consistent living?*

I shake it off because my daughter is looking at me, and she can tell that I'm holding something important back. I produce a smile that is so foreign that it feels wrong on my face. "Well, here we are! This is my big birthday splurge! Your first high tea!" I suddenly worry about the cost. *I probably can't afford it now.* I'd booked months ago when I wasn't suddenly strapped with the probable reality of sole financial responsibility for myself, never mind my kids.

"Mama, this is so, so nice! You deserve it!"

And she's right. I do deserve it. And it's so lovely here at Brown's Hotel with its *intime* wood-paneled rooms, punctuated with crown molding and wainscoting, overflowing with high tea-ers sitting around white tablecloths and starched celadon-green napkins, canopies of plates full of bejeweled cookies and cakes and sandwiches and shrimp forks, pots of tea—Lapsang souchong for me, citron for my daughter, our cups and saucers tickling along with the piano ivories in a distant room—except that I can't stop crying.

It's a new kind of crying. It's more like a *leaking.* Like tear duct incontinence. The kind of crying that doesn't contort your face or make your chin quiver. You just get a little red around the lids and mime-like tears fall crystalline, one at a time, slowly down your cheeks. The kind that can easily be wiped away with a fingertip or, if you're having high tea at Brown's Hotel, a celadon linen napkin.

"Mom, what's *wrong*?" my daughter says. "It's your *birthday.* We're *together* having the trip of a *lifetime*! You just did a great job on a big television show! We're having high tea! We're in London! You're a *New York Times* and international best-selling author! Everything's *perfect*!"

I have never felt hollower. Bereft. Scared. Sad. Lost. Voiceless. Wonderless. It's like she's turned the faucet handle. "Sorry. I'm not sure what's come over me. I guess doing television makes me . . ." (*wipe, sniff*) ". . . very . . ." (*wipe, sniff*) ". . . emotional." (*Blow nose into celadon-green linen napkin.*)

She winces. "I don't think you're supposed to do that with these napkins."

"Oh well." I shrug. She hasn't seen this me. I haven't either. I was raised to mind my p's and q's in high tea–type situations. But all bets are off.

Then the piano tickles in with the "Happy Birthday" song, and my heart lifts and I smile at her. *That's so sweet,* I think. *I've raised such a thoughtful daughter.* I sort of bat my eyelashes at her, which increases the tear incontinence.

She looks at me like a deer in the headlights and shakes her head ever so slowly.

And with that, a table behind us explodes with a resounding, "Happy birthday!"

I turn to see a plump middle-aged woman stand as the plump middle-aged man next to her does the same, and they embrace. "Happy birthday, wifey," he says, wrapping his arms around her and rocking her a bit, whispering something into her ear, which makes her face redden and contort with non-crocodile tears.

My face promptly does the same. My husband calls me "wifey," too, in honor of his father's pet name for my mother-in-law. It's a legacy of "wifey" that I'm about to be exiled from. It's all hitting home. Will I still be a part of his family? Will I still be able to call my mother-in-law or my sister-in-law for a nice long chat? Will my nieces and nephews still be mine? Will I be invited to his parents'

funerals? What about all the weddings? I love them all so much. It's too much to lose!

"What's *wrong*?" my daughter insists.

"Maybe . . . I'm getting . . . my period," I say, a snot slick flowing from my nose, mopping it all up with the napkin.

My daughter scowls at me.

"I'll tell you one thing . . ." (*sniff*) ". . . if that damn piano player plays 'Laura' . . . I'll totally lose my shit."

"Laura" is my theme song. It's from the movie *Laura*. People who know me well request it for me. When I've had a few glasses of wine, I request it for myself. It's sort of my *thing*. I guess if my name were Georgia, I'd request "Georgia." Or if it were Mary, maybe it would be "Mary Had a Little Lamb." *My God, I'm losing my mind. This cannot be happening.*

And just as I think this thought, out of some distant room comes . . . yep. You guessed it. "Laura." Out of all the songs in all the world in all the five-star high tea joints.

I stare at my daughter.

She shrugs. Deer in the headlights. "There's no way that piano player could have heard you! No possible way. He's like, two rooms over! Whoa. That is so spooky."

*No. That's intuition . . .*

I listen to "Laura" and, for the first time ever, wish I could slam that piano shut, right on its player's fingers.

My daughter isn't easily enchanted, but she's definitely in a mystic quandary. "Remember when I was little and you used to say that you had an eye in the back of your head and it could read my mind?"

"Yep." I'd forgotten about that. It wasn't altogether untrue. Mothers see their children with more than just eyes.

"I believed you. You have magical powers, Mom. You made that happen."

And somehow in that moment, all to the tune of "Laura," something kicks in. Something magical. Something that your grandmother might have called "women's intuition." Looking over her glasses. Sternly, yet still hushed. Time for the megaphone. Intuition wouldn't leave me alone.

Which means it's no surprise that when I have seemingly beckoned a song, I hear this in my head, and it ain't the Inner Critic. It's intuition itself: *If he's leaving you, he's obviously with another woman. And she's probably got a younger, tighter ass. And likes to ski. And wears a white ski parka. (Never trust anyone in a white ski parka.) And doesn't want to do horrible wifey-type things like make a nice long Sunday breakfast and take a family walk in the woods! Or say grace!*

Screw tea and tears. I order a martini and decide to reclaim my birthday. As fast as they came on, the tears are gone. "You know what we're going to do today?" I say. "We're going to go to Kew Gardens. I've always wanted to go there after reading the Virginia Woolf story about it. And I've heard that the Waterlily House is magical. We're going to go to the Waterlily House. And we're going to make wishes on those beautiful white and purple and pink and red blooms that get their power from the muddy, murky depths, only to float gracefully on those huge green plate-shaped leaves . . . as if nothing bad or scary has ever happened to them." I rein it back. I don't want to scare her. "And then we're going to go to St Martin-in-the-Fields."

But she looks a little scared nonetheless. "Whatever you want. It's your birthday."

I wave over the waiter and ask him where I can get a *Time Out*, London's newspaper that lists all the non-touristy goings-on about town. He brings me one with a small smirk on his face. It's possible he saw me on the telly this morning and judges me. Who cares!

I open *Time Out* and look to see what's going on tonight in London and if there's anything playing at St Martin-in-the-Fields. And just like the "Happy Birthday" song and "wifey" and "Laura," there is another mindblower. Not only is there something playing at St Martin-in-the-Fields, but it's my very favorite choral piece: the Duruflé Requiem. I sang it with the Trinity Church choir in Boston when I was writing my first book in 1988. In my mind, it is the soundtrack to my wildest writerly whys. How perfectly perfect. It's like my music director friend is orchestrating this day. Telling me to choose love over fear.

"I can't believe it!" I explain to my daughter how significant this music is to me, and she smiles. "It's the perfect birthday present! We're going. If you hate it, you can fall asleep. But we're going."

She doesn't dare object. She notably sees something new in my eyes that she wouldn't touch with a ten-foot-long shrimp fork. She reiterates, "Mom! Whatever you want to do! It's your *birthday!*"

In the cab I tell my daughter and the cabbie, "There's a story by Virginia Woolf about Kew Gardens. There's a married woman in it, wandering the gardens, thinking about herself as a little girl, twenty years prior, when she was at her easel by a lake, painting red water lilies. She'd never seen a red water lily. And suddenly, as she's painting it, she feels a kiss on her neck. She looks around and sees it's a kiss from an old gray-haired lady with a wart on her nose. She calls it 'the mother of all kisses' and never forgets it."

The rain is coming down in sheets now.

"Do you know what I think that kiss really was?" I say, speaking loudly over the rain. "The mother of all kisses?"

My daughter looks at me like I'm really asking her. As if she really knows. But she slowly shakes her head. I catch the cabbie looking doleful in the rearview mirror.

"I think that gray-haired lady didn't exist. I think that the gray-haired lady with the wart on her nose was the old lady she would become, beaming in from the future to tell her that the mother of all kisses is a kiss you can only give yourself.

And it's not something you wait for, or expect, from someone else. Not even a husband. It's something you give yourself every moment of every day if you let yourself."

The rain rains harder and I'm leaking again. "It's *self-love*. Loving yourself in all of the phases of your life: who you were and are and will become, warts and all. The 'mother of all kisses' is the act of loving yourself more than anyone else could ever love you. That's what I want for my birthday. That exact *mother kiss*." I don't say *It's the kiss of intuition*. But I feel it in my gut.

My daughter looks sad. "Even more than your own mother loves you?" she says.

"Even more than your own mother loves you," I say.

She looks out the window, and I think I see tears in her eyes in the reflection. But maybe it's just rain.

I do see a tear in the cabbie's eye.

And now, here we are, walking in the rain toward the Waterlily House.

"Whoa," my daughter gasps, stopping herself at the doorway. She breathes it in—this humid air, this place where fairies must live: a big round reflecting pool, giant lily pads and iridescent fish, and purple, blue, pink, white . . . and *red* water lilies. The rain patters on the glass and drips down the sides like my high tea tears. She takes out her camera and does her thing—she's always had an eye for beauty.

I go the other way around the reflecting pool. I want to be alone. I want to receive whatever it is that I am going to find here. Maybe it will be that mother kiss.

I stop at a small scene: a rotten sunken lily, losing its white to brown, a small orange koi swimming in it. At first I think it's caught, and I pity the fish—caught in the rot amid all this beauty. Then I realize that it's feeding off the rot. Feeding off the rot is both a smart way to survive and a great way to perpetuate suffering. I watch it a little longer, willing it to find better food. But it is content, even excited about its dying fuel.

And it occurs to me: I have been this fish.

Just then, I feel it—the kiss on the back of my neck. It feels like a fingertip brushing my skin. I actually put my hand on the exact spot to meet it.

I hear that voice again, the same one I'd heard earlier at high tea. Intuition. It says, *In the shape he's in these days, there's no way he'd have the courage to do this without another woman prodding him, pushing him, taking the helm, making a case for him to get out of his horrible rotten sham of a marriage to his horrible rotten wifey . . . and come to her. His wifey who knows him better than he knows himself. Yes, there absolutely has to be another woman. And if there's another woman . . . who would it be?*

Maybe intuition lives in the nape of your neck, because a woman's name comes to me. In the same voice that talks to me at 4:00 a.m. The kind voice. Maybe she's my Inner Crone. She speaks a first and a last name. I hardly know the woman this voice has just named. I only have a blurry image of her face. She was at my house once for a baby shower I threw for a friend a few years back. But we never saw each other again. I doubt my husband would even know her. I'm not sure she still even lives in our town.

I cast the thought, and the voice, into the rotting water lily. More fish food.

My daughter joins me. Looks at the fish. Takes a few photos of it. "Did you get the mother of all kisses, Mama?"

"Maybe. But I *did* see a red water lily. How 'bout you?"

"I saw a really cool dragonfly."

"That was in the Virginia Woolf story too. If memory serves, the husband of the woman who feels the *mother kiss*, is walking around Kew Gardens, reflecting back on a time from his past when he wanted to ask a woman to marry him but he wasn't sure about it. So he took her to Kew Gardens and bet it all on a dragonfly. If the dragonfly landed on the water lily, he'd ask her. If it flew away, he wouldn't."

"What happens?"

"The dragonfly never lands."

We both look into the pool.

I say, "You should read Virginia Woolf. Especially *A Room of One's Own*. You should always have a room of your own, even if it's a small one. You should always remember to take care of yourself, no matter who's in your life—kids, husband, family, friends. It's not selfish, no matter what people tell you. It's self-*preservation*. Okay? *Okay?*"

She just nods. Something's the matter, and she's onto me.

Just then, a dragonfly buzzes into the little-fish-and-rotten-flower scene, hovers, and leaves.

I touch the nape of my neck. And I look at my reflection in the water and picture a gray-haired-crone version of myself. *Thank you,* I think. And I know what I have to do when I get home, whether or not the name the gray-haired woman has kiss-whispered to me is true. I know that this is a time for radical self-love. Not from anybody else. Not a man. Not a publisher. Not a reader. Not even from my children or any family member. Not from anyone . . . but me.

On the way back to the hotel, we pass a shop with a poster in the window that says, KEEP CALM AND CARRY ON. I haven't heard this before. We go in and the shopkeeper tells me that was what the queen ordered to the people of England during World War II, in anticipation of the air raids. *I'll need this poster,* I think, and I buy it with the express intention of hanging it on the back of my office door and referring to it often. If it's good enough for air raids and royal mandate, it's good enough for me.

Back in the hotel, my daughter in the shower, I see an email from my husband. I quickly click on it while I have this birthday courage.

He says he's in love. He's never felt this kind of love. It's springing from him in a way he's never known. It's his truth. He's in love with a person whose name is . . . you guessed it.

In an *email*?

I am utterly done with this man. I have given him enough of my precious life. Too much, some would say. In this moment, I feel like I am linking arms with the gray-haired lady I will become, who knows that I will find my way to the mother kiss.

But I cannot stop the eruption of rage that rises up from my deepest being. I want to stand on my bed and clutch my fists to the ceiling and scream, *Good riddance!*

If it weren't for my daughter in the next room, maybe I would.

That night, I sit in St Martin-in-the-Fields listening to the Duruflé Requiem (a funeral mass somehow part of this whole intuition intervention), my daughter asleep with her head on my lap. I know these moments will be fewer and fewer as she gets further into her teens and beyond. I put my hand on her head. With her asleep and this beloved music moving the room and my heartbeat along with it, I can cry if I want to. I don't have to answer any questions. I don't have to bridge to any high-road messages. I can just sit here and be sad.

It's a full house. I'm not the only one who knows what the Duruflé Requiem can do in your bones. I scan the balcony, looking at people's faces. Postures. Companions. These are my people the same way the publishers are my people: hearts wide open to beauty and excellence.

There is one couple that stops my scan. A man and a woman. About my age. She's in a dress with a nice scarf. He's in a suit and tie. They are both leaning forward on their knees, rapt, holding hands. He wipes tears off his cheek as they spill down his face. I smile. These people exist. I am not in a culture all my own. I bet they have been to the Waterlily House. I bet they knew what they truly wanted in a partner. And found it.

And the tears come full faucet now. I don't have to do this anymore: love my husband as my husband. I can love what there is to love about him. From afar. I have done my best. Better than my best. More important: I can remember the things I love most about me and rejoin in that celebration. I can be happy again. Happier than I've ever been. I'm forty-five. I have time. At least I hope I do. Even if I have to reshape my family and lose my beloved home, even if it's excruciating . . . I know what I need to do.

Back in the hotel, my daughter asleep, I lie in bed feeling all of it, including the kiss, the kyrie, the chance to truly love myself like I never have in my life. To give that kiss to myself. All I have to do is touch the nape of my neck. I know that the *beloved* . . . is me. And from now on, my intuition is my guide. I may come kicking and screaming, but I know that it is time to step into the mystery and learn to dwell there. And find wonder again.

And I'm going to have to do it alone.

## your wild why . . .

Start an Intuition section in your journal. For one week, carry it with you everywhere. If your journal is too big, find a small journal that will work. The goal is to start tuning into your intuition in your everyday life. To pay attention to what your intuition is telling you. To honor its wisdom. Do this by writing down what you hear in your mind's eye and even feel at the nape of your neck.

As writing prompts, ask and answer these questions:

*What does my intuition tell me about the current state of my wonder?*

*What does my intuition tell me about self-love?*

*What does my intuition tell me about where I have been looking for love outside of myself?*

You can add to this list of questions. At the end of the week, read over your answers and write about what you have learned.

Then write a promise to yourself about the role you want intuition to have in your life. About how you want to learn to listen . . . and believe.

I hope that you can find your intuition at your fingertips whenever you need it. But it takes practice and letting go of where you thought you wanted to go or were *supposed* to go. Once you live by your intuition, the world looks and behaves a lot differently. That is if you are *ready* to refind your intuition. Which is to say that you are ready to refind your wonder. And why wouldn't you be? Your intuition has been calling you to refind it for years. And the child you're twirling too. And the gray-haired lady. Listen to them. They know the way.

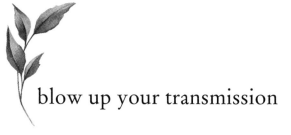

# blow up your transmission

I have found that when we are in active pursuit of uncovering our wonder, stories happen to us as if we're the main character in a book. The stories are pointed, symbolic, and lesson-rich. I have also found that these stories often present themselves as before-and-after moments, testing us, calling us through to the other side. These stories often show us a clear end to one chapter and a solemn but sturdy nod to our next.

Sometimes, however, these moments dare us, taunt us, and even feel like cruel punishment. And yet, these can be the exact invitations to the rest of our life that we dearly need. That we know we must say yes to in order to grow and become. Invitations that appear in the form of taxation to an already-wonder-taxed life, yet invitations that wake us up to our best form of personal creation and transformation and reinvention. Mostly, these sorts of invitations are the ones that jolt us out of the illusion that we are ultimately in charge.

I have learned to see these seemingly powerless moments for the choices they demand and to convert them into some semblance of sway. If I'm tuned into my intuition, sometimes I can even feel these defining moments coming. Because, in so many cases, these moments confirm what we already know intuitively.

Still, these moments often present themselves as brutal insult to injury, arriving when we are most bashed and bloodied by too much stark reality and too much to lose. We stand before them, numb. *Take me. Grind me up and spit me out, new. I'm ready.* These are the exact moments when wonder has the chance to seep in. If we allow it.

There was a Montana moment that matched my Waterlily House moment . . . in which life appeared so symbolically that I simply couldn't ignore the message: My power wasn't in my past. If I was going to truly give myself permission to reclaim my power and my voice, and to regain my wonder, I had to own my present. Who I'd been or who people perceived me to be on the outside wasn't where my power lived. It was in my ability to create my life. It was all *inside* me. It was in the unending flow of creativity, imagination, intuition, curiosity, and awe, and let's not forget self-love, that I possessed in my own unique way. No excuses.

This moment offered itself to me on the day of my divorce.

I'd gotten dressed in my nicest "I am an upstanding citizen" skirt with a neat sweater and "don't mess with me" boots. I'd pulled my hair back into a tight bun, the way I imagined Elizabeth Taylor dressed for at least two of her divorces. It wasn't like I was going in for a fight. We'd managed to do the whole thing with a mediator. It was just a paper to sign in front of a judge. Still, I wanted to look . . . upstanding. I didn't feel upstanding. I felt like a failure. Plus, my soon-to-be wasband emailed me the week prior and said he was leaving town. He wished me luck.

Luck? That word floored me. For some reason, I'd assumed he'd be there to sign the papers. That we'd do this together. He was there when we started this marriage, wearing a proper morning suit, tears in his eyes. He made a charming toast and we gazed into each other's eyes and called it a "perfect moment." But now wasn't a time to think about togetherness. I was officially about to become a solo act. And I was running late. There's nothing like hauling ass down a country road to get to your divorce signing on time to make you look down the barrel of reality.

In a 4:00 a.m. sort-of kind voice, I heard: *It's time to move on. I'm going to make you move on. Just you watch. I'm going to make you find your wonder again. I don't recognize you. Nobody recognizes you. You don't recognize yourself.*

It was true. One of the most painful things my wasband said to me in mediation was that people had come up to him in the streets of our small town and said things like, "What's happened to Laura?"

I couldn't disagree, though it wasn't lost on me that his point was: *You've gained weight.* What it meant to me was: *Your wonder has almost run out of you.*

Did people only recognize and *like* the wonder-full me? So much of my wonder had been sapped after my father, my original advocate, died, but years of marital ups and downs hadn't helped. Still, I'd been the one who didn't know how to ask for help. I was the one pretending I was fine when I wasn't.

Even so, I was hurt by it. Were people only there for me when I was on top? Didn't any of them see the pain I was in? Or if they did, was my pain too scary? I'd been there for my loved ones' scary pain all my life. Where were my advocates? A small, and enormously patient, few had shown up. But still, very few. I felt betrayed, but more than that, I felt rejected. And rejection was my age-old wound. Which meant it was more of a reason to hide. Only now my personal hiding places were all up for grabs unless I could figure out a way to make a substantial living and secure my house from being sold off.

I tried to wipe the worry away. At that moment, I just needed to finalize this thing called the "dissolution of marriage." It felt like a death nell instead of what some hear as freedom bells, and I suspected him being one of them.

I pushed harder on the accelerator and touched the nape of my neck. The pep talk continued: *It doesn't matter anymore. What's past is past. You must create your future now. You've got to find your essence and the engine behind it: your wonder.*

Well, as my grandmother used to say, "God sure has a sense of humor!" Because next thing I knew, as I was screaming down Farm-to-Market Road in my old-but-fully-paid-off Suburban, a tractor pulled out in front of me, going about ten miles per hour.

*Please, Jesus! I need to get to the courthouse!* My mediator had said it to me point-blank, knowing my habitual five-minutes-late tick: "Don't be late!"

So, what's a woman gotta do when a tractor pulls out in front of her on a country road and she's already running those five minutes late? She passes his ass, even though it's a double-yellow line and there's a hill in front of her with potential oncoming traffic, even for a back road. Of course she does. She does not, however, flip him the bird. He's just doing his job. She's too busy shocking herself with reckless driving, which is not her style.

As I pressed the accelerator to the floor, the universe surely on my side, wanting me to get to the next chapter of my life, something told me this wasn't going to go the way I'd planned. I could feel it at the nape of my neck. And sure enough: surprise, surprise. In the full engagement of this V-8 engine, the power ran right out of my truck. It was like I was in neutral, right there in the left lane, with the tractor only inches behind me and an oncoming car coming straight at me.

So I did the only thing I could do: I steered myself back into the right lane behind the tractor. It wasn't lost on me that the tractor driver chose not to flip *me* off, even though I deserved to be flipped off. But I was also pretty sure the universe was flipping me off altogether because now my truck was also billowing black smoke. I knew that I had no other choice but to cut the engine and coast onto the shoulder of the country road.

"Fuck" was the word that came to mind.

Things went from slo-mo to breakneck: I reached for the copy of the divorce decree I'd brought with me because, while I tend to run five minutes late, I'm always prepared. There at the top was my lawyer's phone number. *What are the chances he'll answer?* He didn't, but his coworker Claire did. I liked Claire. Out of all of them, Claire was least freaked out by my tears. It's nice to have someone like that around when you're spending the sum total of your time in someone's office bawling your eyes out.

"Claire! My car just died and I'm on the way to the courthouse. Help?"

Claire's voice was judge-gavel steady. "Hang tight. Be right back."

I sat there in a shroud of black smoke, feeling what was left of the will and the false power and the real power and the dread and the hurt all drain out of me. Total adrenal activation now dissolved into total deactivation. There was no possible way I'd get to the courthouse, not on time, and possibly not that day at all. I couldn't even hitchhike. The road was empty. The tractor was long gone. This wasn't the sort of place where you could grab an Uber.

*I'm not only going to be late, I'm going to miss the whole thing.*

Waiting for Claire, I wondered: *If the divorcing parties don't show up, does the divorce happen? If a tree falls in a forest and no one is around to hear it, does it make a sound?* I've always held that it does.

Claire came back on the line to tell me that the judge could probably do it over the phone. "Sit tight," she told me. "I'll call you right back."

"You can get a divorce . . . on the *phone*?!" I was utterly shocked. But my mind started to loosen to the humor of this moment. *It's funny, really. All the buildup. The skirt. The bun. The boots. My wasband's good-luck wishes.*

I was overtaken by a smell then—a smell that said *danger*. Maybe my car was going to blow up. Wouldn't that drive home the irony stake? What I didn't know yet was that I'd blown my transmission. And the transmission is what gives power to the engine. My truck had lost all its power to move forward. And I didn't know yet that I would spend the next year of my life becoming my own personal transmission in my own personal postdivorce life. But in that moment, all I knew was that I needed to get out of my truck.

So I stood on the shoulder of Farm-to-Market Road, holding my cell phone, waiting for Claire. I couldn't stand it. I needed to do something within my control, so I called the towing company.

"Hey. It's Laura Munson. The one with the old green Suburban."

"With the crazy driveway?"

"Yeah, that one."

"Oh, hey, Laura. What's up?"

The range of answers was limitless, but I kept my focus. Plus, it was one of those times that make small-town living worth the "What happened to Laura?" comments. We know each other. We take each other personally. We are parts of a whole.

"Well . . . my truck just died. And I'm on the way to the county courthouse. To get a divorce, actually. And . . . it looks like I'm not going to make it. So I guess I need a tow. But when you get here, I might be . . . on the phone, actually. In the middle of it. So just go ahead and put my truck on the flatbed." That was my version of a short answer.

"Oh okay." He'd seen a lot.

I hung up and paced.

Claire called back. "Okay, the judge has agreed to do it on the phone. He'll ask you a few questions, and you'll be done. He'll put the decree in the mail today. You'll have it tomorrow."

I was deeply appalled by this whole situation—that my wasband wasn't going to be there, that I was on the side of the road in a cloud of black smoke, that I was about to get divorced by phone, that I was getting divorced at all. For some reason, I stepped to the double-yellow line, ready to take my medicine. Not unlike going on live TV.

The clerk came on the line, and we were in it. I saw the whole thing from a bird's-eye view: *I am about to raise my right hand and vow to tell the truth and nothing but the truth, so help me God. Right here in the middle of Farm-to-Market Road with a broken (but paid-for) truck.*

I raised my right hand. *How do they even know that I'm raising my right hand? This is all so bizarre.* And then I said the bookend "I do" from my wedding day.

"Is your marriage irrevocably broken?" asked the judge.

*Irrevocably broken?* It would be a lie to say that anything is "irrevocably broken." Not even my truck was irrevocably broken.

My lawyer had instructed me to answer with yes or no . . . but there was so much more to say. This was not black-and-white. Not by any stretch. I wanted to talk about intuition and how we ignore it. I wanted to talk about wonder and how we almost lose it. And find it. But I forced myself. "Yes," I said, in a voice nothing like my own.

Even though the proceedings continued, everything got blurry. There was a truck, and a guy I recognized who winked at me, and there were loud cranking metal sounds as my truck was pulled out of my peripheral vision. *Am I still on the phone? Am I doing everything I'm supposed to be doing? Does it matter?*

While all of this was unfolding, guess who I was thinking about? Guess who I was worrying about? Yep. My soon-to-be wasband. I was actually worrying about how he was doing. I was worrying about his mother and father. I loved them dearly. I felt the weight of our whole extended family. His family. Was it no longer my family too? Would the four of us, our nuclear family, ever be able to sit around a table again? *Good luck?* What did that mean? Good luck with today, or good luck with the rest of my life? *I can't take this. I just can't.*

In a matter of minutes, before I even knew it was over, it was over. The judge undid the last two decades of my life. Right there in front of the cows and the white-tailed deer and the tow guy. I got off the phone, and I exploded into a laughter so pure that it billowed its own smoke and grew until I was doubled over in belly-laughing eruptions, standing on the double-yellow line of Farm-to-Market Road. I hadn't laughed like that in so, so long.

The tow guy waited until I was done. Underwhelmed.

I got into the passenger seat, truly happy to be a passenger, and I said, "Thanks for coming so fast. Sorry I was on the phone. You're not going to believe this, but I just got divorced right here in the middle of the road. Now you can officially say you've seen everything."

He smiled. "I sure have seen a lot." I loved him for being so totally unshockable.

"Tell me some stories. I could use a story right now."

He told me some dark ones. Really dark. And they made my little side-of-the-road divorce seem like small potatoes. That's all I wanted to hear—his tow truck stories—until I was at the mechanic shop in my upstanding-citizen outfit at a desk that wasn't the desk I'd dressed for, explaining what had happened to my truck, not my life, to a young man who was eager to throw out the little pet name I'd hear a lot in the next couple of days, and it wasn't "dissolution of marriage," or "irrevocably broken," or "irreconcilable differences." It was "tranny." I'd blown my tranny. And it was gonna cost me.

When the tow guy offered to drive me home, I almost fell into his arms but didn't want to embarrass him. He didn't need to offer me a ride. It wasn't protocol. But I suppose he thought I didn't have anyone to call. And I didn't. Not really. Not in the shape I was in. I was sick of being an emotional wreck around my close friends. In that moment, we both knew that he was the only one who understood my current reality. Small towns can be so beautiful in this way.

I wanted to wax philosophical but spared him that too. That my truck lost its power on my way to my divorce was of course symbolic. I had turned over so much of my power to being a wife and a mother. It occurred to me, sitting in the passenger seat, that there was perhaps more power in being alone than in being coupled. And if that was true, then was I whole all by myself?

And with that wild why, I realized that my bladder was about to burst and I asked him if he wouldn't mind stopping at the gas station. I loved this gas station. I'd never once walked in without the jolly attendant, Murphy, greeting me in his New York accent that sounded exactly like Frosty the Snowman in the classic holiday TV show. I waited for it.

"Munson! I was hopin' you'd come in! I got somethin' for you. You like horses, right?"

"Yeah . . . ." What else did this day have to offer? It seemed like anything was possible.

He pulled a brown grocery bag from behind the counter, his eyes smiling through huge bifocals. "Sorry it's not wrapped."

I felt shy. And suddenly I didn't have to pee. Instead, I reached in and pulled out something heavy, wrapped in newspaper. This man, who seemingly had so little, had gotten me something? In that moment, a brick would have made me cry. Never mind what my eyes beheld. It was a horse.

A hand-blown glass figurine just like the spotted amber one I'd gotten at the glassblowing factory with my daughter in Venice. Only that one was on its knees, struggling to get up, its head raised to the heavens in a wide-mouthed petition to what looked like the gods. This horse was a soothing cobalt blue, and it was in a state of repose. Its head down. Happy to rest on the solid ground of which it seemed so sure.

I couldn't hold back this time. I burst into tears and went around the counter to hug him. "Thank you, Murphy. You have no idea how much this means to me."

"Aw, shucks, Munson. You've seemed like you could use a little cheering up lately." He shrugged. I wondered when the last time was that someone did a random act of kindness for him. Maybe my hug had been that for him. By the time we got home, now the tow guy was tearing up with the ripples of this story. So much kindness in the world, we agreed. And I thought: *Wonder is kind. Only kind.*

I went straight to my journal:

I am officially divorced. I wish I felt good about it. Instead, I feel so powerless and desperate and afraid. Mostly for my kids but also for me. What if the bank won't trust me to be the responsible owner of my mortgage? I don't want to have to prove myself. I want my childhood home's Munson brass door knocker to be already nailed to the front door. I want to tap into some sort of high astral plane that will vibrate financial security toward my children and me. It doesn't have to be in excess. Just enough to bring us stability. And I have absolutely no idea how. I am so terrified of losing my house. It knows everything about me . . . and loves me anyway. Maybe it will find a way to help me keep it. I wish I could skip the holidays this year and just hide.

I felt pathetic as I pulled the calm blue horse out of the paper bag and set it on my desk, next to the struggling, fighting, keening amber one, as if they'd been long-lost and rejoined. As I watched the light dance in their glass bodies, I felt the deep knowing of the Waterlily House. I was going to keep my house and my children safely in it. Myself included. And it didn't need to be a fight. It could feel peaceful. I felt it. I knew it. What was before me was a voyage of true power. Curiosity and awe, indeed. But now . . . intuition, tranny fully loaded. I touched the nape of my neck.

## your wild why . . .

Answer these questions:

> *What is my real power, and what is my false power?*
>
> *How does each behave in my body?*
>
> *What are the lies that my false power tells me?*
>
> *What are the truths that my true power tells me?*
>
> *How do I feel when I am in my false power?*
>
> *What do I fear about my false power?*
>
> *What do I hope for in my false power?*
>
> *What would it take for me to step into my true power and live there and use it?*
>
> *What do I know deeply and intuitively that I just need to remember?*

# the tiger in the room

Do you ever feel like you're giving your life everything you have—and even so, you're about to get into a lot of trouble for it? You might even be killed for it? I call that killer the Tiger in the Room.

Throughout my childhood and into adulthood, I was chased by that feeling. Like there were fangs about to bite the back of my neck. Especially when I asked a lot of questions. And that's because my whys so often resulted in angry discourse, which so often landed in my nos, consequent trouble, and hiding. Sometimes I was hiding from the adult world, but at some point in my childhood, the perpetrator took vicious form.

The Tiger in the Room wasn't my Inner Critter. She was dangerous, yes, but only with her *words* on constant repeat in my mind. The Tiger in the Room was different—something outside of myself. I hadn't named her yet. It was just a very visceral feeling that had me wanting to fight, freeze, or flee. Mostly flee. It took me until somewhat recently to understand that I've spent a lot of my life, unknowingly, in adrenal blowout, anticipating this attack. It's not lost on me that I ended up living in mountain lion territory. They say that you won't be aware of them until you feel their fangs piercing your skin. So a mere walk in the backyard can go terribly wrong. Talk about a literal wonder-kill!

The Tiger has been consistently blood-hungry for my wonder. It took issue with my wild why and didn't need soap and Tabasco or dog collars and wig brushes. It had fangs and claws. So especially in the darkest times in my life, I've kept my wonder in very safe and private places where the Tiger wouldn't think to look. Again, I didn't know to name it. Only to run from it. Or prepare to fight it. And so there have been times when my wonder has been a tiny, hidden thing.

The Tiger went away for a while when I became a mother. Maybe in being an authority, teacher, and caretaker to two little wonderous, innocent beings, I was getting my own innocent wonder back in full swing. All the bedtime stories and star-gazing into the Montana night sky, all the romping through the woods in pursuit of Calypso orchids and knots in trees where gnomes or fairies must live, all the stopping to watch the birds, dragonflies, and butterflies landing on sweaty summer limbs. All the hunting for heart-shaped rocks on the banks of Montana's mighty rivers. All the answering of their whys and the new, wonderous questions that would emerge. There was so *much* wonder. I was steeped in it and so were they.

If my definition of "wonder" is "curiosity and awe mixed together," those years were heavy on the awe for me. And heavy on the curiosity for my children. Together, we were truly wonder-full.

Awe: "Wow, kids. Look at how you can see the rain passing across the valley. Like the clouds are smearing downward. I love that."

Curiosity: "Why can you see the rain when it's far from you but not when it's right in front of you?"

Awe: "Let's sit here on our front stoop and watch it until it's upon us. Maybe then we'll know."

Wonder: "It'll be cool either way."

So curiosity and awe would inevitably merge, and we'd sit there and stare into the rain, watching it move closer and closer, feeling the air cool and cool, until we'd lose sight of the rain altogether, and that's when we knew we were about to get wet. Still, we wouldn't move. We'd stay there until we understood something new about rain. "Now someone can see *our* rain from across the valley!" one of us would say. Another would say, "Most people wouldn't sit here in the rain." Another: "It's summer! I don't get why people don't like to get rained on when it's hot outside. I mean, they take showers. Doesn't make sense." We prided ourselves on not letting resistance ruin our wonder. Or fear: "Most people would be too scared to sit here in the rain. Because maybe there's lightning." We didn't let fear in very often, if at all.

During those precious years, I discovered something life-altering: wonder is bigger than fear if you let it do its job. Like love. And I loved those little children with such a *pure* love. When they came out of my body and were placed in my arms, I said, "You can be whoever you want to be. I will hold that for you as you go." Something deep in me healed in those moments, holding my babies, more soul than flesh. What I was really saying was, *I will hold your wonder in case you forget.*

But as the years went by, life got hard, and my wonder spell got broken by death and divorce and single parenting, and the fear of an empty nest and living alone in rural Montana, and financial instability and losing my house, and the sometimes bottomlessness of human existence. And the fear-mongering Tiger returned.

This time, chasing the ambulance of my reinvention as a single person and single mother, knowing it was time to somehow find financial security . . . the Tiger wanted real blood. And it knew exactly where to look. In my bank account. In my kids' lunch boxes. In my stack of bills. At 4:00 a.m.

That's why I needed to stare the Tiger down, whether I wanted to or not. It took a long conversation with a good friend at a hole-in-the-wall bar to finally name and retire the Tiger.

Here's the story:

It's February 10, my father's birthday. I don't like this day, even fifteen years after his death. I use it as a day to observe pain, loss, grief, survival. And I generally like to do it alone.

But today I'm standing at a bar in the middle of Montana, waiting for my friend. She's taken a hiatus from her job as a high-profile journalist and is driving cross-country to interview everyday people in everyday small towns to tap back into the heart of humanity. She also needs to clear out her brain from all the wreckage she's covered over the years: tornadoes, hurricanes, floods, airplane crashes, gang riots, kidnappings, school shootings. Unthinkable etc.

I'm on hiatus from the speaking circuit, which has become my bread and butter. I need to clear out my brain from the plot twists of my professional life and the wreckage of my personal life. Divorce wreckage. Family wreckage. Future wreckage. Stability and security and hopes-and-dreams wreckage. Lesser wreckage than the sort of devastation she covers on her major-network news program, but wreckage nonetheless, and I'm sick of trying to understand how it all happened. Sick of trying to salvage what's left of my last chapter and rebuild. Sick of trying to explain it to my loved ones.

"I'm going to be in southern Montana. Drive down and meet me," she said in a phone call last week. "You can just be *you*."

What she meant: Not a mother. Not an author. Not a speaker. Not an ex-wife. Not a responsible citizen of the human heart, nor a blood bank donor, nor a borrower approved by mortgage lenders.

"Okay."

"Bring your journal. And bring your guitar."

We all need friends like that. Especially when we're reinventing our lives.

The drive through Montana is one long breath in and one long sigh out. Windows down. Ninety miles an hour with not another vehicle in sight. Singing loudly to tunes hardly anyone in my life would want to listen to. Like requiem. Like musicals. Like Irish sea shanties and Hindu *kirtan*. My kids are with their father and they have fun plans, so that's covered. And I don't have to be alone in my house without them, which guts me every time. I have two days to myself with this dear friend. I'm proud of myself for saying yes. And a little scared. I haven't socialized in a long time. Who knows what will come out of my mouth? I'm either on the stage, mothering, or being a writerly hermit.

But the Montana road casts its spell, as it always does. For six beautiful road-trip hours, I've been feeling the topography of my professional life melt away as lush mountains become arid high desert, replete with tumbleweed. I am far from the speaking circuit—the women's conferences and wellness-world stages that have tried to Eliza-Doolittle me into being an expert with a brand, wielding a PowerPoint clicker, in a pantsuit, full hair and makeup, attempting her version of the Ten Easy Steps, Tips, and Tricks that the speaking world is blood-hungry for. (The Tiger is good friends with this stage.) I've been delivering my messages my way, and it's not their way, and that's a problem because I've tried to adapt. I really have. But I can't take one more minute of it. It's just not . . . me.

It's like the wind in my ears and hair and face, the bugs going kamikaze against the windshield, and the deer standing sentinel on the side of the road are bringing me back to my senses: I've been taking stages all my life, but really, I'm a writer. What I have to say is in my books. And lately there's been something about these speaking gigs that feels bad. Really bad. Like there's a dangerous creature threatening to attack. And I don't know why. I'm good at speaking. I'm an extrovert with a theater background. I care about my messages, and I don't mind being the messenger. I care about the women who spill their guts to me afterward. I see their pain and I recognize it. It's not going to kill me to have a PowerPoint clicker in my hand, as long as I don't sell out, and I haven't. And the money is good.

But it takes me away from time with my kids and time with my muse. And time in the woods. The speaking circuit, and all its planes, trains, and automobiles and crowded airport-sized conference centers, is sucking at my wonder. And my wonder is how I breathe. I used to think it was my writing. But it's more than that. It's what's *behind* my writing. It's what's at the root of who I am. I need my wonder, but I don't see a way out. I am financially responsible for sustaining a stable family-of-three life. And that seems to be my dangerous attacker's best bait.

As I roll into town, I feel a romantic stirring in my gut. I'm in a free zone. I'm not going to run into anybody. I'm not going to hear anything about what my wasband is up to. And tourists don't come to a place like this, so it's just a smattering of locals. It's dusty and dry and flat. Not everybody *gets* this Montana, this ghost-of-the-one-pony-town Montana, but this friend does. She's chosen this town for exactly what it is: small, liberating, spacious . . .and, well, a playground for *fuck-it-if-they-can't-take-a-joke*. If you don't live there that is. In the small-Montana town where you *actually* live, it's best to keep the joke to yourself. I long for this anonymity and for the conversations I know are in store for me in spending time with this dear, wonder-worn friend.

She's booked a room in one of those iconic old western hotels with the lone smoking woman at the front desk, and the photo of the famous person who once stayed there ninety years ago, and the taxidermy lording over the lobby. When you've lived in Montana for decades, you learn to respect taxidermy like that, never mind the hotel and the woman smoking. I love this piece of Montana. Getting a little lost on purpose and nobody caring. I need *a little lost*. I need to *play* a little. Especially on this tenth day of February when I miss being able to call up a man back there in Illinois and say, "Happy birthday, Dad! I love you! I am grateful for you!" My father truly accepted me. He listened to a lot of my pain and mopped up a lot of my tears. And his birthday every year guts me for perhaps that reason most. It's a day when the wonder wound is loud and mean.

My friend knows this. She's a talker/thinker/wonderer too. We've missed how we hammer away at a theme, taking every angle we can think of until we are sated. We might not have answers by the end, but we will have found some relief in our questions and mind-meanderings. And I'm positive that we will be better in the wonder department, at least I know that I will, and that's what I need.

She walks in. We give each other a long hug and then another even longer hug. Then we get to business. We each order a beer and a shot of whiskey.

She looks down the bar and says, "Shots for the house on me," and the bartender clicks into action.

The belly-ups look at her sideways and grin. They've seen this before, and they're not that enthused about being anybody's social experiment. But they're happy to oblige, free booze being what it is.

"Not sure if you knew this, but my father was from a small town in southern Illinois," I say. "He loved a small town, even though he ended up in a fancy suburb. He used to say, 'People are the same everywhere.' I feel like my whole life's journey has been a field study in seeing if he was right."

"Was he?"

"I think so. Definitely. We all just want to love and be loved. Seen. Understood. Respected. Worthy. We all just want to be able to express ourselves and have it be received. Don't you think?"

"I agree," she says. "It's one thing to do that field study in a large metropolis but another to observe it in little town after little town all across America. It's been an enlightening road trip."

The bartender brings us the shots, and my friend raises her glass and says, "Here's to small-town living," and we all say, "Cheers," and drink.

The belly-ups go back to watching TV, and I look at my friend's bright, producer eyes and say, "What have you learned on your road trip?" Of course what I'm really asking her about is the thing I prize most: empathy. The outcome of wonder.

Without hesitating she says, "I've learned that we're all waiting for the Tiger in the Room."

I was expecting something more along the lines of *kindness, grief, fear of mortality.* "The Tiger in the Room?" I say, sensing its pounce, feeling those speaking-gig stages encroaching. "Tell me more."

"C'mon! There's *no* way you don't know about the Tiger in the Room."

I look around, looking for an actual taxidermied tiger— that's how long I've lived in Montana. I see dusty antlers, too many televisions for too few customers, old signs from businesses that have gone under, rows of shining, mid-shelf booze bottles. I don't see a literal tiger in the room, though I do see a few guys who look like they might have killed someone and gotten away with it.

She continues, "You know. I'm sure you do. It's when everything seems perfectly lovely. Nothing's going wrong. There's nothing to fear. The sunset's perfect. The wine's chilled just right in your glass. You're in your favorite chair. You've had years of therapy, and you've healed and forgiven, and you're in an excellent place mind, body, soul. And still . . . you feel these fangs on your neck. You look around, anticipating. Always anticipating. Ready to kill or be killed."

"Oh *that* Tiger in the Room," I say. It's the exact topic I know I need to parse, and she's named it within five minutes of us sitting down. "I've never called it by any name, but yes, I know it well. Just the *anticipation* of the Tiger is enough to take you down. Half the time, we don't even know we're doing it. When I catch myself bracing against those fangs, I try to live in the wisdom of the Dude from *The Big Lebowski*: 'No, man, nothing is fucked here.'"

"Does it work?" She's serious.

"Of course not."

Now she laughs. "*Half* the time? I think it's *most* of the time, if not *all* of the time. For a lot of us."

I know what she means, but I've been working so hard to come back to myself since the dissolution of my marriage. I say, "The misconception is that the anticipation of the Tiger makes us smart, or prepared, or like nobody's fool. Like it sucker-punch-proofs us. I can't live like that anymore."

"Exactly," she says. "People think you're living the dream if you're moving and shaking in the world of media, or if you're a best-selling author on the speaking circuit, free and clear of the Tiger. But what they don't see are all the personal fires you've put out, or how little sleep you're running on, or what happened on the way to the gig. Or where self-doubt reigns supreme."

I add, "Or worse, how you sometimes feel like a complete imposter. Or like the audience is going to boo you offstage and write mean things about you on the internet."

We clink our glasses and drink.

She smiles. "You're the one who is on the stage, my dear. I'm behind the scenes, so I don't deal with as much scrutiny as you do."

"Well, you have your reputation. Just as much to lose."
She shrugs and knows I'm right.

"Even though I can keep it together onstage, I don't think I've given one speech without thinking that someone is going to come in with a megaphone and say, 'Cut, cut. Munson, what are you doing on this set? You're supposed to be on the solo-writer set, in a farmhouse in Montana.' There has never been one time up on those stages that I haven't felt like I was about to get into big, big trouble. Like that Tiger you're talking about was ready to pounce and eat me alive with the lethal words I heard throughout my childhood: 'You talk too much.' Took me a long time to figure it out, but it's right there in my fourth-grade journal. It's my childhood wound. Do you have that too?"

"Are you kidding? I feel that way *all* the time. I think a lot of people in leadership positions *especially* feel that way." Then her signature churlish-but-kind grin spreads across her face. "This isn't meant to be a jab, but I'm curious: If your oldest wound is that you think you talk too much, then what are you doing on the speaking circuit?"

"Good freaking question! Because I'm good at it? Because it helps people? Because it pays well and I need a steady income? Because it's immediate? Unlike writing and publishing books?"

Her eyes light up, as they tend to do. "I think the longer you tell yourself all of that, the more it keeps the Tiger in the room. I think you're sick of being in a leadership role. I think you need to dish. Right here. Right now. Where you can talk as much as you want. And it'll be safe."

Bless her. But *dish*? I try not to complain about this subject. It's not like anyone is *forcing* me to do the speaking circuit. There are other choices.

"Come on. Go for it. Let it rip."

So I do. "Sometimes I just want to say, 'Become your own guru. Take this message and make it your own! Fly! Be free! There are no good Tips and Tricks. Not that ultimately matter. It's time to live your *life*! The thing that's in your way . . . is *you*! And what's in your way is that you think that the answers are *outside* of you. They're not. They're *in* you. That's all you need to know!'"

She puts her hand on her forehead. "Woman, you need to get back to your writing."

"Believe me, I know. The Tiger can't find me there. But every writer I know has to have some sort of side hustle. And I really do love connecting with the women who come to those conferences. If something I've said helps somebody, what's better than that?"

"I believe you." She pauses and looks at the belly-ups as if they're a living litmus test. "But you really need to get back to your writing. You can find a balance of both."

"Yeah. I'm sure I can. Just seems like a lot to balance these days with my kids about to fledge and so much uncertainty ahead."

"The Tiger loves uncertainty." She looks like she's talking about a serial killer that's on the loose.

"Let's talk more about the Tiger. I'm more familiar with the Inner Critic. I call her the Inner Critter because why not? It disembowels her. The Tiger is different. The Tiger is outside you, and the Inner Critter is *in* you. I feel like I'm better at controlling the Inner Critter, but the Tiger is elusive. The Tiger can pounce at will. At least the Inner Critter has to announce herself. The Inner Critter is very chatty."

My friend thinks for a moment and then leans in like she's about to tell me a dangerous secret. "The Tiger is what runs our society. So it makes sense that we're always waiting for some serious shit to go down. We're always waiting for Tigers. They're lurking everywhere. But that's too scary to admit. So we distract ourselves with work and more work and screens and social engagements. Busy, busy, busy. Rather than staying present. And what's more important to our emotional health than staying present? That's what we're talking about here: emotional health, whether it's an Inner Critter or a Tiger. They both are the enemy of emotional well-being."

We give each other knowing nods.

I say, "I mean, that's pretty much what I'm trying to teach in my speaking gigs. But am I *living* it right now? You'd think that I'd be free from that sort of lifestyle, living out here in Montana." I look into the liquor bottles, so shiny. "But lately, I suck at being present. I didn't used to. When my kids were young, I was totally present. But now there are so many distractions. I have a theory, and I haven't really shared it with anyone, but I think that our distractions have to do with the fact that we've lost our wonder."

Her eyes shine. She clearly knows all about wonder, but as if it's newfound. The road has changed her.

So I keep going. "Does the Tiger eat our wonder?"

She doesn't skip a beat. "I think the Tiger *hates* our wonder. I think our wonder is the Tiger's *kryptonite.*"

As if we need relief from our conversation, we simultaneously spin around on our bar stools and take in the room. The ball caps and dollar bills on the ceiling. The dart board that looks like it's only lonely on weekdays. The B-minus health grade posted unapologetically over the kitchen fryer.

I say, "So it begins with becoming aware that these Tigers *do* exist. They're not just figments of our imaginations."

"Yes. And knowing that they shape-shift. Sometimes they're people. Sometimes they're places. Sometimes they're events. Like your gigs."

"But do we have power over them?" I ask.

Her eyes are on fire. "Yes. Even if the Tigers shapeshift, even if they're inevitable, they're not necessarily *bad*. They might be excellent teachers. It's what we *do* with them that counts."

"I think that the *fear* of the Tiger is always worse than the *actual* Tiger."

"Truth," she says.

We catch eyes and we're smiling at each other. I love that about us. Then we spin back around to the bar.

I say, "I wonder if there wouldn't be Tigers if we didn't *expect* that there would be Tigers. That anticipation we were talking about is something else that the Tiger loves to feed on. Because we've already given it free access to pounce. If we didn't believe in Tigers, quite likely, they wouldn't be able to pounce on us. They'd go find other prey."

"I think that takes a lot of practice. Especially if you've been hurt by a lot of Tigers."

Neither of us says, *And we have.* Who hasn't been hurt by Tigers?

She says, "Yeah, and especially when the Tigers are in our personal world. Professional Tigers just give us practice for the real shit."

I whisper, "I wish I could pick up and drive away from the personal Tigers in my life. But I can't."

She knows I don't want to talk about divorce. Or my career for that matter. She gets me. "The Tiger in the Room is sometimes very quiet," she says. "Or camouflaged so that you can't see its stripes. Sometimes, it looks like something to play with, like a kitten. Or someone to dance with. Like a lover."

She's road-trip-wise, and I'm real-life-weary.

"I once went into schtick during a speaking gig. It was like I'd said yes to dancing with the Tiger. And to turn heart language into schtick is a depressing trajectory."

She nods and orders two more beers.

I look around. It's a sunny day. The bar patrons are happy enough. There's nothing bad going on. I check in with myself. I can feel the Tiger lurking. Even the Inner Critter seems scared of it.

My friend leans in again. She's onto something, like my golden retriever on an old gut pile that's melting in the March thaw. "The Tiger has swagger."

I lean into her. "So do we need to become Tiger *tamers*? With a good chair?"

She pulls back. "God, I hope not. That's giving the Tiger's swagger way too much power."

"Well, what other options do we have? To try to kill it?" I realize that my words are flawed as they come out of my mouth. Of course there are options. I just can't think of them in this moment.

"What would happen if you just opened the door to the cage and walked out? Because you do realize that you are in a cage with the Tiger. If you believe in Tigers. Which we both do. What if we left the door open and kept walking and never looked back over our shoulder?" Her eyes are as wide as I've seen them. "And . . . what if we didn't run?"

"I'm always running. 'You want me to have it all done by this afternoon but it's a two-week job? Sure, I'll deliver.' My Inner Critter can be a relentless taskmaster: *You can handle it. You can handle it.* And who is she talking to? Who is she being run by? By George, I think it's the *Tiger!* It never occurred to me to just open the door and walk away. It never occurred to me that I've been in a cage with the Tiger, saying, 'I can handle it!' What am I trying to prove?!" I feel so suddenly free.

"What's the alternative?"

"To stay in the cage, I guess." I look at the row of booze bottles—all that distraction in liquid courage. "That sounds much more exhausting. And more dangerous."

"Yeah, and here's another thing to consider. What if the Tiger doesn't want to leave the cage? Or maybe the Tiger doesn't know how to leave the cage? Even with the door open. It's spent its whole life in there. It doesn't know what's on the other side. But you . . . do. And you won't be free until you at least try to walk away. Even if it's dangerous. You just might be *braver* than the Tiger. Ever thought of that?"

"Huh. Is that why you took a hiatus from your job?"

"Yup. I'm sick of *handling* it. I want to play. Like a child. In a sandbox. Or a bathtub. With wooden spoons and a steel bowl. And measuring cups to measure nothing but maybe bubbles. And everything I want those nothing-bubbles to be."

"You want your wonder."

Now she smiles even wider. "My dear, I don't think it's possible to lose our wonder. It's just that it gets buried sometimes, and we need to work at resurfacing it. And saying, 'I can handle it, I can handle it,' doesn't work in the end. All that *handling* is a wonder-suck."

"A wonder-*kill*!"

We sip on our beers.

I say, "I hate that the world asks us to lose our wonder." And then a darkness flickers inside me and I name it. "What we're really talking about is anxiety, isn't it? Aren't we saying that most of us live with a certain level of constant anxiety? Because of outside forces? Not necessarily inside ones."

"Yes, I think that's what we're looking at. We're run by the anxiety-inducing Tiger. So we practice distraction to try to give ourselves the illusion of safety. Like messing around on the internet. Or day-drinking at a bar. Or any number of things that society serves up in the way of numbing options. And I mean . . . sometimes we need to just have a *fuck it* day." She straightens herself on the barstool and switches to her journalist acuity. "But distraction is still a way of trying to tame the Tiger. Staying in the cage. And now it's manifesting in our society as anxiety and depression and death by suicide. Because no one is talking about what's really going on inside them. I mean . . . very few."

Something opens in me then. It's the kind of thing you go to a small town like this to have happen. I breathe, and it opens even bigger. "If people would take the amount of time they spend managing their stress and replace it with practicing wonder, I think the Tiger would go find someone else to mess with. Maybe even another Tiger. Remember *The Story of Little Babaji*? The tigers are all messing with him, and he outsmarts them by playing to their egos. And they all end up chasing each other and turn into ghee. And he eats the butter tigers on his pancakes. I want to be like little Babaji. That was my daughter's favorite book when she was little."

She smiles. "Little Babaji knew he had to open the door to the cage and walk away."

"So true. Scary as shit, but I suppose true."

I gaze into the row of booze again, especially at the bottom shelf of rotgut whiskey and rotgut rum. "Who do we think we are, anyway, trying to tame Tigers? Constantly waiting for them to pounce. It's a completely ludicrous way to live life."

"That's why I hit the road," she says. "I wanted to find other wonderers. People like you. Who want to play."

"I love that you did that. And I love that we're here talking about this because I don't feel the Tiger in the Room. But when I get home, I'm afraid that I'll feel those fangs back on my neck."

"I wonder the same thing. I mean, I can't just live on the road, interviewing people in small-town USA for the rest of my life. I'll have to go back to work at some point. But not to the way I was. Maybe I need a new career."

"Yeah. Me too. Let's help each other with our next chapters."

"I'm all in." We smile and clink our glasses. Then almost to herself, she says, "But don't we owe the Tigers an explanation? Can we really just walk away? Say nothing?"

"Something tells me that the minute we explain ourselves is the minute we walk back into the cage."

Our smiles fade and we look like the rest of the belly-ups.

"I think it's time to open the door to the cage and just walk away," I say. "Even if the Tiger chases us and tries to kill us. It's become that dire, hasn't it?"

She nods. "We just have to promise ourselves that we won't look back. Especially when we feel like the Tiger might chase us. Especially when the Tiger tells us that we're going to lose everything. That's its favorite ruse. But if we don't look back, the Tiger knows…it's lost."

I think about all the Tigers I've let hunt me. Likely in the name of *I can handle it*. Or worse, *I deserve it*. And how I've contributed to that.

Then it comes to me, crystal clear: "It's not about making ourselves Tiger-proof. It's about walking away and walking *toward* a life of ease. It's about releasing ourselves from the things that have hurt us and that we've let hunt us. The things we enthrone and empower by giving them so much attention."

"We've gotta learn how *not* to feed the beast. And we have to walk away if we're going to be the messenger of *that* message."

"The beast can feed itself. I'd take the stage for *that* message."

"This is the conversation I've needed to have," says my friend. "This exact conversation. Thank you."

"Me too. Thank *you*."

I look out the window at the wind in the cottonwoods along the river. The cottonwoods were how the settlers knew where to find water. Homing. I feel an extreme homing sitting here with this friend having this long, wonderous conversation. Why are so many people so quick to end conversations like these before they even start? Where has all the wonder gone?

For a few beats, I feel hopeful, horizon-full, wonder-full, free from the Tiger. I lean my head back and open my mouth for a deep breath that feels more like a wild gasp for air that then slowly releases back into the bar until I feel empty. Empty of anxiety, empty of fear, empty of anticipation of what needs to come next, empty of worrying about handling it.

I look down the bar at the faces which seem suddenly sad. Not at all distracted.

"Tigers, Tigers everywhere," I say. And a new thought hatches. "Maybe we need to forgive the Tigers before we walk out of the cage. Maybe that's the very thing that won't have them chase us. Whether or not they *accept* our forgiveness isn't our problem. Because the trouble with Tigers is: they never see that they've done anything wrong. So they'll never apologize."

She puts a hand on my knee. "Don't you think you've given enough of your life to those Tigers, Laura? I think that if you're going to forgive anyone, it's you."

This hits hard. I pull back. Look out the window again. Hoping for a bird.

She pulls me back. "Hey. You're safe with me."

"Yeah. I know." Tears spill down my cheeks. "I'm mad at myself for giving those Tigers so much power."

"I know. Me too. What would it take for us to shed that anger?"

"For me?" I wipe my tears and let myself dream. "A month in Costa Rica, watching birds. Following a hummingbird migration. Especially the calliope hummingbird. The smallest bird. Who migrates from Montana to Costa Rica . . . *alone*. I wrote that into my last novel. At least my protagonist gets to do it. I need to travel. When my kids fledge, I need to fledge too. Somehow, I need to go see who I am out in the world. How about you?"

"Costa Rica sounds like exactly what you need. For me? Well, traveling across the US has been life-changing." She gets her grin again. "And do you think that fierce little calliope hummingbird gives a shit about Tigers?"

I have nothing to say to that.

So, that's the place to stop this story. For now. At a small bar. In a small town. In a big state. Two friends talking about things that matter to them, exploring their wonder safely, rolling around in the questions and not necessarily needing answers. With nowhere to go. And nothing to fear. And nothing to fight. And no one to tell them they're lingering too long in their words and ideas. And no one to tell them they're making a big deal out of nothing. That they're too dramatic. Too sensitive. Too much. That they should stop talking. Feeling. Wondering. Just two good friends who believe in miles and miles of endless road and forgiveness along the way. And a whole night to talk and get a little lost with no one paying attention. No one needing their wisdom. And no Tigers.

## your wild why . . .

Let's wonder about our Tigers for a moment, write into these questions, and see what lessons there are to learn:

*What is my definition of the Tiger in the Room?*

*What does it look like? Characterize it.*

*When does it like to pounce? When my life is going along smoothly? Does it hate for my life to go smoothly? Is it at a family reunion or at the Thanksgiving dinner table? Is it when I'm alone?*

*If it had a voice, what would it say to me?*

*Is it possible for me not to believe it has any power? That it's really a helpless stray kitten?*

*Do I need to forgive it or just walk away?*

*Is it possible for me to forgive myself for giving it so much power? For letting it rule my life?*

*Is it possible to forgive it?*

*Who would I be without the Tiger?*

*Can I open the gate and walk away?*

**Extra invitation:** Find a friend with whom you feel safe in the realm of self-expression. Pick a topic that you need to parse but that scares you. Ask your trusted friend if they would be willing to sit with you for a stretch of time and look at it from many angles, not necessarily looking for answers. If you find answers, that's a bonus. This is an opportunity to roll around in wonder with someone you trust. See what you find. Write about it.

# "what can I create?"

L et's go back to the most powerful and wonder-full question
I know: "What can I create?" I've gone back to it all my
life. It's the question that holds my heart together. The hope.
The possibility. The freshness of it.

Asking yourself this question is an opportunity to keep
front and center the possibility of reinvention. Sometimes
those reinventions will be small. In my case, I've experienced
many that nobody would notice but me. Maybe it's a thought
pattern I'm transforming that doesn't serve me and never did.
Or maybe I'm creating a new idea altogether—a new invention.
But all of it builds on the original moment when I ask, "What
can I create?" That question begets profound answers, some
that work and some that don't. Even so, I know I am always
better for having asked this question in the first place. It's been
a fifty-year-plus passion play of invention and reinvention,
all rooted in that question and mostly for my own good use.

So when my life's trajectory totally changed and I was
staring down the barrel of losing my twenty-year-old Montana
dream, I was glad that my passions were in a row, even though
my ducks weren't. I'd given up a lot for that dream, and I

wasn't anywhere close to having fully lived it. There were many more moments of mothering and growing what was left of our family on the land and in the house where we'd hatched it all. My house and my hearth and my land were my safe haven. I created it all from scratch. It's why I live in Montana and why I stay here. Leaving this place would have meant leaving much of who I am. It's never healthy to have your identity so wrapped up in a place, but it happens—and it happened to me. My home is my terra firma, my grounding, my container. My children's legacy. And I worked hard to create it in all its glory for many pivotal years.

But now push had come to shove, and the odds were against me. I'd been told by almost everyone I knew that I was going to lose my house and move into a condo "like all the other divorced people in town." Everything in my being was opposed to it. Why would I ever pack up all that we'd created in the way of house and land? And our town wasn't like other places where you can just move to a new comparable neighborhood. There just weren't houses like the one we'd designed and built. It bore our scars, our hopes. We belonged to it, and it belonged to us.

Plus, we're just not condo people. We need land. We need privacy. We need solitude. Otherwise, what's the point of living in rural Montana? If we had to leave our home, then I might as well just move my brood to a city where there were more opportunities for reinvention.

I hadn't even put the subject on the table with my kids. We'd been conditioned to live moment by moment, breath by breath. It didn't feel fair to move them away from their school and their friends. And there was another large piece: when you don't have extended family around you for support, then your home, in ways you wouldn't want to admit . . . becomes your mother. Your father. Your keeper. They needed their home as much as I did.

The day the push shoved me into reinvention was "normal." I'd managed to say yes to coffee with some old friends who had called, intervention-style: "You need to get out! Join the living! Nobody's seen you in *months*!" I've learned that you know you're at the end of triage when people start to knock on your door again. Like you've somehow proven to be a decent human again. Fit for public consumption. Just by being spotted in the grocery store as looking "okay."

So I was at the café having a perfectly okay cup of coffee when the condo subject came up. Again. *So* convenient. *So* close to town. *So* much easier for the kids with school and sports and social life. *So* much better for me for those same reasons. And all the singles to meet! Instead of being *so* stuck out on my property, all alone in my soon-to-be-empty house.

It felt like a witch hunt, though it was meant as a friendly ducks-in-row-getter inner.

All self-promises of "light and polite" fell away. Instead, tears broiled in my eyes. I stood up, red-faced, and pointed at each of them. "Just . . . you . . . *watch* . . . me!" It was a direct echo of something I'd said in mediation months prior, but today, the triage had yielded enough room in the realm of reinvention that I meant business. I marched out of there, and I shouted every swear word I knew all the way home.

As I crowned my driveway's hill, I shouted, but now like a bodyguard, "I am not leaving you! And I am not losing you." The white-tailed deer scattered from their roosts in the high grass. "I'm going to figure out a way to keep all of this if it's the last thing I do!"

But I was terrified.

I paced the front porch, the pulse of so many birthday parties, so much late-night stargazing, so many jam sessions, singing into the wee hours. I would keep this dream alive without my wasband. His exit strategy was not mine. Not in the least. There'd been enough damage done to the three remaining members of this household. I would not allow any more. No way! I just had to figure out how to mine my talents and passions. This time I was going to go full throttle into my intuition and any wisdom available to me.

I tuned in. What did I know how to do that was monetizable? Being a best-selling author didn't mean the royalty checks could float the boat, and per my conversation with my friend about the Tiger, I'd decided to leave the speaking circuit. Plus my kids needed me to be home. I had piles of unpublished work, but that all took time, and time wasn't on my side.

I didn't want to do just anything. I wanted a side job that I loved and that would help people. I wanted a life in balance. I wanted to model that to my children. How could I be of service in this world, build on my successful platform, and monetize it? What need could I fill in myself and in others? How could I transform how I had been showing up in the world into a business that would fulfill my needs while still being congruent with my integrity?

I brought it to my journal. "What can I create?"

And as I wrote, it occurred to me: even though my career had been built on retraining the mind by finding new self-awareness in our thought patterns, the bulk of what I'd heard on the road from my readers, audience members, and interviewers had to do with something else. What I'd heard, like a broken record, was: "You wrote your way through a rough time. I've gone through a rough time. I'd like to write about what happened to me. I want to help others know there's light on the other side. Plus I think it would be good for me to write it all down."

And then, predictably, their gazes would drop to their shoes and the qualifiers would come in: "Who do I think I am? I'm not even a writer. It's already been done so much better than I could ever do it. It's self-indulgent at best. I'm not creative anyway. I don't even have a voice to begin with."

Over and over I had told people, "Yes you do! Of *course* you have a voice! Of *course* you are creative! Everyone has a voice that is unique to them. Everyone is creative. You choose the clothes you're wearing. You choose the words that come out of your mouth and probably the furniture in your living room. You're creative! Just ask yourself the most powerful question I know: *What can I create?* You will find your answer if you're serious about that question. It's the mightiest way I know to transform your life!"

A spark would ignite in their eyes then fade. *My God*, I'd thought. *They've lost their wonder . . . . How have I possibly kept mine?* The answer was obvious: Writing.

My pen started moving fast. What if I could create something that would support these people? What if I could teach them, whether or not they were writers, to find their way to the essence of what they had to say through the brilliant and transformative practice that is writing?!

I wrote, "What can I create that would help people find their voice, using what I know and who I am? What would that look like?"

An hour later, I had a plan. And alongside it, the wonder-full elation of creativity bubbling inside me that I'd been missing for months. Maybe years. I could see a future.

I called a few friends who led retreats. They'd told me in the past that I'd be skilled at it. But I needed confirmation. It was a unanimous "What are you waiting for?" That's the sign of a good retreat leader: it's a generous, supportive, more-is-more sort of space.

It all came to me then. I would lead writing retreats that focused on finding true self-expression through the written word. I would teach people that they each had a unique voice and that they were creative beyond their wildest imaginings. I would show them how to bring that practice into their lives, whether they considered themselves writers or hadn't written anything since their school days. Whether they were best-selling authors or just starting. Whether they had book ideas burning inside them, or personal essays or poems, or messages, or just needed to find permission to honor their original thoughts in the first place in a journal, for their eyes only. In all cases, I would remind them of their wild why.

At my retreats, no one would get in trouble for their self-expression or feel like they had to hide their light. I would help them heal their childhood wounds in this realm through the power of the written word. They would learn to *delight* in their voices again! They would learn what writing meant to them, in process and project, based on exactly who they were, what their responsibilities were, what their habits and their dreams and their stuck places and their flow places were. And I would keep those circles safe, with the best boundaries possible, in the most beautiful place I knew: Montana. The place that had fed my muse for decades.

I had these exact skills in spades! I would create community and support and a program that would hold their hearts and not let them go. I would create a place of curiosity and awe and imagination and storytelling and learning and even intuition. I would call it Haven. I had no idea where it would be, but I felt a deep knowing that it was the answer to my "So now what?" *Not* a condo.

So, with a sketch of a program and passion now erupting from my deepest wonder, I put it on Facebook: "Hey, anybody want to come on a writing retreat with me in Montana?"

Mind you, at that point, I had a lot of trusting fans who had written me, saying that they felt like I was writing my memoir directly to them. That I felt like an old friend. That I'd helped them to not feel alone. I suspect it was for this very reason that within two hours, twenty-four people signed up for a retreat that had no place, price point, design, or reputation. I couldn't believe it! Maybe I wasn't that far off track. Maybe this was a plot twist that would even be a surprise gift.

I had a kind of supernatural confidence in this Haven pursuit because it didn't come from my mind or my fear or my coping or *handling*. It came from my sixth-ist sense. My deepest gut. My truest knowing and wondering. I trusted everything about this pursuit. This creation. It was perhaps the most honest of any of my creations outside of my books—and I couldn't have done it even five years prior. I had to live into the success myth. Bust it. I had to live into the false power myth. And bust that too. I had to live into the myth that intuition is nonsense when it is, in fact, *all* the sense. It's the sense that is the very best guide when you allow yourself to believe in it and co-create with it. I was ready. My life had made me ready. I could have turned the other way. But instead I asked myself, "What can I create?" And it all fell into place. With ease. And with wonder.

Twelve years later, Haven Writing Retreats and Programs is ranked in the top writing retreats in the US with four different programs, an online ongoing community called Haven Nest, an eight-week online course called Haven Home, a Writer in Residence program, and the Haven Foundation nonprofit, which offers partial scholarships to those who need financial support to make Haven possible. I also lead one-day workshops, both live and online, for those who can't make Montana happen. I've worked with over a thousand people from all over the world, in small circles of six to eight attendees, who have come to northwest Montana to do this work. I have looked into so many tearful eyes upon departure and heard these words: "This just changed my life."

I can say all this because it's not about me. I designed the retreat that I knew would meet people where they needed to be met. The retreat that I would want to attend. It works in its wonder-full way because the program holds the attendees.

I hold the program. The people at the ranch where I lead the retreats hold me. It's a mind-blowingly healthy symbiosis. I have to believe that all of this happened because when I asked, "What can I create?" I was in a place of pure creation. So it makes sense that this purity runs through all things Haven.

I believe that anyone who's at a crossroads has their own version of Haven inside of them. It's there waiting for you. Step into your wonder about it: What's burning inside you that could profoundly change your life? What would happen if you lived into it boldly? What would it take to call yourself to action? No one is so lost that they can't be found.

It may seem too hard to handle. Go easy on yourself. Begin by going inside yourself with love, the way you would speak to a child. Remember the child in the meadow. Hold her extra close. Try to contact her wonder if you can't find your own. What would it ask that child? Here are some good questions I asked myself in creating my next chapter:

*What am I curious about?*

*What awes me?*

*What is the one thing that is holding my heart together right now?*

*What do I love to do?*

*What is the one nonnegotiable belief that I hold and will never let go of?*

*What do I know how to do that could be of service to others? Of service to myself?*

*How could I merge those places of service into one entity?*

*How am I already showing up in my life, and am I being called to take a leap into an even higher calling?*

*When am I truly wise?*

*When am I in my intuition?*

*When am I in my true power?*

*What lights me up?*

*What causes me to live in wonder?*

Over all else, that's what I've found in Haven: my wonder. As much as mothering, and writing, and even speaking have been my callings, this work is the perfect confluence of who I am and how I've always shown up. The little girl in me who asked all of those questions has a place to meet other seekers now and use the tools she's used all her life to help them move forward in their lives with their unique, true, and essential voices!

This work, in many ways, is the work of my life because in giving this program to others, I've allowed it to give itself to me. It's healed my childhood wound. Mostly. In fact, the ones who inflicted that childhood wound on me have apologized. They've even said things like, "I stand in awe of you and your talents and all that you have become. How you've helped people."

And I've said true thank-yous. In fact, I wonder if I would be where I am today if I hadn't needed a place to retreat, starting as a small child. To safely express myself, without judgment, in the haven that has always been mine: to write.

So in that sense, a heart-full and wonder-full thank-you to those people.

As I tell my Haven attendees, "Notice when what flows from you comes naturally. Easily. Not necessarily because the subject is *easy*. But notice where the *ease* is—the natural flow. That's when you know . . . you are in your voice."

I can say the same thing for your next chapter. If you tap into your wonder, you will find your true purpose. Maybe you are already living in it. If you are, you know that you don't have to look very hard if you give yourself permission to be who you already are. All you have to do is remember. And ask, "What can I create?"

## your wild why . . .

Answer the questions that I asked myself, as listed above. See where they lead you. If I can reinvent my life and answer my Free Child's call, so can you.

*part IV*

wonder-found

# my wondering: how do I allow myself to be "spelled differently"?

There is a line in a poem I love by Emma Mellon. It says, "Allow yourself / to be spelled differently." To me, that's one intoxicating invitation. To revisit the core of my identity. To see what's left of that little girl hiding in leaf piles and trees and charming birds in the grass. To allow myself to wonder about where I am in this moment of my life. To see where I might have become too used to living in a way that I recognize. To dream my future alive perhaps much differently.

My way is almost always by asking questions. Who am I at this stage of my life? Who am I without my daily motherhood? Who am I outside the comfort of my own home? Outside of my usual roles? If I allowed myself to be "spelled differently," what would I find? Would I recognize myself? Would I *like* myself? Would wonder follow me?

To return to wonder means that you have to really want it back. And to believe you had it to begin with. It might require you to leave home. Go out into the world. Learn some things. Come back with more wisdom. Hopefully. Or at least with news to share with the village. Only "home" is different than it was when you left it, and so is your wonder. Maybe you forgot that it existed, but now after spelling yourself differently you find that your wonder is wiser and deeper because of the living you've done. But its essence is the same. You have to believe that. Does it serve you not to?

It's like a baseball game, and I've watched plenty of those, thanks to my son. I look at baseball like a hero's journey and once my kids were both out of the house and my new calling as a teacher, editor, and retreat leader was stable, I knew that it was time to attempt my own version of that journey. But I resisted it. There was balance to my life. The home front was safe. The retreat-leader life suited me. I had time to write again, but I also had time to step out of my life and see where I was with my wonder. Had I been hiding, riding the waves of my life when I had to, but ducking under them perhaps too much? Like I had as a child. Only not in my tree house or in leaf or pillow forts, but in my adult home, and in the woods around my home in my Montana. Where it was hard to find me. Just like when I was a little girl.

Like my good friends had leaned hard on me to say yes to coffee in town on the tail end of triage, now my fledged kids leaned hard on me to rejoin the wider world. "Mom, you talk about all the solo travel you did when you were in your twenties. Why don't you do that again? You need to have some real adventures just for you! And not as the leader."

Just for me? Permission? I didn't know I was looking for it, especially not from my children. But I think they were the only people who I would have received it from.

I gave them a list/litany of why traveling was a bad idea. It was too expensive. I needed to finish and publish and promote my books. I needed to hold down our fort. What about the dogs?

Turns out, I created stubborn-ass offspring.

And so I began my own fledge. I joined my twenty-year-old self and began my Wonder Trips.

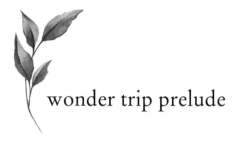

# wonder trip prelude

It started with a trial run just before my nest emptied. I got invited to speak and teach at a writing conference in Mexico. My son was still a senior in high school. I didn't want to leave him. His father no longer lived in Montana, so I was a full-time mother again, only a single one, and that had different demands.

"You need to do this, Mom," my son said. "It's only a week. I'll be fine. You need a break!" He meant, *I'm of age. I'm strong. I make good decisions. I can do this. Give me the chance.*

Against my motherly better judgment, I took him up on it. I trusted my son. And our neighbors were like family. He was safe.

He was also right: I needed a break, and I was in between retreat seasons. I'd finished a book and was waiting on beta readers before I submitted it to my agent. Maybe I should see a preview of who I was going to be without my daily motherhood, only out in the world. *That* girl. Florence girl. Blue Mosque girl. Was she still in me? In less than a year I would be on my own. The conference was only for a week, including travel days. He convinced me to take two. So in a way, I left him before he could leave me. A person does that sometimes when she's running scared from who she is without the roles she's used to.

The conference was in the small hill town of San Miguel de Allende. I'd wanted to visit it for years. It's famous for its artists. Writers. Dropouts. Lost souls and found ones. I had collected places like that in my twenties when I was a warrior for my wonder and worshipped my restlessness.

I booked my flights so that I had a whole week to myself before the conference began. A week alone in a foreign county seemed almost impossible to imagine. I needed to make it count toward truly allowing myself "to be spelled differently." So I found a room in an artist's home turned boutique hotel, which was in its day a hotbed for eclectic parties with artists and dignitaries, right in the center of town, surrounded by church bells tolling every fifteen minutes and nightlong fiestas.

I promised myself I would leave work at home. There's a lot more to being in the retreat business than leading retreats. Same with being an author. You can work 24/7 if you let it run you. But I promised myself I would lollygag. Wander. Bump into things. Look down alleys, see things happening in small spaces, and go to them, moth. Instead of racing by, on to the next thing. I needed to get a major change of scenery. I couldn't seem to shake my fear of empty nest at home, the fear of passing by now both of my children's empty rooms in a matter of months, with their baseball trophies and children's books. And that had me ashamed. I'd been so adamant about not defining myself by my motherhood. But I had. And I knew that if I went somewhere new and stopped, I stood a chance at staring down this abject and unadulterated piercing fear of an empty nest. To get real. *My second child is leaving home. Good for him! That chapter will be over in six months. What will I do next? Who will I be? Who will I become?*

It was time to get back to my wild why.

The Inner Critter did not like my exodus. I was changing the rules. She was loud and mean the whole flight. *What is your problem? Why are you so scared? You have a life outside of your motherhood! You knew this was coming when you had kids! You want them to fledge! But I can't believe you left your son at home alone in the eleventh hour! What kind of a mother are you? Maybe he's better off without you!* She did not want me to even entertain the thought of being spelled differently.

I wept with my forehead on the airplane window, thinking about the sweet years when I held my babies in bed, reading to them, singing, praying, talking. Back then we were all that mattered in the world and all was safe and all was well and all was peaceful. But even then, there was this fear, this knowing, that it would end. And the thought of it was so excruciating that I ignored it. Instead, I'd dip my nose into their heads and smell their hair and hold back the fear and tears and just . . . *be* for that borrowed moment. All too fleeting.

As we made our descent through the bitter yellow smog of Mexico City, I wondered if the Inner Critter would leave me alone for a few weeks. Maybe she wouldn't know what to do with me so far from home and my mother role. She'd dogged me to the edges of myself, desperate, reminding me that in just months I'd be up against the edge and the only way forward . . . was over.

I knew I would be hearing from her at 4:00 a.m., whispering: *You are nothing without those babies. Your most important job of your life is done. Over. You are empty and your house is empty, and your heart is a home for nothing and no one, so why do you try? Stop trying. I'm not going away either way. I'm here to haunt you until this house finally dies and you finally die to the last two decades of your life.*

Looking through the plane window, I said to my Inner Critter out loud, "Can you please stop? Just . . . *stop*. I need to get away from you and be twenty again. Maybe *that* girl has answers. She's really good at not being run by fear. It's just that *that* girl didn't have a lot to lose. This girl . . . does."

And as the wheels hit Mexican ground, I wondered, *Who*

*am I now? They came and they took everything I had and then just left. As children should. That's the whole point. So why does this feel so excruciating?*

As if my honest wondering and my Inner Critter petition had beckoned the kind voice, it whispered a warm, *Life doesn't stand still, but you can stand still in it. This is just the end of a chapter. It goes like this. Chapter by chapter. You never come to the end of anything. Everything is a beginning. It's beginning by beginning. By beginning. Until the end. Life is daily. Don't you see? Don't be scared. Stop running so fast that you can't hear me. Come to me. I will hold you during this. And I will hold you after.*

"I wish I believed you. I'm ashamed that I don't," I admitted.

*You are going to have to start trying. Right now. You have two weeks to practice what's going to be your reality in six months. Your son has a posse of families watching over him. He's confident, smart, and shrewd. He'll be just fine. This is good for him too. What are you so scared of?*

"I'm afraid I'll be so lonely after he leaves . . . that I won't know how to live."

*You have everything you need. And always have. Stop trying to find what you already have. Be gentle with yourself this week. Go slowly. Sit. Watch. Your hard work as a mother is done. And you can rejoice in that now. Fall in love with yourself again.*

I had come to Mexico to sit. To be still. To smell jasmine. And hear church bells.

What I didn't expect was that I would make friends. Real friends. I was swept up into a throng I'd forgotten existed, hiding in my Montana. Doors flung open. People were asking me to link arms in a perpetual dance I'd forgotten. Invitations flowed. "Come to our house for a glass of wine!"

I said yes.

"We couldn't help but notice that you're dining alone. Would you like to join us?"

I said yes.

And then on the last night of my week, sitting at an outdoor café, a woman in a white veil and a scarlet dress came up to me with who were clearly her bridesmaids celebrating a bachelorette party and said, "Come with us!"

I said yes!

And they took me to a local bar with an old man playing traditional songs on his guitar, and they got up on the stage with him and sang and danced, linking arms with every woman that joined them from the crowd, as if they were all family.

I sat at the table, holding down a fort that didn't need to be held down.

"Laura, now you take the stage!" they shouted, laughing and dancing.

I shook my head.

"Laura! *Venga!*"

"I don't know the songs! I don't know the dances!"

They didn't care. They pulled me up onstage and put me in the center and they clapped and stomped and hollered for me to sing and dance. *Especially* since I didn't know the words or know the dance.

The old guitarist smiled at me. And I danced. And sang. Even though I didn't know the words or the dance, I did it anyway. I sang and danced and drank wine from a bottle and hugged these women and staggered home along with them, wearing a yellow star piñata on my head. Back to my little hotel. Where I climbed up to the rooftop and lay on a hammock under the stars that winked through a pink-dark sky. And went to sleep.

When I woke a bit later, there was a man lying on a lounge chair next to me, looking into the stars. He had total kindness in his eyes.

He said, "I've been admiring your hat."

I remembered the yellow star piñata on my head, and I said, "Thanks. I had a really lovely night. The loveliest in a long time. I'm really happy. I love this town."

"Me too. I love this town too. You know yourself here." He was an American. He lived there. I wondered if he was divorced and empty-nested. Whatever he was, he was free in a way that I wanted to be free in six months, rather than weeping on the floor in my children's rooms.

Then I told him about my fear of empty nest. "I came here to be alone. I'm not good at being alone. And all I've found here are friends."

"San Miguel is like that. What do you love to do?"

It was the question that I always asked a new person. No one had asked me that in a long time. "I like to write books. What do you like to do?"

"I like to paint."

Then he invited me to come to his studio the next day, and I said yes to that too. He showed me a watercolor of a hummingbird in flames who wouldn't die. "Like the goddess Apollonia who jumps into the fire rather than let her oppressors push her," he said. And he pointed to the words around the frame. "Hildegard von Bingen. Twelfth-century mystic." And translated: "*Tu rubes* ('You glow red') *ut aurora* ('like the dawn') *et ardes ut* ('and burn') *solis flamma* ('like the flames of the sun')."

"So I have to jump?" I said.

"Yes." Then he looked at me the same way my mountain-man friend looked at me in the woods, building the sixty-second fire. And he whispered, "And . . . there isn't any fire. There never was." And he gave me the painting. Just like the man had given me the "Breathe, believe, receive. It's all happening" goddess print. I knew to receive them as divine gifts.

I took the painting and went to the cathedral steps with all the children blowing bubbles, and then there was a processional in the street with a small child in a white gown atop a donkey and all her family singing behind her.

"*Primera comunión,*" a woman on the steps said to me, or to herself, or to no one.

And I spoke to myself but maybe to a bubble. But most definitely to the kind voice in my mind: "Well, there were some really bad moments. All my life. And my motherhood held sway. I'm afraid to believe in my future."

There it was again, saying, *You have a future. Your future is on these cathedral steps. Just like when you were on the steps of the Blue Mosque, realizing that you were a writer. Sit here in the sun like you're a hummingbird in flames. Not dying. See that cat over there. Preen like her. It's time to be a selfish cat.*

"I'm allergic to cats," I replied.

*Sit. Feel the sun on your face. You are a good girl, Laura. It's time for you to start believing it. It's time for you to return to your wonder. It's safe now.*

I watched one bubble float into the sky, purple and pink and shiny like a jellyfish that is so beautiful but you know that it will sting you if you touch it. And I said to that bubble, "I forgive you." And then . . . it popped. Like it had never existed.

## your wild why . . .

What does your Inner Champion sound like? Could you give her a kind voice? Could you let the Inner Critter surrender her meanness and allow the Inner Champion to tell you what you *truly* want to hear but are possibly too afraid to believe? Try it. What would she say to you?

Can you forgive the Inner Critter and yourself for co-creating for so long?

Can the Inner Critter become the Inner Champion?

## empty next

My time in San Miguel de Allende confirmed for me that I wanted more of this spelling myself differently. This "me" outside my motherhood. This newly refound wonder. So as soon as I dropped my son off at college I booked another trip. I wanted to challenge myself to go someplace less safe, less charted, less a given for a woman traveling alone. A place where I didn't speak the language. Where the culture would be very different from my own. So I went to Morocco. This time for a month.

I galloped a Barb Arabian mare on the beach in the seaside village of Essaouira and felt true bliss for the first time in a long time. I rode a camel, which wasn't that blissful, but it was new. New was what I wanted to feel and be. I walked through the labyrinthine Marrakech medina in the dark, knowing that I would get lost and liking it that way. I learned about empowering young girls in an after-school program inspired by the Michelle Obama–incentive to end the practice of child brides. I hung out with a local goat cheese maker for Friday afternoon couscous, and he asked me to write in charcoal on his white stucco wall. I chose Rumi:

Out beyond ideas of wrongdoing and rightdoing,
there is a field. I'll meet you there.

He smiled wide, as if touting his dearth of teeth.

In Fez, I hired a guide named Kamel and toured with him
for nine hours in the medina one day and nine hours around
the medina the next, learning more about what "civilization"
really means than ever in my life. I mean, do you know who
makes your buttons? Your bread? Your pots and pans? Your
shoes? Is it your grandfather? Your daughter?

I wandered into a restaurant and met one of the top chefs
and restauranteurs in Africa and sat with her and talked about
the book she needed to write about being a woman in northern
Africa with her prestige. But with no rights to her child.

I rode another Barb Arabian—this time a stallion who
was more interested in the mares along the beach than listening
to me. It ended in an emergency dismount. Which I couldn't
have planned better in the way of symbolism. Isn't that what I
was doing there? Emergency dismounting from my fear of an
empty nest? Leaving my home like it was on fire, terrified that
I was going to die in it alone? Was I trying to prove to myself
that I could put myself out into the burning *world* and live?
I realized that everything I'd done in Morocco was to prove
myself to myself. That I had power and courage. But what
about being taken care *of*?

That's when I realized that one thing I had yet to do in
Morocco was to get a traditional hammam. The local kind.
I'd avoided the traditional hammam because it required me
to be completely naked with one woman scrubbing my entire
body, with nothing to hide behind, my skin sloughing off
onto the hot, wet marble. Was I ready to finally let it slough?
To be naked and that new? Not hiding behind my motherhood? Not being a teacher or retreat leader? Not pouring it
all into books? Not even my journal could hide me in that

olive-branch-fired room. Did I even know how to ask to be taken care of?

Here's what happened when I finally did:

It's the last day, and I am in the basement of the *riad* with the hotel manager, Fatima, who calls me "darling" and tells me how good it is to be scrubbed once a week in a hammam. "To feel new." She holds out her hand to lead the way, but I hedge.

"Does it hurt?" I ask her.

Her chocolate-drop eyes dance. "Ah, no, darling." She smiles like she has a secret and that we'll both know it together in a few hours. I suspect: it hurts. I follow her anyway.

This is not a touristy hammam. I'm doing it the way the locals do it, fired by olive branches from below, by men who have done this for generations, shoveling the wood in an underground oven from the street.

I walk in, and a woman is there in a tank top and shorts and flip-flops with her hair in a bun on top of her head. She speaks to me in French, and I say, "*Je ne parle pas français,*" which I've been saying a lot, and so it's charades again. She touches my shirt and my yoga pants and points to a hook on the wall and stands there.

*She's going to stand here while I take off my clothes?* I'm very modest, so I take off my shirt and pants and bra and put them on the hook. I point to my underwear. She does a traffic-cop stop with her hand, and I'm relieved. She drapes a towel over my arm.

Then she opens a door to a room and quickly shuts it behind us. It's hot and wet and slippery and I reach for her hand and she supports me down the steps. It's not a large room. It's surrounded by pink and gray marble with two raised marble slabs on either side and a fountain at the end. I wonder if all hammams are this beautiful.

She points to the slab on the left, and I wonder if I'm supposed to put the towel down or sit directly on the marble, but she takes the towel from me and rolls it up and points at the slab, so I sit. It's hot and wet. She puts the towel at the top of the slab and I realize that it's probably for my head, for later. I am sitting there with my knees together and my head bowed like I've done something wrong. Somehow, the Tiger is in this room. The Inner Champion says, *Walk away.* I will my mind to walk away and not look back. I feel five years old. And also fifty-two. I stay there, at the age I am. As the woman I am. Appropriately naked.

Then she turns on a copper spigot coming out of the wall and fills a silver engraved bowl and puts my finger in it. "Okay?" she says.

I love my hot baths, but this is pretty hot. Still, I say, "Okay." When you can't speak the language, you realize how many extra words you use in life to keep yourself comfortable, especially when you're scared.

Then she dumps the water over my head and it runs down my back and drips into my ears and it's really hot water, truth be told. And the five-year-old comes back. I feel like I'm being punished. And like I deserve it. And I feel like crying. And hiding.

That's when she puts the bowl down and puts her hands on my shoulders and gives them both a hard downward shove, and I realize that my shoulders have been so tight and raised and braced. Probably for longer than I've been aware.

I look up at her, and she smiles. "Okay," she tells me. It's not a question.

I practice this line of thinking: *She's right. I am okay. I am going to be bathed. She does this all the time. I am not disgusting to her in this body of mine that has too many pounds on it. She doesn't know what I looked like when I was twenty. She has nothing to gain or lose by me being in this exact body, right here, right now, getting this bath. That's all that's happening. I'm getting a bath from a professional bather. And it's been this way, in this room, for hundreds of years. Who am I to let my shame get in the way of her job?*

So I let my legs go slack and relax my shoulders. Still, I am scared.

*I know how to do this. I know how to be bathed. I am not a little girl in trouble. I'm being cleansed by someone who wants me to be cleansed. Receive what she is giving. Feel good about it. You loved it when your mother or your grandmother gave you baths. No one is going to be mean to you.*

She puts her hand in a bowl of black paste and scoops out a palmful, shows me, smiles, and says, "*Savon beldi.*"

I close my eyes while she rubs it all over me, lifting my breasts to get every bit of my body surface, hiking up my underwear to coat my butt cheeks. Then she points for me to lie down on my back. She puts the towel under my head and leaves.

I don't know what this paste is. Maybe I should have done some research. I don't know what makes it black, but with so much of Morocco fed by olives—for breakfast, the pits used to fire the ceramics, the wood firing the hammam—I suspect it's olives. I love olives, so I decide to love this paste all over my body. I keep thinking about Fatima and how much she loves this, and I suddenly wish there were other women getting hammams here, too, so I could hear them gossiping in Arabic, their hijabs doffed, their skin exposed in sacred sisterhood. Bathing together.

I miss women.

My left leg is wedged up against the marble wall and it's hot, but if I scoot to the right, I'll fall off the slab. So I just lie there against the hot marble, figuring this is normal so I need to be normal in it. To receive. That's why I'm really here in Morocco, I realize. Not to prove. Not to lead. Not to win. Not even to give. I'm here to receive.

I close my eyes and lie there. I imagine the mask sinking into my open pores, purifying my skin, and going deeper into my organs and deeper into my bloodstream. Then the woman comes in and motions for me to flip over. So I do. She gives me the towel to put under my face and rubs more of the paste on me, buttocks and all. Then she leaves again.

My forehead is flat on the slab, and I'm hot and uncomfortable. I turn my face toward the other slab and picture a girl there. Nineteen. In the Cağaloğlu Hamam in Istanbul, where Florence Nightingale bathed, and so many others, including me, in my young-girl body, lying on a marble slab with a woman in black underwear and pendulous breasts, like mine now, rubbing her down. I don't remember the process. I just remember feeling like I was an exotic bird and I'd never be anything else ever again when I walked out of that marble temple of women. "Hi," I whisper to her. "I've missed you."

Then the woman comes back and shows me a loofah-like glove. "*Kessa*," she says, with purpose in her eyes. And she motions for me to sit up.

I do, and there begins the deepest scrub I've ever known, almost to the point of extreme. But not quite. I figure she knows that I need it to be this hard. So I tolerate it. *Receive, Laura. The nineteen-year-old in you knows how. Thirty years of living and loss needs to slough off. Let it go.*

She makes the rounds while I sit, then lie down, then flip over. She covers every inch of me other than my pubic area. Under my breasts. *Please, not my nipples.* Yes, light on my nipples. Under my armpits. Even my face. She pulls on my arm and shows me the *kessa* and says, "Skin."

"Sorry," I say. "It's been a rough year. A lot to shed," knowing she doesn't speak English.

"Normal," she says, smiling, pleased with how this is going. I love that she knows this word. I do not know what my new normal will be. Perhaps it will have more receiving in it.

I smile. Yes, the pain of life is so very normal. And none of us really knows how to do it. So we stay busy. We pretend we're fine. But in hot rooms with women caring for us, naked, we can't lie.

I start to weep, my cheek to the hot marble, face to the wall so she can't see. But I bet she can tell. And I bet . . . that it's "normal" too.

Then it's a pumice stone to my feet, which tickles in a bad way, and I want this to be over and I pull back my feet. I can't take it.

"Tickle," she says, laughing.

"Yeah." I am not laughing.

She stops and fills up the bowl and it's pretty much a car wash after this. She splashes bowl after bowl of water over me, rinsing the dead skin off. Then soaps me up and rinses it off, and then takes my hand, puts soap in it, and points to my pubic area.

*Oh Lord. I'm going to have to wash myself with her standing there, and just exactly how are we going to rinse?* But I remember: This is my bath today. Everything must be clean when I leave this room. So I obey, and she drops a bowl of hot water down my underwear. But it's still soapy, and I'm not going to walk around Marrakech with soap in my nether regions. I motion for another bowl of water with the confidence of nineteen-year-old me, and she's quick to deliver.

And just when I think it's over, she sits me up and tilts back my head and washes my hair. She washes my *hair*. Then dumps bowls of water on it so that it all drips down my back until it rinses clear. It's over. And I don't want it to be.

That's when another woman appears and says, "Massage?"

I nod with an emphatic up and down of my shiny-clean head.

The first woman takes my hand to help me from slipping and puts my other hand on my arm. "Smooth," she says.

"So smooth. *Shukran*," I say, smiling.

Now I'm lying naked and wet with the smoothest skin of my life, and this new woman is rubbing argan oil all over me. My hair even. For twenty minutes. It's not really a massage. It's a serious rubdown to make sure that this miracle oil that Moroccans love so much is in as many pores as she can touch and from the roots of my scalp to the tips of my hair.

When it's over, she gives me a robe and I'm glad for cover, finally, and we go back to the little room, where my clothes still hang on the hook, and she puts my clothes in my hands and says something to me in Arabic. And I guess that's it. She leads me to a back stairway of the *riad* and points up. She puts her hands to her heart and smiles. And then she puts her hands together and presses her cheek, slowly dropping her face into them and closing her eyes.

She is telling me to rest now.

I put my hand on my heart and say, "*Shokrun,*" and I walk up the stone steps of the *riad*, cross the green and white and mustard diamond-shaped tiles to my room, put the big antique key in the hole, twist, and go to my perfectly made bed with the crisp, cool sheets. I climb into bed in the robe holding in my new skin, soaked in argan, by women who have cared for me. And I let them. And I rest.

However it is that I got to a place where I no longer know how to ask for what I want, nor receive what's being lovingly given to me, I don't know. And I don't want to go back. It's a wonder-kill, not allowing yourself to be cared for. It's time to start being honest with myself and the world around me. My nos need to mean no. My yeses need to mean yes. I need to remember how important it is to take care of myself, by letting go of the layers that accumulate and keep me feeling anything but new. And sometimes that takes someone else's loving care, and maybe from a stranger. But it begins with asking.

## your wild why . . .

Where in the world would you go, all by yourself, where you just receive? Where you let go? Where you go with the flow and allow the world to show you its wisdom and care for you?

Maybe it's somewhere very close to you, like a nature preserve, where you can go and sit and write in your journal. Or maybe it's as far away as a hammam in Morocco is from Montana. Maybe it's booking that appointment with that massage therapist you've heard so much about but never seem to make time to pursue. Or maybe it's time spent with animals that you long for but never give to yourself. The possibilities are as limitless as your longing to be cared for. It starts there. Sometimes just admitting that we long to be cared for is the biggest obstacle to bringing that care into our lives. I'm inviting you to give yourself permission. To know that it's not selfish. It's necessary.

Imagine a scene in which you are being cared for but only because you asked to be. It can be physically, like my example, or emotionally, verbally, whatever is your longing. Maybe you resisted asking at first but you mustered the courage to finally do it.

Write the scene out with every detail that you can imagine. Be generous with your imagining, and be receiving of it all as if you are living it as fully as possible.

Now invite yourself to live it in real life with a one-line written statement that begins with "I give myself permission to . . . ."

And make it happen. Book your flight. Make the appointment. Whatever it is, near or far. And please, show up. Your wonder needs you to.

## wonder loves community

My nest had officially emptied. My kids were fledged and thriving. Even though it was excruciating at first, I'd gotten used to it. We made sure to still go on family vacations and make the very most of our time together. I had my annual Wonder Trips to look forward to and the consistency of my writing and my retreats to rely on. My life was full and balanced. I liked my own company. Steady was a relief after too much ride.

But then the COVID-coaster ride came, and my nest refilled to the brim. For four months, my twenty-one-year-old and twenty-five-year-old were back in the house. We called it our "Long Spring Break." Time stood still, every moment of it so precious. We knew we were living through an unprecedented time in modern history and that we were doing it in a magical place. Together.

But this morning, just like that, they left. I took off my apron, washed their stripped sheets, and made their beds, too stunned to be sad. The house is quiet again. Just a fifty-something-year-old and two white dogs staring into one another's confused eyes.

What. Just. Happened?

Mid-March 2020 marked the premature end of my book tour for my novel *Willa's Grove*. On March 13, in a hotel room in Minneapolis, the West Coast on lockdown, I knew it was time to go home. So I canceled my thirty-eight remaining events across the US, went home to Montana, and bought beans, rice, and toilet paper like everyone else. The world was reeling from a global pandemic, but we were all privately mourning our own losses. Mine: finally getting a novel published. My longest-held dream. The novel I loved most out of all of them sitting in my closet gathering dust. The novel that had taken me eight years and nineteen drafts to write. The novel that was the living branch of what happened on every single one of my retreats, as each group created a sure and sacred space for pure self-expression. A novel about community, released on March 2, as COVID rolled out, making community almost impossible for two-plus years.

I knew there wasn't time to get lost in self-pity. I had to get my children home. That was the only community that mattered to me in that moment of my life. As I scrambled to book what flights were left to our remote part of the world, it all started to un-blur: not only was my book tour canceled, but I also didn't have a job. No one was going anywhere.

But once we were all sheltered in place, my worries fell away upon those of my adult children. Both of them were in the middle of such wonderous lives, full of so many dreams being dreamed! And now it all spilled out through their fingers: no baseball season or a college life for my son. Online classes. Back to his childhood baseball bedsheets and early-glory-day trophies. No office culture for my daughter in her dear San Francisco. Remote work from her childhood bedroom, still replete with Pottery Barn Teen decor and plastic Breyer horses. And me, in my office, trying to understand whatever this Zoom thing was all about. Somehow I had to figure out how to pivot like everybody else was and bring my book tour online. And maybe even my retreats. And I had no idea how to make any of that possible. *Really? Here again?* So much for balance.

But none of us complained. The mood in the house was instead sunny. Full of gratitude. We knew that it could have been so much worse. We saw people stuck in small apartments in large cities, catching a glimpse of their neighbors, never mind the moon, from small windows or, if they were lucky, a balcony. We had twenty acres and all of Montana to wander in. And we had each other.

That first night of our Long Spring Break, we sat at the kitchen table and I spoke to them like a football coach—loud, strained, focused, and severe. And afraid. I'd never used that voice before.

"We're a team now. Not three solo acts. Every decision we make needs to ultimately be for the team. Who knows what's about to happen with this virus. We have to think of how to fortify who we are so that we can be of service to others if need be. Now is a time for community. And the three of us together . . . are a firmament."

They looked at me like I was an alien.

But I felt like something was talking through me. Something like intuition. This time, I believed in it and applied it.

Because suddenly I turned around and there was a flowing, thriving community of twentysomethings living in my front yard and eating around my firepit. Local twentysomethings that I'd known all their lives, who needed a spot to shelter in place for various reasons: immunocompromised parents, no local housing, obliterated plans. Not long ago, we were having our goodbye parties and talking about the big wonderful world out there. Not long ago, their small hometown under the big sky was something second to their future.

But now the only thing that made sense to them was land. Montana land, old friends, and a familiar house where they could hang their socially distanced hats for a while "until things get back to normal."

They came with tents and sleeping bags and dashed dreams that they wanted to talk about. They were smack-dab in the middle of their happy college and postcollege years. Some of them had planned to go abroad. Others had hard-won internships in cities. Some of them were loving their classes and teachers and academically illuminating conversations. All denied.

They sat around the firepit staring into the flames, scratching their heads like they were serving time for something they didn't do. Was it a dream? How was it possible that they had come full circle when they'd been so forward-focused? I watched them from all windows of my house because I was adamant about keeping my distance. No COVID tests available, and I'd surely been exposed to it in a host of major cities and airports. I watched them in a new way. Not for regular teen and twentysomething shenanigans. This wasn't a party. This was their new normal, and they were lost. They stared at trees like they'd never seen one in all their lives. Ran their hands through dead grass, remembering bare feet to green lawn like an ancient kiss. Dropped their heads back to study clouds until it looked like it hurt, but that was part of it.

"Thank you for this," they each said in their own way. "Sorry about your book tour."

But I didn't really care about my book anymore. It was finding its way on its own. And my income? It was too over-whelming to think about, but deep in my gut I knew that another reinvention was possible if need be. No, it was these kids that I cared about. Who were they going to be now? What if they wouldn't get the chance to follow their dreams at all? I'd had years to pursue mine. What if this living community was what mattered most? These kids needed what I had to give. And I supposed I needed them in this way too. It seemed to me that the most important thing I could do for these young people was to help activate their wonder.

So I asked my most reliable question: "What can I create?"

Years of wonderous birthday parties rolled through my memory. Scavenger hunts for magic pebbles, and pine-cone-upside-down-cake mud pies, and fairy houses in woodpecker-pocked river birches, and field days paddling in the pond, and doing the limbo to Caribbean music in the backyard. I could see it so indelibly in my mind's eye: these exact kids running around with *Lord of the Flies* sticks in their hands, self-selecting leaders yet working together as a team. All for one and one for all, with still-high voices, some needing help in the bathroom. Who were they now, in these grown-up bodies but with the vulnerability of children?

I watched those big children moping around my yard. They needed to remember the little people that still lived inside them. The ones with muddy feet and water balloons in their hands who didn't care about five minutes from now unless there were birthday cake and ice cream and presents involved. These kids needed to play. But the "big" in them also needed purpose.

So I asked for help. Truth was, I'd let things fall into dis-repair, living alone on the "ranch," and the twentysomethings were more than happy, relieved even, to offer their services, especially in return for my sheltered place.

A few of them knew about trucks. Others were skilled with axes, mauls, and hatchets for wood that hadn't made it into the woodshed the prior fall. Some knew how to use chainsaws on the felled trees around the property. Some had worked in forestry and knew what trees were showing disease and needed to be removed. All of them were strong at making burn piles for the slash and hauling the good wood to the woodshed to stack. And all of them knew how to make a mean bonfire in case it got cold. It was still March in Montana, after all. We had basic human needs on our minds. There was no reason not to think it could come to that—living like homesteaders. I was buoyed by the fact that a family had homesteaded this land in the late 1800s and had made it here for many years.

One day I called over to them from the front porch, still socially distancing because now I had a bad cough. "You know, there are two natural springs on this property that the homesteaders used. If we needed to fashion a pump and carry water, I have full faith that you all could figure that out."

Their faces took on preternatural Montana pride. They could suddenly see how everything came down to having water, and they were not immune to that fact. And by virtue of this land, we were lucky. A few months prior, that fact wouldn't have gotten a blink of eye contact out of any of those kids so steeped in their screens, classes, sports, jobs, and first-world stresses. Now they were looking at survival. Daring it, almost. "Where are those springs?" one of them asked. I'd never seen such essential curiosity. I was sure that there would be awe soon enough.

"I know where one is!" said my son.

"Me too!" said my daughter.

And suddenly the whole group was off in two directions, led by my children. I wished my grandparents were around to see this, both children of homesteaders. Their genes were kicking in, clear out here in Montana!

If need be . . . we were going to survive. We were a community. I was their Ma Ingalls. And it occurred to me that the things I knew how to do suddenly had purchase. So when I was better, and ostensibly COVID-free, I offered what I knew best in the way of practical life skills. (Insert "just in case" after each question that follows. That's what we were all thinking but not saying.)

"Who wants to learn how to make bread?"

"Who wants to learn how to garden? Let's turn the flower garden into a victory garden."

"Who wants to make arnica salve? It's great for bruises and aches!"

"Who wants to make conifer-tip syrup? It's full of vitamin C!"

"Who wants to learn how to make Bolognese sauce?"

Eager takers for all of them!

I didn't dare mention writing.

But one of them came to me in private one day and said, blushing, "I'd really love to learn how to write. I've always had an idea for a book. About a kid who can fly but all he wants to do is walk." I tried to contain myself. He'd had the most wonder of all of them. Yet a lot of hard knocks. I'd worried about him when he was little. But there it was! His wonder was alive and intact! And he wanted to write!

"Seems like this is the perfect time to write it. With the world on pause." That was the most vital "just in case" that I knew.

So I went back into teaching mode, and as I saw writing giving its life force to this young man, I realized that there was a world out there, yes, on pause, starved for community and storytelling. Only not old stories. This story. This story of life on pause in the midst of an unforeseen global pandemic. We weren't superheroes after all.

That night, I started an online, free writing group, focusing on using writing to get through the pandemic. I took all that I'd learned from my community of twentysomethings—what they needed, feared, longed for, mourned for—and created a writing practice called So Now What. It was inspired by my novel but brought to life by the young people living on my land. For one hour every Friday night, I would lead a group of people through this practice on Zoom. Who knew? Maybe people would say yes. What else was there to say?

Hundreds of people joined from all over the world. They met loved ones on the screen who they couldn't see in real life. They wrote together and they healed together every Friday for two years, with the exception of one Friday that fell on Christmas. I needed it as much as my students did. It made me realize how much I missed leading retreats and being in those small, miracle communities.

I kept waiting for my kids to roll their eyes at me or to say, *Calm down!* (which never calms anyone down) or *Easy on the Montessori, Mother.* But they seemed to love my educational offerings. They realized that they'd profited from them, whether they had liked it back then or not. Now, with their friends chomping at the bit for this knowledge, my kids liked their purchase too. A few of their friends even joined the weekly writing sessions. Our house was now so alive when recently it had felt so dead.

It was hard not to be a bit smug. I'd always told my kids, when they'd complain about where we lived, "Someday, you'll actually *like* living out of town. Someday you and your friends will love this cozy house and this firepit and our land. They'll *want* to be here. Mark my words." Their eyes would glaze over while I went on and on about this house that we built with all its happy scars from country living: the floors scratched by dozens of dog nails, dents from highchair-flung sippy cups, handprints on the ceiling from post-mud-pie couch traversing. Good clean fun. And here . . . we . . . were.

Our Long Spring Break was the definition of "good clean fun." The kids were now voluntarily doing things like hauling cedar chips to spread around the firepit and positioning camping chairs around it to "make it nice." They put beauty into this thing called "sheltering in place." They said please and thank you. They cleaned up after themselves. Sometimes when I joined them at the firepit with my guitar they chanted

"Laur-a, Laur-a," and that made me deliriously happy. They wanted to sing the old folk tunes I'd sung for them at school and at the birthday parties and bonfires of their youth. "Black Socks." "The Fox." "Crawdad." "This Land Is Your Land." Especially they wanted to sing "This Land Is Your Land." I'd lost them to high school. But now they were back. Just as silly and dewy-eyed as they had been as wee, wonder-full ones.

Each day ended in stories of new adventures. Some of them were accompanied by their college- and postcollege-inspired red-cup adventures. Yet still so much of it was full of a child's wonder. They found what was left of the winter snow at higher elevations, and they slid around on it. They were happy to uphill ski and take one long, luxurious, and deserving ski down instead of hopping obliviously on chairlifts, constantly checking how much "vert" they'd gotten after a high-speed quad lift up the mountain and super-fast "shredding" in the "pow pow" down. "It's nice to go slowly," my son said. "You really appreciate the work it takes to get to the top. So you want to make it last, going down."

Music to my ears. The sort of thing he used to say when he was six.

As the weeks went by, I loved their bonfire conversation most. Now they spoke like soldiers, knowing exactly what they were fighting for and who their victory was ultimately for, knowing they were living in an extreme time in extreme beauty, and never had they felt such gratitude for it. It was in every word, every action, every breath.

It was an ultimate gift, watching and fortifying this parade of young seekers. They needed each other, and they needed this land to hold their loss and their fear of their futures. And their fun. And it became obvious that these young adults needed *me*. What a surprise diversion from the way my life had been going. No online community could ever be better than this community.

When it was time for them to move on, our grateful, loving pandemic pod knew that they'd forged memories they never would have made if it hadn't been for this uncertain time. They'd made their world certain and taken it to the mountains, rivers, lakes, and, yes . . . to my twenty acres. They laughed and played and had long talks and real thank-yous and tearful goodbyes when their colleges and workplaces opened up and it was time to go back to their other "real" lives. We all knew that what we'd lived through together was the definition of "real."

Now that the house is empty, I know that I'm going to miss being Ma Ingalls. I know I'm going to miss *them*. But I'm glad they are out in the world again, whatever that world has to offer them. I know that they will seize it like they never would have prepandemic. But I also know that they are better for having had each other during this time. And this land. And even me. I know it because just now, I found a circle of heart-shaped rocks by the firepit. Their wonder intact, I would like to think for good.

## your wild why . . .

Were you alone or in a community during the pandemic months? What did that time bring up for you? How did you respond? Did you pivot? Reinvent? Create something new? Did you learn more about what it is to be in the flow? Did you learn to *be* more than *do*? Were you grateful for small things? Did you reconnect with your wonder and your wild whys? Or was it a time of extreme stagnancy and loneliness? Was it a time of grief?

What were the lessons? Did you lose those lessons when things normalized afterward? *Did* things normalize for you again, or did those years change you in ways that are permanent? If so, is that a good thing? Or not? Write about it. Go deeply into your truth. Your feelings. Your curiosity and awe. It requires you to look in the rearview mirror, but the lessons that we learned in those years need to be put to use. We were different then. Sometimes for the better. Sometimes not. And we need to admit it and process it. Writing our truth helps. Especially if it connects us to our wonder or the threat of losing it.

# the inner champion

The world opened again, and so did my retreats. People who come to Haven are always grateful by nature, but I had never seen such gratitude like I did in that first post-COVID lockdown retreat. We all wept, strangers starving for their wonder and each other. I knew that I needed to bring back my own personal Wonder Trips, especially to preserve the *being* I'd experienced versus the *doing* during the pandemic.

There was a place in the world that I knew was as high in wonder as it gets. A place I'd wanted to go since sixth grade when I wrote a paper on Darwin: the Galapagos Islands. I wanted to unscrew my head all the way this time and let in all the wonder that I could. To be in the world of blue-footed boobies and swimming iguanas and flamingo flocks. I wanted to sit with hundred-year-old tortoises and go just as slowly as they. I pictured myself floating on my belly while sea lions braided around me. I pictured white-sand beaches with only a smattering of humans and me and my binoculars watching Darwin finches. I trusted myself to travel solo after my month in Morocco, but this time I wanted to be silent. I wanted to see just how silent I could be. I'd devoted my life to self-expression in multiple forms. I knew I needed to practice silence, so I fashioned my own kind of personal silent retreat.

Then came the plot twist. After a solid year of planning and saving and juggling, the day before I was scheduled to land in mainland Ecuador for one night, Galapagos-bound the next, terrorism hit. One of the country's top gang leaders escaped from prison, and a news station was stormed during live programming, as well as a university. Hostages. Horror. Hysteria. State of emergency. Curfew. All in the mainland city where I had planned to stay before heading to the islands. So why not an airport or a hotel? I knew that this wasn't my year for blue-footed boobies and swimming iguanas. Or silence.

Instead, I found myself grounded in Mexico City, a place I'd been warned was "dangerous." Much more so than Ecuador. I'd flown through on my way to San Miguel de Allende but had never spent any time there. I could have taken the next plane back to the US, but Montana was experiencing forty-five-below temps without a break in sight, so I asked myself if I might be able to turn this massive, not-silent city into my respelling ground.

The Inner Critter awakened from what had been a nice long summer and fall nap and made herself known, loud and clear and mean. Like she'd been activated by the terrorism itself. She oozed: *You should stop this nonsense. Go home and get back to work!* But I told her no. If I wasn't going to have the opportunity to share molecules with flora and fauna found nowhere else in the world, then maybe one of the largest, highly populated, museum-full, culinary meccas in the world would deliver the same personal unspelling and respelling, the unscrewing of my loud mind, and create an urban place where the Inner Critter couldn't find me.

What was she going to say to me?

*You need to go to another museum! At least three a day!*

*You need to eat another taco al pastor and at an even-more-local taco stand! Who do you think you are? Anthony Bourdain?*

*Do you realize that some of the top restaurants in the world are in CDMX? You haven't done enough tasting menus!*

*By the way, your Spanish is embarrassing! Your beloved grade school Spanish teacher would be so ashamed of you!*

*Don't you know how reckless you're being? Don't you know that this city is dangerous? Especially for a woman traveling solo?*

Was it? More so than other cities? I was more worried about my urban unspelling. Even though I've lived in rural Montana for three decades, I hail from Chicago. Cities are within my comfort zone. I know how to "do" cities, even really big ones. The point of this pilgrimage, however, was not to "do" anything. But, rather, to "be." I knew I'd likely not be silent in this huge city, but what if I changed my goal to just "being"? Would I be able to "be" in a city of this magnitude? Would I be bowled over by awe, which had been my plan? Or would the Inner Critter's voice follow me and dog me to *try try try* and *do do do* and *want want want* and go back to my pre-COVID lifestyle? I was worried about that danger more than any other.

What I knew for sure: no matter where I was going on my annual solo wonder pilgrimage, the answer would rest in my ability to stop. To stop and allow curiosity and awe to wash over me. That would be my ultimate goal. Only now, it would be as urban and as loud as it gets. Maybe that would help the unspelling to happen at an even faster rate, especially given the surprise plot twist.

As the taxi drove through stop-and-go traffic, I looked out the window at that colorful and loud and large humanity dance. Street musicians in the middle of the intersection. A young girl in a school uniform picking out ice cream from a cart vendor with her mother. Women proudly selling handcrafted blankets, pillows, purses, scarves, laid out on the sidewalk. I decided I would focus on stopping, especially for the little in-between moments that happen precisely because of so much human energy in one place all at once. I would keep my guard up, urban-smart, but I would keep my heart open, human-ready. But would I even be able to smile at strangers along the sidewalk in a huge city like that? It's one thing in a small town in Montana. But in Mexico City? I mean, did a smile scream, "Mug me"? I hoped not.

Just what were the chances that I would really be able to stop in a city like Mexico City at all? Not a tortoise in sight. From my taxi window, I figured slim to none. And so did the Inner Critter. She taunted me: *I dare you to sit on a museum bench and look at one Aztec artifact for five full minutes instead of taking out your phone and letting its lens see it. Click. Move to the next Instagrammable photo op. You're going to fail at stopping.* So mean. So scared.

So I started at a place where I was certain I'd find wonder and where the Inner Critter would leave me alone: the Frida Kahlo museum. The Casa Azul, her childhood and later adult home and studio with (and without) Diego Rivera. As I wandered through the rooms, looking at her artwork, her letters and photos, her elaborate clothes, her wheelchair and easel, her paints and books, I could feel her there. A woman interrupted—that's what it felt like. I stole a good glance into the mirror she'd looked into as she created her self-portraits. Into the mirror in the ceiling of her canopy bed where she'd watched herself heal from her near-fatal childhood accident and painted her way to living life again. Into the plaster body casts she painted after her operations. Into the courtyard, once festooning with her famous parties.

I spent hours looking into all of it as other tourists passed by me, with likely two other museums to fit into their day of "doing Mexico City," and wondered if Frida had her own mean, scared Inner Critter. And if so, I wondered if her Inner Critter tried to kill her wonder. If it ever succeeded. I suspected that it tried to. I hoped it didn't ultimately win. She seemed to have such a sad ending. There was so much brokenness and pain in her paintings and in her life.

I sat in the courtyard and began weeping uncontrollably. How was it possible that we allow our wonder to be so starved? Our civilization needs it to thrive, and if the artists are susceptible, then who isn't? I felt a deep sorrow. But I also felt that her wonder must have been intact in a magical courtyard like this one, with her pet monkeys and her studio wrapping itself around her. And her famous quote after the amputation of her feet: "Feet, what do I need them for if I have wings to fly."

That night, I dreamed that Frida Kahlo, in her traditional Tehuana regalia, emerged from behind a blue wall and said, "You must take your love seriously." It woke me up, and I sat up in bed. My *love*? What did that mean? My love of life? My art? Myself? I decided to stay in Mexico City for as long as I'd planned to be in Ecuador. The city had something to teach me. Something big. "*Viva la vida*," Frida painted on a canvas of bright, sliced watermelons that hung on her studio wall.

I decided to bring my city pilgrimage into finer focus and obey my Frida dream. What I didn't expect was the weeping. With every museum I visited, I sat on benches before a painting or sculpture or ancient artifact, weeping like the tide of wonder itself was washing over me. Every wildly delicious piece of food I was served brought a tear to my eye, and I ate *slowly*. When I was walking, I was tearless. But when I stopped and sat, I wept. It felt uncontainable and it felt foreign. These weren't my normal tears. Were these the Inner Critter's tears? Was this her sadness, and had she been afraid to feel it? If she was made of fear, then was she also made of sorrow? I stopped and sat and wept even *more* with the conviction to find out.

And that led to the smiling. One day, I started smiling

at people from my perches. People smiled back. Every one of them. More weeping. More smiling. I think of myself as no stranger to smiling, but the Mexicans *really* love to smile. To catch an eye and honor it with a loving smile of recognition. As if to say, *We're all humans. We're all in this together. In some way.* Had those smiles been there for me all the time and I'd just forgotten how to stop to see and receive and give them? No wonder I had been weeping. What was Mexico City doing to me? This had never happened in any other city I'd visited or lived in.

Soon, the hugging started. I felt this overwhelming gushing of love for humanity. Myself included. Every new person I met became an immediate friend, and interactions ended in mutual hugs. The historian/anthropologist tour guide who took me to the Aztec pyramids of Teotihuacan and helped me feel the radical empathy of the ages and to see how little we've changed. The hotel manager who brought me chicken and rice soup when I was ill, with extra broth in a little white pitcher. The artist who sold me ex-votos, words on art, something I love and collect whenever I'm in Mexico. Ex-votos are all about stopping to honor blessings and, in their case, to thank saints. She invited me to her studio for coffee and we talked about the sacred nature of an artist having *a room of one's own.* The man playing a classical guitar version of "My Way" on the terrace of my hotel, singing it directly into my eyes as if he knew it had been my theme song for years. My way. That's how I've done it. The Inner Critter hasn't liked that. But the Inner Critter wasn't there, for all that weeping and smiling and hugging.

Instead, I felt this sort of prophetic, magnetic urge growing and growing inside me. Like I could feel Frida in her home, it got so that I could feel the smiles and hugs of strangers coming on, and my tears subsided with all of that hope. It felt like those people wanted smiles and hugs and maybe tears too. Maybe they needed to spell themselves differently too. Maybe they had big, mean, scared voices in their heads too, and maybe when they saw someone stopping and smiling, even weeping, it gave them some sort of permission to not let it lord over them.

One day I had to do some unexpected work from my hotel room. And my Inner Critter saw an opening: *What is your problem? Why are you crying? Why do you need to hug everybody? You don't need all this time in a big, polluted, dangerous city. You're spending too much money. Go home and get back to work. You're acting like a delirious, spoiled brat, not a responsible adult. Plus, do you seriously believe that you are special enough that Frida freaking Kahlo would come to you in a dream? Get over it. She didn't. Plus, you're a chicken that you didn't risk it and go to the Galapagos.*

Just as I was about to agree with the Inner Critter, suddenly, the kind Inner Champion voice was there in that hotel room. Soft but stern. Loving and kind. Not unlike Frida's voice in my dream. It said, *Dearheart, don't listen to that mean, scared voice. Listen to this one. You are brave, finding your way around this huge city. You are brave to stop. To smile, and weep, and hug, publicly. You are doing exactly what you need to do. Keep stopping. Keep going slowly. And weeping. And smiling. And hugging. You are almost spelled differently. And when you go home, I will be your lord. I am you. That other voice . . . it's time to let it go. It's not you. Not anymore. Fear was never your friend. Love is the only lord.*

Maybe I was closer than I thought to quieting that mean, scared voice once and for all. Would I have had this experience of inward and outward resplendent love toward humanity in the Galapagos? Likely for flora and fauna. But what I didn't know that I needed was to fall madly in love with the human being. Myself included.

## your wild why . . .

Make a promise to yourself: go someplace very different from where you live, far away if you can swing it, or nearby. Either way, it should be out of your comfort zone. Take some time there. Stop and sit. Exile the mean, scared voice. Allow in the loving one. Smile and weep if you need to. Hug if you are moved to. Be part of the throng, wherever you are. Follow the plot twists that will surely come. Take your love seriously. It will spell you differently.

And then, when you return, I encourage you to do the following:

For one day, every time you hear that mean, scared voice (because back home, you most likely will), respond to it with love. Like a mother getting in the way of a bully, not by sending it to the principal but by bringing it into her lovingly and claiming the mic. But still acknowledging the voice's fear. Try some of these affirmations:

*Dearheart, I know you're worried that you are going to be late. But right now, you're on time. And if you end up being a few minutes late, that's okay. The sky won't fall.*

*Darling, comparing yourself to other people never works. Look at your individualism! Can you see it as the miracle that it is? I can. I'll see it for you until you can too.*

*Look at what you've created and take a bow!*

*Enjoy the infatuation of your ideas. Don't worry about the result. Bask in the process of co-creating with them!*

*You're doing your best and it's a beautiful thing. I am so proud of you.*

*You are special, just as everyone is special. Know that.*

It takes practice to cast away the scared, mean voice and to cultivate this brave, kind voice—this voice that is purely committed to self-preservation. This voice that takes her love seriously. And for me, the practice is almost constant. But I'm getting better and better at it. And not because it wields its fear-propelled bullying: *You need to be better at being good to yourself!* No. The Inner Champion speaks in invitations and possibility. *Could you lovingly move through your to-do list today? What would it take for you to feel good right now, even in this career challenge?*

I'm not going to pretend that I've loved the mean, scared voice into submission. Believe me: I haven't. If I pretended, that wouldn't serve you or me. I do promise you this: while this new voice may be exceedingly kind, it's no sucker and it's no fool and it's not going to punish you for being bad. This voice simply sees the true goodness of who you are and takes it seriously. Isn't it time that you do the same?

Whether you have been told that you are "special," or that you need to be "normal," ultimately you have to decide for yourself who and what you are. And please . . . let it be special. And please . . . let that process be simple and loving.

## to love

I suppose that if you look at wonder in a certain way, it's really *love*. It's the will not just to *live* but to live in *love*. To see with your imagination, empathy, intuition, curiosity, and awe. And also to see with your heart. Your loving, wonder-full heart.

In the years after the end of my marriage and as my reinvention unfolded, I had started seeing with my heart again in the way of self-love but not in the way of loving a partner. I wanted to be in love. I wanted an equal, kind, wonder-full partner. I just didn't admit it to anyone and barely to myself.

Outside of my retreats and my Wonder Trips, I had turned into a hermit. I wasn't proud of it—pretending I was "fine." I wasn't. I was as personally lonely as I'd ever been. My wonder felt like it had run dry in the realm of ever loving again. I thought I was keeping it well under wraps.

Apparently I wasn't. Not to my adult children.

"You aren't meant to be alone, Mom. You thrive in a relationship. You need a partner. And you live in a tiny town. You need to start online dating," they both said in different iterations.

"No way," I told them.

Before I could pretend to know how to stop their quick-fire button pushing, they had signed me up for three dating sites. "Humor us."

I feigned a modicum of interest. In fact, the only real thing that was interesting to me was answering the questions these sites asked. It was like a sociological field study. Maybe I'd get a personal essay out of it to submit to *The New York Times*. I mean, do I brush my teeth every day? Is that a *question*?

And what was with all the profile pics of guys in their *cars*? Was that supposed to be a bonus—that they had a *car*? And taking shirtless selfies in their bathroom *mirrors*? Was that supposed to be a *turn-on*? And holding a fish in a trout stream? And thick-fisted grips on the antlers of the deer they'd shot? *Oh good, you like to kill things.* What were the chances of finding any Montana men who wanted to spend a Sunday listening to NPR and reading books?

I polled women who actually *liked* online dating to see what was in it for them.

"You're overthinking it," they said. "Have some *fun* for a change! It's not like you have to find a *husband*."

"I'm not *looking* for a husband."

"What *are* you looking for?"

I didn't know. Was there something in between a hookup and a husband?

What I did know was that it was a game to these friends of mine. A game I didn't want to play.

But were my kids right? Was I in massive denial about a key piece of my basic needs? So I told a non-game-playing divorced friend that I'd signed up for online dating and had hit an immediate wall. I'd watched her navigate those waters, and I liked her style. She'd said, "I don't even know if I *can* be in love again." But she'd gone forth despite her trepidation. And she'd found the love of her life.

She was happy to help. "If you could be in the loving, dedicated relationship of your life, what would it be like?"

"Just . . . ." I couldn't find words. And this from someone who so prizes fluency in her self-expression.

"Come on. Tell me. What do you really *want*?"

I remembered the list I'd written in Italy of what I wanted in a partnership right as the marital shit was hitting the fan. Maybe it was time to revisit that list. Or write a new one. So much had transpired since then.

I let myself ramble, and she listened. "I want . . . someone who is really *kind*. And who is a healthy communicator. Who can actually express themselves authentically. Someone who's emotionally responsible. And who's passionate about making their life matter. Helping others. Someone who loves beauty and lives to create it. Someone who really wants to be in an equal, loving relationship with me. I mean . . . someone who really is *for* me. Someone who might even want to take *care* of me. Is that such a bad thing? Who might even . . . *fight* for me. I don't mean physically. But who would stand between me and anyone who is trying to mess with me. And someone who is funny. But not mean-funny. And never, ever passive-aggressive. And who doesn't have a gaslighting bone in their body."

I took in a deep, exposure-embarrassed breath, but I thought of the couple at St Martin-in-the-Fields in the balcony, loving each other and the Duruflé Requiem. I wanted that. Was that possible? I doubted it.

"There's no reason in the world why you can't find a partner like that. I mean, if *you're* in Montana, then why can't there be other people in Montana who love the things you love? You just have to be open to it."

Open to it? I wasn't sure what that meant. Did I have to learn how to kill things?

I emailed my dear godmother and asked her. She always had a voice of reason, along with a penchant for play. She responded right away: "Prince Charming isn't coming to a ranch near you on a white horse! Get thee back to the literati of your Seattle days! You belong in a place where there are more people than cows!"

I was not about to leave this place I'd worked so hard to keep. Plus, it had proven itself to be our family headquarters. The kids made me promise never to sell it. They wanted it as their legacy. I'd make my peace with being solo. I'd take my Wonder Trips. Maybe I'd have a lover in every port? Ha. I am so *not* that woman. The *hammam* had been a challenge!

I called a writer friend. "Would it be so bad to want someone who loves literature? A seeker? A world traveler who's lived all over and settled in the West? And heck, I've been thinking about getting back into horses. Maybe a guy on a white horse. Ha ha."

We both chuckled. Being rescued by a guy on a white horse was so not me.

"Be as honest with yourself as you have been with your writing life," she said. "You never know what might be around the bend."

Honest? It all felt so false. How was I supposed to honestly respond to comments like "Nice smile. You look intriguing. Pretty hair." Ew. Gross. Yuck. Go away, Kenny, the pest-control expert from Libby. (Nothing against Libby. Or pest-control experts. Or guys named Kenny. But what were the chances that he listened to NPR?) Apparently I was in high school.

Mostly to get my kids off my back, I started to talk to select friends about what I wanted, even though it felt like the stuff that sinkholes are made of.

I heard iterations of, "You're too picky."

Too *picky*? Weren't we *supposed* to be picky? Especially after the decay and demise of a long-term marriage? A marriage that I believed in?

"I refuse to settle," was my response, even though it was true that I'd looked at plenty of the profiles and thought *Maybe I could get into ranching. I mean . . . I binge-watched* Yellowstone *even though I've never met a Montanan remotely similar to those characters. Maybe I could get into NASCAR. Paul Newman drove race cars. Right? Love me my Paul Newman.*

I felt like I needed to take a shower. Who was I kidding? Finally, I gave up. I mean, I hadn't even really started. It was a relief. I canceled all of my accounts. I liked my own company just fine.

About a month later I was looking over my credit card statement and realized there was one online-dating membership I had yet to cancel. So I went onto the site, and lo, a photo of a guy on a white horse popped up. In an English saddle. Guys I know out here in the West don't ride in an English saddle. And why was he even on my feed in the first place? He lived hundreds of miles away from me in western Oregon, and I'd set my profile geography to a hundred-mile radius of my town. Which by Montana standards was not all that long-distance. Five hundred miles was another story.

My eyes scanned his profile and my mouth dropped open. An American *Literature* major? Who loved Joan Didion and the plays of Eugene O'Neill? He loved to *cook*? And *dance*? And loved *bluegrass*? And of the character traits he most valued, the top one was *kindness*? And get this: he led *wellness* retreats. Using a form of equine therapy. For men dealing with the trauma of *divorce. Whaaat?* Who *was* this guy?

So I did something I hadn't done before in the online-dating arena. I wrote him a short note, not even attempting to be clever or cryptic or flirty or anything, really. I genuinely wanted to know who this guy was. That's all. Maybe we'd be friends. Maybe we'd commiserate about this online-dating bullshit with Didion snark.

So I wrote, "Something tells me that you know what

Equine Assisted Learning is," which is a lesser-known form of equine therapy and something I'd worked with personally and used on my retreats.

In seconds, he answered me back. "Yes." And he went on for a few more beats about how he used it in his work.

He must have looked at my profile and seen that I was from Chicago because he added another beat. Guess where he was from originally? Yep. Mentioned that he'd spent some time in New England. Moved west and never looked back.

I smelled socioeconomic twinning mixed with rebellion. Nothing more seductive.

So I wrote him back.

In one more text, we realized we had mutual friends. In another, that our mothers knew each other. And then the icing: that his stepsiblings were in my mother's carpool!

"Holy shit. We need to get on the phone," I wrote.

"Yes. Immediately," he wrote.

Five minutes later, that's what we did. For six straight hours. We were in love. We just didn't know to call it that. Yet. Don't roll your eyes—I've done enough eyeball rolling for the both of us.

There began marathon phone calls, which begat months of road-trip relay races back and forth from Montana to Oregon. We were both nervous the first time we met in person. He'd driven nine hours and surprised me with oysters and a Weber grill because I'd told him I loved grilled oysters and didn't have a grill anymore. We folded into each other's arms like old lovers. It gutted us that we'd likely been in many of the same rooms at the same time all our lives but had only now met. His plan was to stay for a few days. He stayed a week. Then drove home. And forty-eight hours later, he came back.

"I love you, Laura Munson," he said, standing in my front yard like he'd been practicing it for the whole drive. He said that he was "swinging for the fence." That he was committed to "living in the Big." He'd been traumatized by his divorce and the loss of his children. He'd been through hell, lived to tell the tale, and had devoted his life to helping men in his position find their way back to a place of thriving.

"I love you, Laura Munson," he said over and over, without a smidgeon of vacillation. He was all in.

Was I? We'd only been in each other's actual presence for a matter of days!

What was sure, however, was my nonexistent willpower when it came to the force of his love. I couldn't resist him in any way. The only other place in my life that garnered this sort of behavior was in my writing cocoon. Now, there was *this* cocoon. I didn't know what to do with it except for just to be in it. And to not overthink it. To let my heart be my guide.

We were love-blind, I suppose, and we kept it private. I barely told my children. How would anyone believe us? So fast and furious in just a matter of weeks. But we were certain: a beyond-beautiful thing was happening to both of us. Neither of us had imagined what a dream new partner could really be, never mind such an equal and loving one. And here it was. Was there actually something to those online-dating algorithms? Or was it some sort of divine intervention, a phrase neither of us were the types to proffer. No matter. It felt reckless to resist it. We tried not to let the past define us. This was the present. A beautiful, bountiful present. We told each other we were brave enough to receive it.

And yet we were both terrified.

Life didn't seem to care. Instead, life defied our fear and became a world of color again. The gloom that neither of us had been willing to admit had overcome our everyday lives was lifting fast and furiously. The wonder started to seep back in. We'd had such similar stories. We'd *started* in such similar places and *landed* in such similar places, taking our pain and learning from it and devoting so much of our lives to helping others through their own. He with horses. Me with the written word. And our mothers *knew* each other? We had handfuls of friends in *common*? It was just all too, well, in his word, "serendipitous." He'd just about quit online dating too.

A man on a white horse. I'd never fancied myself a princess awaiting her knight in shining armor. Quite the opposite. I don't even really *like* white horses. I'm a sucker for a bay. Oh, and he had a bay too. Turns out.

I'd had an excerpt from a Wallace Stevens poem taped to my bedside table for years. I'd forgotten it was even there. Like it had become part of the wood. But then I woke up one morning, solo, in between his visits, and read it as if some spirit had put it there in the night. It was about living and breathing again. About time flashing again.

I was living this flash. Maybe the poem had brought me to this love, subconsciously, working on me in the night while I slept. Who knows. Sometimes things are so perfect that you just can't try to find the cause. Only to receive what is happening as an enormous and pure gift that has come your way. And it most definitely had come mine.

My kids were curious, but I played it down. This was between the two of us until it made sense, if it ever made sense. I wanted no one to touch it. Tarnish it. Doubt it. Even root for it. It was all ours. And dare I say, both of us deserved it. We took it as a severe case of something that people like to name. Manifestation? Law of attraction? Kismet? A will being done? I didn't want to think about it. I just wanted to receive it. Maybe wonder itself had brought us together. We decided to call it that.

He kept saying, "I love you and I *like* you too."

I could say the same, yet words came less easily to me. That's because there was a problem. For the first time since 1988, I had no urge to write.

I shrugged it off. This was *living* time. Living was its own kind of writing. I'd said that many times before. The writing would come back. This was a time to learn about love. To *live* love. Because in a matter of minutes that turned to months, I'd fallen in love with the most giving, kind, and, yes, hilarious human I had ever met. A human who was my definitive equal. Truly, like we were made for each other.

We'd both lived over half a century in almost the exact same way, circling around each other from coast to coast and in between, the first decade and a half literally thirty miles down the road from each other. We'd left that road and gone west. We'd suffered similar excruciating losses. Had almost the exact same dreams. Had actualized those dreams in almost the exact same way. And yet we'd found each other, needle in a haystack, with absolutely none of the above factors connecting us.

One day, in a small crabbing boat on Netarts Bay in Oregon, with tears choking his throat, he managed to say, "I didn't know how to dream you. And yet, here you are."

I could have said the same. Yet I was seemingly unable to find the words. I didn't recognize myself in this way. Me? Tongue-tied? I plunged into the task at hand, pulling up the crabbing rings for us to sort out the keepers, squealing like eight-year-olds at the skittering, clawed crustaceans. He seemed okay with my emotional reserve. Instead, we laughed at how inept we were yet felt proud that we were trying something new. Together. That was our theme: trying new things. Together. Wasn't that enough for now?

But where I was stoic, he was a fountain. He couldn't stop talking, mostly about it all being "the living definition of 'serendipity.'" "There's no other word for it . . . if there is a word for it at all," he said later that night, shucking local oysters for dinner on the deck. He was finding his words. Where were mine?

Is it possible for two people to fall in love in ten minutes? It happened to us. When we'd both stopped looking. What words were there for that? The ones that came to my mind weren't mood-appropriate: *I'm scared.*

Sometimes I attributed my loss of words to the fact that I had only recently started to speak what I truly wanted for this next chapter of my life. Having the twentysomethings around had been life-altering, and the Wonder Trips had been too. They'd opened me up to my genuine self-expression and self-love and the wonder behind it. And I'd bravely claimed it. But it seemed that my words hadn't caught up. The fact that he had such access to his words made it feel recklessly one-sided. I needed to write. To go into myself and have a look. But my journal just lay there, dormant. I had no interest in it. Only in this man and how I felt being with him. That would have to be my "journaling" process for now. I told myself that it was just temporary.

As my heart opened to this surprise feeling with this surprise human, the giving and receiving of a surprise love, I realized I had been living in a closed and unavailable inner world for far too long. I couldn't blame it on the pandemic. In fact, I'd used the pandemic to hide. My book tour stopped flat. My retreats stopped flat. The world (not flat) stopped. Insanity was brewing in our population, and the future was completely unclear. So I'd drawn within. Made myself unavailable to others and maybe even to myself.

But now here was this man. And this massive and delicious world of possibility and connection. And it was clear: in losing what I'd believed to be an intimate, loving, sacred, and secure relationship in my marriage and in spending ten years holding on to my little family and my little life with all that I could create, I had created my way into an emotional fortress with high walls and a moat around it with wild, terrifying fake monsters that breathed fake fire as they roared a fake, "You shall not pass!" to anyone who tried. But his loving kindness was breaking through that fortress. Fast.

As my heart flung open to loving and being loved, it was wildly apparent to me that my fortress had been a place to belong to myself and myself only. It was where my writing lived. And not a whole lot else. My fortress had served me. Even when it leaked and smelled and fell into disrepair. I belonged there, just me, and I felt safe. Like my tree house. But now, being loved for the woman I was, walls and all, I knew it was time for the walls to come down and the monsters to be released, to let down the drawbridge, and walk into the warm, wide-open countryside. And be safe there. Even if he didn't meet me there. Even if his job was only to get me out of the fortress.

Whatever the outcome, I promised that I would not make the same mistakes twice. My safety and belonging would never again be contingent upon a relationship. I would risk loving and being loved, but the ultimate belonging was inside myself. Period. Which meant that I needed to take a ferociously honest look at how I'd arranged my sense of identity, especially when it came to writing.

That's when it got really scary.

With all of those walls coming down and this burgeoning new love illuminating the way, I knew I needed to become a student again. How could I love this man, and my writing, and myself in a healthy, nonnegotiable way?

I went back to learning from my old teachers on the page. To Meister Eckhart. Thomas Merton. Hafiz. Kabir. Rumi. Rilke. Julian of Norwich. Hildegard von Bingen. E. E. Cummings. I opened my heart to what these elders had to teach me now. I'd been in Rumi's bright, wide-open field when I'd read them in my twenties. I was in the bright, wide-open field again. I marveled at my twenty-year-old underlinings and notes in the margins, reminding me that I used to be such a starved and sated seeker. How had I locked her away in a fortress?

My relationship with this man continued to bloom. The problem was, the more I loved him, the less I wanted to show up for my writing. And that had never, *ever* happened. It had always been the other way since childhood. I couldn't *not* write. But now I had no hunger for creating the space for my words. Usually I *fought* for that space. Tricked life into giving it to me and then locked the door behind me so I could sit down and let what was gnawing at me out. Now there was nothing that needed out. I wanted things *in*. I was processing this great love in my *heart* but not through the written word.

Did I have a dysfunctional relationship with my muse? The more love I felt for this man, the more the muse seemed hell-bent on swimming to a distant shore. She wanted nothing to do with me if I was going to behave this way. And my relationship with her had been the one sacrosanct aspect of my life, *all* my life.

I woke in the night, sweating, mumbling myself off of dream cliffs: "My writing is not me. It is *of* me. But it's not me. My writing is not me. It is *of* me. But it's not me." But short of truly dying, I'd never felt so close to a dying inside of me. Who was I without my writing? How could I process life? How could I be *okay*, especially with so much newness in my life? The walls were down. My heart was open. And my muse had left.

"Fuuuuuuck!" I screamed into the 4:00 a.m. darkness. How was that for fully self-expressed? It was about all I had.

I didn't know how to verbalize what I was going through to others, and was I really a sympathetic character anyway? Not likely. No one asks us to write. But my books had always been the container for my muse. Just what *is* a muse anyway? No one asks us to have a muse. And certainly no one asks us to take *care* of our muses. That was *my* job. Just like it was my job to take care of myself. Maybe taking care of my muse had historically been *how* I took care of myself. How would I take care of myself without her? I knew not to assign that role to this man. That would be a recipe for disaster. The stakes were high, and I was out of answers.

One morning, after a particularly dark, muse-less night of the soul, I stood on my front porch as I did every morning and tried to call my siren back to me. Where was she? *Who* was she? Was she wonder itself? Had loving this man killed my wonder? I needed to wander in the woods.

I stepped out into my yard and continued into the trees, thinking about the sixty-second fire, my ambition, and my wonderless cabin, all for show and, yes, maybe for sustenance too. But now wasn't a time to pretend. I needed to create a true Wonder Cabin in my mind that would hold me whether I was in the woods or in Midtown Manhattan. But I couldn't let it be a hiding place. Not a fortress anymore. Instead, it needed to be a safe inner structure that could include both my writing and my love.

As I kicked rocks and pinecones I wondered: *How can my heart be so full, loving this man and receiving his love? And yet so empty in this other way? My way. My writing.* Was writing my ultimate way of loving myself? That seemed like a dangerous equation and one I'd worried about off and on for years. And if it was the case, how had I backed myself up into that corner? It was suddenly clear to me. This love had built a raging bonfire, sap be damned, but I couldn't see for all the heat and glare.

A dirty secret seeped from my essence in the way of wild whys: Had I told myself all my life that I'd found myself in my writing when really it was my place to be lost? To hide? Was it just a lie I'd told myself to keep myself safe?

I sat on the stump that I'd sat on countless times when I needed clarity. The scariest question of all hit me then: If my writing wasn't "me," then who was the self I'd lose without it?

I was so scared and so confused. And so in love. Everything was colliding and so quickly. Again . . . *fuuuuuuck*!

The kind voice said, *Let it flow. Let it teach. Stay open. Don't run scared. Stay in the bright meadow. Hold your Free Child in your arms. The muse will come back. This is living time.*

But the Inner Critter came in violent: *You're being idiotic. Falling in love in ten minutes? Giving so much to one person and abandoning your muse? How fickle are you?*

Maybe I was delusional. Maybe this love wasn't even real. Maybe I wasn't meant to love at all. Maybe the wonder wound was too deep. Maybe I was letting myself be steamrollered for fear of being alone, back in the dark, leaking, dilapidated fortress. At least there . . . I could write.

*Fuuuuuck! Fuuuck fuck!*

I started to backpedal.

"I'm madly in love with you and I want to spend the rest of my life with you," my love said again and again.

I had no response. Just a shy smile. My heart wanted to say yes, but did that mean I had to let go of what had been my life force? My writing? It seemed like I couldn't have both. All the ancient voices came flooding in. I was being "too dramatic." "Too sensitive." I couldn't even defend to myself that I had simply lost the ballast of my life. I felt like I was falling with no hope for a net to catch me. Somehow I'd managed to pit the two great adult loves of my life against each other. But I knew that really I was in a war with myself.

And the oldest version of the Inner Critter roiled up inside of me: *Just be like the everybody elses. Fall in love. Couple. Let go of the writing. Did it ever really serve you? Seems to me that it's a liability more than a life force. All of the inherent rejection. All of the inherent criticism. Why would you put yourself through that for one more second when you have so much acceptance and support from this man? Hasn't your writing always been . . . an inconvenience for the people who love you? This guy would probably be happier if you divorced your muse and married him.*

She spewed lies, but I didn't have it in me to put the Inner Critter down for her nap. I was a mess. A mess who was in love with a man I hadn't known how to dream. A mess who had been afraid to dream just like he had been afraid. And it was true: I couldn't imagine the rest of my life without him. I couldn't imagine the rest of my life at all. I couldn't even feel my Free Child. I'd abandoned her in the field.

And then our love became even more beautiful. And terrifying.

We'd devoted the month of November to him living with me in Montana. To get into a rhythm. Not just to play on the Oregon coast, lollygagging all day, shucking oysters, crabbing, and drinking rosé over Netarts Bay. We were going to "live in the Big" in the little ways and see how it went. So far our time together had been seamless. So joyful. So easy. So much laughter and sharing that I was hoarse all the time. What might "real life" look like?

He wanted to see Montana, and not just the touristy spots. He wanted to see the surprises. After all, we were living a surprise. I hadn't shared with him that my muse was AWOL. We went to a place I'd wanted to experience for years, set along a country road near Missoula. The Garden of One Thousand Buddhas.

The Buddhist monk Gochen Tulku Sang-ngag Rinpoche, a Tibetan master of the Nyingma school of Buddhism, created a shrine, which he completed in 2012. Following a traditional Buddhist method, Sang-ngag Rinpoche chose the location immediately upon seeing it, recalling a prophetic dream from his youth that corresponded to the garden's landscape. People came from all over on pilgrimage to be in its midst. It seemed in keeping with the mystical elements that surrounded our relationship.

He'd heard of it. Of course he had. So we went.

We walked the mandala, signifying the Buddha's Noble Eightfold Path, life, death, and rebirth. We walked it clockwise and from the left, as we were told. We were both silent, taking it in. And taking in what had grown between us.

At the end of walking the mandala, I wanted to take a moment to climb the hill to the prayer flag shrine while he opted to stay back, one week short of a knee replacement.

I stood in the middle of the prayer flags flapping in the wind, asking for guidance from the souls of writers and their muses through time. The seekers and word wanderers and wonderers. The kindreds from the beginning of civilization who knew that without their pen they would not thrive. The ones who could love and not put down their pen but love more and better because of it. I was sure I was such a being. Sure of it. But not sure how. And again, this was a hellacious shock to me. A woman who didn't believe in writer's block. Who had lived a life of making her self-expression through the written word absolutely untouchable.

Into the howling wind, I yelled, "Do I have to choose between this man and my writing?" Of course I could love both. They weren't mutually exclusive. The *love* wonder was bowling me over. But where was my *writing* wonder?

I sat down in the dry brown November grass, the wind in my ears, trying to listen to echoes of my longing. How did all of this happen?

I looked into the wide, wise, but not-so-forgiving Montana sky and yelled, "I want my writing back!" Then my voice turned to a whisper: "But I want him too. Can't I have both?" And it made sense, suddenly: he filled the same longing, and belonging, and wonder . . . that my writing had all my life. That was more terrifying than all of it. No one had ever done this in the realm of a loving partner.

Sitting there among the flapping hillside prayer flags, a nameless, desperate plea emerged in me. *Please, help me!* I opened my mouth to offer it to Montana, but only a groan came out. The wind took it just the same. The wind seemed to know what to do with my plea.

When I came down the hill, more confused than when I'd gone up it, he was seated at a small table. His face was solemn, like he'd heard me scream, but maybe the wind had delivered my groan too.

"Sit down," he said, pulling out the other chair.

I sat.

Then he took my hand, under the table, looking so wholly into my eyes, and slipped a ring onto my ring finger. "Will you spend the rest of your life with me, Laura Munson?" he said, tears welling up in his beautiful blue eyes and spilling down his pain-carved face.

I wanted to scream, *Yes! Yes! Of course I will!* But the part of me that had abandoned what I had just realized was my lifelong lover could not utter those words.

Instead, I put my head between his neck and his shoulder and said a small, "Let's give it a whirl," ashamed that I could not offer more.

That's what fear sounds like. And love. All at the same time.

He took it as a yes.

He wanted a photo of us in front of the Buddha shrine. The sun came out of the steel-gray clouds and flooded the one thousand Buddhas surrounding us. I wanted to be happier than I felt. Instead, I felt like a prayer flag flapping in the wind. When I look at those photos now, it shows.

But something happened on that hillside. When you're out there on scaffolding like that, and you open your mouth to your heart's deepest desire, I believe there is a cosmic echo. A calling in of the saints and sages and ancestors and all the powers that be. Maybe even the muses. Because that's the time when you don't know how to pray. And it's when what some call the Holy Spirit comes in to carry your pain and fear. The Holy Spirit that convenes with the divine when all you can do is groan. The Holy Spirit that groans for you with an under-standing of your soul's language. I'd left the church a long time ago, but I'd never left the messages of love and compassion and, mostly, the holy mystery. I'd studied mystics in all world religions. This was a time for the mystics to come in on the wind. The *that which we do not know*. The mysterious yet essential root of all love. And that day, the Holy Spirit seemed like the wind itself, sweeping away my fearful, pleading groan into the wonder of the Montana hills so that I could find my yes to both loves. But in that moment, I didn't know that I would ever find two yeses. I was as scared as I had ever been.

On the ride back home, I was stone silent. All I could think about were those two yeses. I'd always believed that writing was the closest thing to co-creating with the divine that I knew. And I'd lost it for love? Was I going to lose both? In that moment, I didn't know how to say yes to either.

In the days that followed, I was alone again in my house. He went back to Oregon to get his knee replacement surgery. I was leaving for a long-planned trip to Ireland, this time with my children for the holidays and then solo for a month.

I sat in my bed, staring at my dormant journal. Staring at this unfinished book on my computer screen. Not hungry for it anymore. And now not hungry for him either. At least that was what I told myself. I had things to do. Practical things. I had to get my business ducks in a row. Get my mail held. Pay my mortgage and bills. Make sure the driveway would get plowed and the pipes wouldn't freeze and the dogs would be cared for and all the things that seem so dire before you leave home that are instantly forgotten once you are in a faraway place. Especially when you are terrified. I needed to be swept away by something other than this surprise and deep love. And this surprise and deep loss.

As I packed my carry-on, I eyed my journal. I decided to leave it be. Too much pressure. Too much heartbreak. Maybe I needed to find new heart fuel. New wind. Then maybe the writing would come back. Then maybe I could say a true yes to this man. I was told that the west coast of Ireland had the purest wind around.

## your wild why . . .

Take some time to step into your wonder when it comes to love, especially if you find that the things you love are in conflict with one another. You can translate "love" as it pertains to you. Maybe it's a human that you love. Or a creature. A calling. Ask yourself these questions, but be sure not to make yourself wrong for your answers. Be honest with yourself:

*What would I do for love?*

*How do I identify myself by who/what I love?*

*Am I hiding from love?*

*What am I afraid of when it comes to love?*

*Would I let one love eclipse another?*

*What are my rules when it comes to love?*

*How am I expressing myself when it comes to love, both to myself and others?*

*Am I being honest?*

*Am I saying yes to love?*

*Do I mean it?*

*Is that yes to the exclusion of my truth and well-being?*

Now consider this: What if love is the outward expression of wonder? Write into that question most of all. See what you find there that is your utter truth.

## the thin place

I looked out of my airplane window and into the emerald
fields of Ireland—like a kind giant's mother made quilt,
squared off by stone stitching. I felt small in a way that I
needed to feel small. Everything had felt so big lately. I just
wanted to be one stone in one wall, astride green fields where
maybe I would find my Free Child, sit down with her, and get
some things figured out in the way of love and words.

As we descended into this green expanse, I felt the
locked match of wills between my Inner Critter and my Inner
Champion start to come apart. I hoped that I was far enough
from the war zone for them to leave me alone, even though I
knew it lived inside me. I hoped that there wouldn't be fuel
for it here, in this place where I was without any identity. I'd
shed the inner terrorism in San Miguel de Allende and Mexico
City. I'd shed it in Morocco and other places recently, too, like
Costa Rica, finally, to track hummingbirds. But I'd never done
it with a great, new love calling me to say yes. And with the
words not coming to me—not on the page, not in my mind,
and definitely not out of my mouth. I needed a mantra, but
it felt more like I needed a battle cry. Maybe Joyce, Yeats,

Wilde, Beckett, and, heck, Bono would rub off on me—*one* love and all.

My friend who lives in Ireland says you should choose a theme and travel the country following it. I chose, small surprise, *wonder*. Not the word, but the state of being. Ireland was full of cause for this state of being—in its fairy-ring forts, high Celtic crosses, rising cliffs, and crashing coasts. But it was the legendary ancient stone circles that I was attracted to most. I loved that they were likely a Bronze Age way to track the sun and moon patterns but were still a modern mystery, abiding by time, set in the stillness of stone. I was far from stillness. I had never been more restless.

*Do I say yes to this man? Does outer love beget inner love? Or is it that love must start inside in order to love outwardly? And either way, if I find a way to fully love, will the writing come back?*

How was it that I was here again, at this intersection of wanting and being? Would I ever escape it? I had tried to practice self-love in so many ways by becoming aware of the Inner Critter and Inner Champion and choosing to fuel the latter over the former. But understanding a concept is different from living into it, especially when the stakes are high, fear and love are duking it out, and they both want blood. Clearly, there were major holes in my practice because all too often my attempts had landed in self-loathing. I didn't want self-loathing on this trip. I wanted freedom. And I had zero faith that I could find it. I felt ashamed.

I tried to shake it off. Looked out the airplane window for a circle of stones. Thinking wasn't the answer this time. I needed stillness. To stop thinking about what I was made to do and love, in body, mind, soul. To instead find within myself not a fortress but a sanctuary. To live in that self-sanctuary far from home, and to bring it back with me. Inside of me. To see who I was *without* all of my outer loves. Including my children. And this surprise man. And even my writing. No matter how wobbly and precarious it felt, I needed to finally come home to myself.

Despite my blurry brain, of this I was sure: now was a time for a silent self-homing. And there was nothing that held that sacred silence more than stones. I peered deeper into the green to try to spot a stone circle. I trusted stones. The patience of them. The presence of them. I'd been collecting stones all my life. I had a garden path made of heart-shaped stones. I often arranged stones in circles in my garden, inspired by the energy I'd felt as a college student while standing in the center of Stonehenge, as well as the replica of it not far from my home in Montana. Maybe I'd find the echo of the groan I'd uttered at the Garden of One Thousand Buddhas in a circle of ancient stones.

I decided that I'd celebrate the holidays with my children, and then I'd go in pursuit of stone-circle stillness. There were hundreds of stone circles all throughout Ireland. I trusted that I would find my way to the one I needed most.

As we landed, my intuition kicked in like a pinch hitter: *To find this self-homing, you need to be jolted out of your mind. You need a wordless, thoughtless place. The place of the soul. You will find it here if you go gently with yourself.*

Maybe all the pondering and pilgrimages and forest bathing were pathways. But maybe I hadn't followed them to the place I needed most: the pathway to my soul. The unseen center of presence. To step out of the wants of the self and to be in stillness, outer and inner.

But then the Inner Critter attacked, loud and mean, even here, suspended over Ireland:

*Stop this nonsense. You have things to figure out. You'll never find that stillness. You're too afraid. You need the life of your mind to be active. You're too afraid to listen to what your soul knows. You're too afraid to say yes. You need to go back to your fortress and trust nobody but yourself.*

I wanted to prove her wrong. Very wrong. But what if she was somehow right? Did I have to be alone in order to finally and wholly heal the wonder wound and love myself? Or could I find this healing with this man in my life? Did we learn to love ourselves by loving another? My mind swung back and forth, like a heavy pendulum. I willed it to stop.

We had survived the divorce, the pandemic lockdown was over, I was taking my children on a lovely and lavish international trip that I had funded all on my own, we could spread our wings again, and it was Christmastime. My solo Wonder Trip would come on the shirttails of all this bounty. I needed to find my way back to bounty. I'd get to the stillness soon enough, I hoped.

Ireland proved its weight in family magic with every stubborn wind-whipped castle we visited, every light-encased ruin, every peat moss fire warming our drenched selves in every pub. Every jig. Every reel. Every pint. Every hot whiskey with lemon and clove and honey. Every busker and bodhran and tin whistle. We found a levity we had lost in the pandemic. The disorientation of driving on the left side of the road with the steering wheel on the right side was a perfect parallel to how we felt inside, but we found humor in it. When we're a little scared in my family, we laugh. And as I drove in almost-disasters through the Irish countryside, my kids and I laughed and argued and laughed about arguing and laughed about laughing about arguing. Being together was the perfect family balm, but I knew it was just a quick fix. I had deep work to do.

My kids were restless too, still in the shadows of a world that had just stopped and restarted. And where I was drawn to stones, they were drawn to cliffs. They are mountain people, used to the lessons of extreme vertical. They wanted, needed, to stand on a mighty edge and look out over the stakes of the sea below and prove that they would not go over. That they could look to the hope of the horizon. They had their sights set on the famous Cliffs of Moher. We'd heard that this place was literally mind-blowing in its whipping Atlantic wind, churning water, and precarious edge.

I was less interested in that precarious edge. I felt too much edge inside me. But I drove them there, in a dense fog, inside and out. And as we stood on the towering cliffs and leaned into the western-blowing wind, we knew that it would hold us from going over, so pure and strong and beguiling. We needed that knowing. But it was all that I could do to stay on that edge. I could barely look down. Or at the horizon. I kept catching myself looking only at my boots.

My children wanted to hike up to a higher lookout, but I forced myself to stay standing in the wind. Trying to stay like I did at the prayer flag shrine in Montana. So I stood there, taking the wind's beating, lashing and whipping against me . . . until I realized that I was back to my old proving: the lonely nowhere of "I can handle it."

I relented, cold to my core and literally shaking in my boots. I needed sun, and I needed it immediately.

Across the way was a field of green, now not for a giant but seemingly for me, because the sun streamed down on a patch of grass up against a stone wall. I needed that warmth. I wanted to be a stone in that wall. It might not be a stone circle, but it was still and safe.

I followed the streaming sun to the patch of grass and leaned back against the stones, a free zone against the domineering wind. I took off my hat and scarf and let the sun warm my face. I felt hidden. Young. Away from peril and disapproving voices. They were not invited into this field. Once and for all. Maybe this was Rumi's "field." Outside ideas of right and wrong.

With that "once and for all," as if from out of the stones, a feeling of playfulness cartwheeled up my spine like I was being invited into a world I'd been missing for all my worrying and trying so hard to get serious about love.

And I felt her. My Free Child, like she'd been playing games with giants and was tired of their big footprints and heavy teacups. She'd missed me. I swept her into my arms and stood, resting her on one hip. We'd get back to the twirl later. I saw my adult children waiting for me at the end of the path but knowing not to interrupt me. I was glad for that.

So, it was with three of them that I walked back to my car, and three of them that I drove back to the hotel, four of us stone silent and spent in the best way. My absolute and undying love for my children had always been easy. And now, for all three of them.

That night, I lay in bed longing to write about how I felt. To write about this search for soul. An in-between place. A wordless place. A nothingness. And an everythingness. That was likely where wonder really lived, and where I would find my yes to both love and my muse. I tried to imagine that version of myself: a woman in love with herself, her writing, and this beloved man. Where would she be? What would her life be like? Good questions welcomed word-full answers. And I tore off a piece of hotel stationery from my nightstand and grabbed a pen, hoping that this image would come in words that tapped into the wordlessness of intuition and even soul. Placeholder words. Writers needed their words, but perhaps they found them in a wordless place.

Nothing. Not even a feeling. Nor an urge. There had never been nothing. If this was nothingness, I didn't want it. Maybe I should just return with my kids and call it good. Go back to the fortress.

It was still daytime in the US, so I emailed a dear poet friend, who exists in the space between the physical and the metaphysical. What some people call *the thin place*. Where the veil between this world and whatever you conceive to be other-worldly is thin. Where heaven and earth surrender to each other. I'd felt it in sacred moments, big and small, all my life. That was where I knew I needed to be, and soon. The thin place. The stakes were getting higher and higher, and I thought of the edge I'd stood on that afternoon. The edge I couldn't stay on.

My poet friend was the only person I could think of who might understand, because she'd loved and written abundantly from edges. And her beloved husband had recently died, so she was thick in the edge of grief. Grief brings with it a certain raw knowing. And certainly silence. I asked her if she had it in her to talk about love and loss. She did. On top of it, she was first-generation Irish and had traveled the country as a local, many times, likely to mystical places.

"I can't write," I confessed. "I've fallen in love. And I can't write. My book is just . . . lying fallow. I promised it to my editor months ago. And I'm in Ireland. Without my journal because I seem to be allergic to it these days. It's that bad. Oh, and I think I've lost my wonder. And, funny enough, the book is about *wonder*!"

"*You* can't *write*?" It didn't help that she had panic in her voice. She'd known me since I was in my early twenties, writing my first books in Seattle. Abundantly.

"It's like I've lost my ballast," I said. "I'm madly in love and I can't write and I've lost my ballast. Please don't tell me that I can't have love, writing, and ballast."

She said, "That's how I've felt. I lost my ballast too. He was my ballast." She paused. "Did you know that I went to Ireland again recently? I found my ballast there. I'd lost my words too."

I didn't have the nerve to ask where. It felt so private. But she offered: "In the stone circles."

My whole soul brightened. At this point, it didn't make sense to linger in the serendipity. Serendipity seemed like it was coming after me the way a mother does for her troubled child. I decided I needed to ride it and see what it had in store for me.

I said, "I feel so called to those stone circles. I'm going to them after the holidays. I'm not sure which ones, and I feel like I shouldn't plan it. I want to just come upon them. And walk around them and sit in their midst. Maybe I'll find my ballast again too. I'm so glad you did, my friend."

And then she mentioned the name. It was a lesser-known stone circle on the Beara Peninsula. One I'd been studying.

"It's over four thousand years old," she said. "It's a smaller circle. Next to a beautiful lake with a waterfall on the other side. I felt a deep inner peace there that showed me that I can go on with my life." She paused. "And there was the most exquisite rainbow there that day. A double rainbow. I wrote a poem about it."

I was so happy for her, that she'd found healing peace, hope, and her words. And a rainbow-inspired poem. Was that where life had brought me? Back to one of my original wild whys? The rainbow? Had I lost my wild why? Had I fastened too tightly to my stories of pain and punishment and loss and failure and loneliness? Was it time to shed it all and finally do as Harrison did in his "Cabin Poem": "swallow myself / in ceaseless flow"? Was that why I couldn't write? Was writing this book, and looking so intensely into my wonder wound, and consequently my past stories, what was in my way? Was exposing it all causing my wonder wound to rebleed?

I thought about what Terry Tempest Williams wrote about writing. "It's a bloody risk."

The message was clear: it was time for a new bloom of self and soul. But not with a busy mind. Instead, a radical move into radical self-sanctuary. Maybe I could find a wild why that was less about curiosity and more about stillness. Maybe then I'd find my writing again. And my wonder behind it. Maybe then I could say yes to this rest-of-my-life love.

That afternoon, I kissed my children goodbye as they hopped into their taxi, homeward bound. It was time for my

Wonder Trip, and I had no confidence that I'd find anything this time. But I was open. I needed to be open.

At my first hotel, the doorman brimmed over with kindness, as the Irish do, boasting a top hat and red-faced smile. "It's nice to have an American here. We missed you during the pandemic. What are you going to be seeing today?"

"I'm not sure, exactly. I'd like to drive the Beara Peninsula. And see some stone circles."

He paused, as if he shouldn't speak what was in his mind. But then he couldn't seem to help himself. "Do you like a rainbow?" he said.

I held back tears but they brimmed anyway. "Yes. I especially love a rainbow."

He pulled out a map. "There's a stone circle there where I've never *not* seen a rainbow." Now his eyes brimmed with tears too. He pointed at the map. "It's here. But go where your heart wants. Better to stumble upon it than plan it. You should get on your way though. You're chasing daylight this time of year."

I looked at his fingertip. It pointed to the same stone circle where my poet friend had experienced her double-rainbow moment. Now the tears spilled over.

He tilted his head in gentle concern. "And mind you, love: an Irish rainbow is more than just about leprechauns and pots of gold. It's about having hope and following your dreams. Even if they feel unreachable." Then he added, "It's a bridge, the rainbow. But you just behold it. Because you'll never get to the end of it. You know?"

"Yes," I said, smiling, but not nearly as brightly as he was. "I know. But you can still believe."

"True, love. No harm in believing." This man was made of wonder. I wanted to take him with me. But I knew I had to find my ballast alone.

I drove the Beara, the rain and wind slamming the land, yet the thick gray sky, somehow in and out of sun, made the grassy fields obscenely green. I decided to try to find the stone circle that apparently made rainbows.

The road was single-lane, windy, and empty. I was sure I was lost. My friend had said to be patient. That I'd know I was there when I rounded a bend and it opened up to fields of grazing sheep. Twisty turn after twisty turn, just as I was about to turn back, there were the fields of grazing sheep.

The rain was steady. Not rainbow weather. Still, a rain walk felt like part of this living into the thin place. A short walk up, and there was the main stone, covered in lichen. *If a stone could talk*, I thought. And then my eyes opened to the fields. The lake. The mountains and waterfall. I felt like I was back in Montana in a way. The thinnest place I knew.

I walked through the portal stones and stood in the center of the circle. There were offerings of sorts, mostly stones and coins, stacked in a cairn. There wasn't anyone there, so I sat. I sat with my lack of words and fear of love. I sat with the stillness and presence of ancient but human-placed stones. And I wondered what it must be like to sit there during solstice and see the ancient astronomy all lined up and in balance. Ballast.

Just then, a sound filled my ears and the space around me. It was as if I were in a cave and it was coming from even further underneath me, gaining in timbre and force, louder and deeper. A low groaning. It was twin to my groaning on the hillside amid the prayer flags. But that had been within. This felt outside of me, like it was asking me to enter into it.

I wanted to run. But I knew I needed to stay, no matter how alone I felt, or how anxious. So I stayed seated. I thought of my friend's sap. I thought of him quoting the Apache proverb: "Wisdom sits in places." Tears broke through what I didn't know had been such a thin veil because I couldn't tell what was rain and what was saline. Until I looked up.

And saw that the rain had stopped.

And sure enough . . . there was a rainbow. Full arch. Not

a single. Not a double. But a triple, mesmerizing, rainbow. If I'd believed in a pot of gold, it would have been within reach, just over the lake. And it occurred to me: Why wouldn't I believe in that pot of "gold"? A pot of dreams. A pot of presence. A pot of possibility. A pot of yes. And the rainbow leading to it? Like Harrison's bridge out over water. One that he was glad to build, knowing it would never be finished. Presence turned into poetry.

I watched it. I looked to the heavens. I looked at my boots on the green grass. I felt the thin place between them. And I lost track of time as if I had, indeed, stepped into my soul. A timeless, wordless, place of nothingness. Like how I'd learned to describe Montana: "the middle of everywhere."

I suddenly had the deep urge to write something and leave it there as my own offering. But I didn't want to write on a stone. I wanted to write on something that would fast disintegrate in this constant wind and rain and mist, as a vote in favor of my future, however it played out.

I took out my favorite pen and my little notebook (ever since Harrison's scolding, I was never without one, even if I'd left my main journal at home) and stared at the blank page for only a second before my pen started to move across the paper.

It wrote these words:

"What makes wonder?"

I didn't need to know. The asking was enough. The asking had uncovered my words, pure and true and finally. And I could trust them. I stared into my question in the red, orange, yellow, green, blue, indigo, and violet until it finally faded to gray. Then I ripped out the page, rolled it up into a tiny scroll, and slid it into the cairn of stones with the other offerings. And I whispered my question: "What makes wonder?"

I knew the answer then. Presence. Presence is what makes wonder. Presence is what is behind wonder, like wonder is behind creativity and empathy. I'd thought it was intuition. But there was something behind even that.

In that moment, I felt like I could leave behind all the scrutiny and rejection and loss that had festered so deep and for so long. I could shed the burden of trying to be "the star of the family" and the need to prove to all the elders that their mean *shhhhh-ing* was unwarranted. The trying to make up for what I had failed at in the way of "supposed to be" and "not supposed to be." I had nothing to prove to anyone anymore. I could stop trying. Total self-love seemed too tall an order for now. But self-sanctuary was there for the taking. It was clear: there was an inner place that the wonder wound could not touch. As long as you found presence. The soul was the way. Not the mind.

Relief softened in my shoulders, through my ribs, and down the rest of my body, all the way to my toes. I decided to believe that I had heard wonder itself in that circle of stones. The echo of my groaning from the prayer flags at the Garden of One Thousand Buddhas in Montana to the soul-groaning from an ancient, sacred circle in western Ireland. It had come back to me. Voice. I was ready to receive its message. Presence is the way to wonder. And the way to self-love and all love. The ballast you find when you leave your old ballast behind.

A song came from me that I hadn't sung in so long. One of Mimi's favorites. *In the Gloaming.* I changed the words to *In the Groaning.* And I sang it as loudly and prayerfully as I could.

All felt calm and clear. I'd opened myself up to loving again, and it had scared me. I was finally realizing that I needed to tend to myself, in presence, whatever the outcome. If I could live in this truth, then how could the writing not come back? And how could I not say yes to love? To loving this man? But also to loving myself?

I felt all of my mentors converge inside me, all ballast. And I pulled out my notebook and wrote this on the opposing page to the one I'd torn out and left as an offering: "Stay in this love, Laura. Be brave. Allow it all. Be gentle with yourself. Be kind. Be present." My pen was moving again. And it surprised me because it wrote a blessing.

"Bless my love and bless my fear in ceaseless presence."

I'd never thought to bless my fear. Only to manage it, shun it, or be overcome by it. It felt so graceful, this concept. It wasn't that I was blessing fear to *worship* fear. But instead to honor that it is part of the human experience. And just like the Inner Critter, maybe I could love my fear of loving this man and consequently losing my writing . . . into submission. If my Inner Critter was fear itself, and it wasn't likely that I'd ever truly get her mean, scared voice out of my head, then why wouldn't I bless the process of acknowledging fear? Was it possible to love fear? And by loving it, blessing it . . . so that it quiets down and stops its haunt? With love, you break the haunt. With blessing, you break the haunt.

So I spoke the blessing aloud: "Bless my love and bless my fear in ceaseless presence."

That night I opened my computer to this book and started writing. I wrote until dawn. I wrote this chapter, in fact.

And when I came home to Montana, I said yes. To all of it.

## your wild why . . .

Where would you go on a pilgrimage of self-sanctuary?

What would it take to say yes to presence? To self-love? To a woundless place in your soul? To the pilgrimage of the root of love? And to bless your love and your fear? What would it be like to say thank you for what you find there?

Can you write a one-line invitation to your soul? Can it start with "I invite myself . . ."? Maybe it's "to know you in presence." Whatever it is that you deeply seek.

And could you then write a one-line blessing, whatever that means to you, as a way for you to say yes to this invitation?

Try. Your wonder needs you to try.

## the wonder cabin

Let's return to the sixty-second fire.

This book hasn't been that. I have tried to build you a bonfire in these pages. A good old-fashioned backyard Montana bonfire of wonder wandering, love, and inspiration. I have given you calls to action, personal stories, concrete solutions, writing opportunities, and food for thought.

But wouldn't you like to have a place for your wonder that you can find in your mind whenever you need it? When someone says to go to your "happy place"? It doesn't have to be something lavish. Just a cozy shelter with a warm hearth that you can rely on. Remember how un-cozy mine was in that scene when I was trying to build my untrue Wonder Cabin? I've since learned how to hold my true Wonder Cabin in my mind and heart. It just took practice.

So let's do this. Let's have you practice imagining your Wonder Cabin. Start in the meadow twirling with your Free Child. Imagine that you stop, let the child slip out of your arms, and gently place her in the grass. She's probably pretty dizzy by now, and likely you are too.

Imagine the two of you lying down in the meadow. Watch the clouds. Maybe a slight breeze will part your hair and you'll feel it on your forehead like a mother's hand.

Maybe the sun will go behind a cloud and you'll feel cool. And then it will come out and you'll feel warm again. Allow it all. Allow whatever thoughts and feelings come flooding in. But don't snag on those thoughts and feelings. Let them move by like clouds. Instead, grasp your Free Child's hand. You have one job. You need to find the Wonder Cabin. Together.

Where is it? Is it in the woods? Tucked into a grove of aspens by a babbling brook? On a beach? High in the trees? Where do you most like to be?

Now imagine what it looks like. Is it made of logs? Driftwood? Is it made of glass? Are the windows square? What color is the door? Is there a pathway leading to it? What is the pathway made of? Heart shaped rocks?

There's nothing foolish about this process. If your mind goes there, hold your Free Child's hand tighter. Believe me, in her mind she's already eating the gumdrops off the walls and having tea in candy daffodils with nice mice.

Now imagine the inside of the Wonder Cabin. Be sure that there's a hearth. A hearth to come home to. Is it a stone fireplace? A woodstove? What does it smell like? How do you light it, this hearth of your soul?

If the refrigerator could be filled with anything, what would it contain? If someone you love slipped in during the day and baked something for you, what would be there cooling on the counter? What does the china look like? Is it blue and white because you love blue-and-white china? Is there a collection of something on a shelf? Like sea glass? Driftwood? Little stones with rings around them? Is there a teakettle? An old cast-iron popcorn maker? Candles that are burned down to their quick and some new ones too? A vase with fresh flowers? What kind of flowers are in your Wonder Cabin? Cornflowers? Peach roses? White sweet peas?

What are the soft surfaces in your Wonder Cabin? Is there an old blanket that someone wove for you? What about the rugs? What do they feel like under your bare feet? Where do you sleep in your Wonder Cabin? Is there a window by your bed? Let there be a window by your bed. What does the sky look like on a full moon through your window? What does it look like on a rainy spring morning through your window? In the fog? In the snow? In the salt air? What seasons are there at your Wonder Cabin?

Now ask: *What's the worst thing that can happen in my Wonder Cabin?*

Hang out here for a moment more. In your meadow. You're still getting un-dizzy. Hold your Free Child's hand tighter. She knows what to be afraid of and what isn't worth the energy.

With love, ask: *What is the very worst thing that can happen in my Wonder Cabin?*

There's no right answer.

There's no wrong answer.

So why not have it be fear? Fear is the worst thing that can happen in your Wonder Cabin. And by now, hopefully, you believe that love is greater than fear. And love is the stuff of wonder. Stop at that because if you make the list too long, you might never get there to find out.

And so, you'd better get up! *Get up!* Even if your head is still spinning. Take that child's hand—and *run!*

See how she's pulling you, how she's in front of you? Follow her. Don't let go! She might leave you behind because she knows what's cooling on the counter and she's hungry from all that twirling! Haven't you realized that she *is* your wonder? And that in these pages, she's been working really hard on your return to her? To be one again?

So:

*Run!*

Even if your heart is burning in your throat and your feet forgot how to run through the woods or on hot sand or wherever your Wonder Cabin wants to be . . . *do not let go!*

Do.

Not.

Let.

Go.

And when you get to your Wonder Cabin, fling open the door. Enter together. Go to the hearth. Make a fire to show your wonder that you will honor it with the flame of ritual. Start with sap. With what you already know. The sap of your wonder. What is all around you. Allow what you already know to be what it already is.

Tell yourself, with love, "It was always here. I just had to remember my way."

And so I ask you:

Why is the sky blue?

# *acknowledgments*

To my children. The best wonder-ers I know. Never stop asking your wild whys. Thank you for all of your abiding love and support.

To my sister. Thank you for my journals, and for showing me divine love all along the way.

To my mother. Thank you for modeling what it is to love your work. For driving the family station wagon from Chicago to Connecticut to hear me sing off-key. For camp in the Rocky Mountains. For Italy. For knowing that when I was in my tree house, I was doing important work.

To Buck, who was there all along. It just took a while, and a lot of wonder, to find each other.

To Brooke Warner, torch bearer, writer's writer, third-eye-wide-open editor and publisher. Thank you for reading in between the lines. To Barrett Briske and her CMOS eagle-eye and heart. And to Lauren Wise for holding it all together.

To my intrepid and loyal agent, Beth Davey, whose wonder has been holding my own for a long time now. Thank you. And to Emi Battaglia and Susie Stangland for helping to get this book into readers' hands.

To all of my Haven Writing Retreats alums. You have touched my heart's wonder and are engraved in it always. And to the Dancing Spirit Ranch, deep bows to you for how you hold my retreaters, and me. Thank you for reminding me that the land does the work.

A wonder-full thank you to all who helped keep my wonder intact. I wonder if you know who you are. I trust that you do. I love you all.

To my father and grandparents. Tell me . . . why is the sky blue? I suspect you know the full answer now.

To Montana. You hold my wonder like no place I know. Deep bows to you.

To wonder itself, high in the thin branches. To every bird. To every heart-shaped rock. To every blue sky. To every setting sun. To every rainbow. To every child. To every wild why.

# *about the author*

L aura Munson is *The New York Times*, *USA Today*, and international best-selling author of the memoir *This Is Not The Story You Think It Is* (Amy Einhorn/Putnam), and the novel *Willa's Grove* (Blackstone). Founder of the acclaimed Haven Writing Retreats, she has been featured or published in *The New York Times* Modern Love column, *The New York Times Magazine*, *O, The Oprah Magazine*, *Vanity Fair*, *Elle*, *Redbook*, *Time*, *Newsweek*, and many other publications. She has appeared on *Good Morning America*, *The Early Show*, WGN, NPR, London's *This Morning*, Australia's *Sunrise*, and other global media outlets. She lives in Whitefish, Montana.

*Author photo © Bader Howar*

## Looking for your next great read?

We can help!

Visit www.shewritespress.com/next-read
or scan the QR code below for a list
of our recommended titles.

She Writes Press is an award-winning
independent publishing company founded to
serve women writers everywhere.